1 00 033643 9

KU-182-729

DATE DUE FOR RETURN

UNIVERSITY
LIBRARY
MA

Adjustment in oil-importing developing countries
A comparative economic analysis

The two oil price shocks of 1973–4 and 1979–80 have been by far the largest price movements to occur in the international economy in the postwar period. The book analyzes the adjustment of oil-importing developing countries to those shocks with a view both to understanding an important episode in recent economic history, and to eliciting lessons that can guide successful adjustment to similar events in the future. Unlike other treatments of this subject, the findings of the study are derived by combining a broad-brush approach that covers a large number of countries with the development of techniques that permit an in-depth investigation into a few selected countries. The study develops quantitative economic methods and applies them to contemporary problems in order to yield useful insights for policy-makers.

Adjustment in oil-importing developing countries

A comparative economic analysis

PRADEEP K. MITRA

Published by the Press Syndicate of the University of Cambridge
The Pitt Building, Trumpington Street, Cambridge CB2 1RP
40 West 20th Street, New York, NY 10011-4211, USA
10 Stamford Road, Oakleigh, Melbourne 3166, Australia

© Cambridge University Press 1994

First published 1994

Printed in Great Britain by Bell and Bain Ltd, Glasgow

A catalogue record for this book is available from the British Library

Library of Congress cataloguing in publication data
Adjustment in oil-importing developing countries: A comparative economic
analysis
    p.   cm.
Includes bibliographical references.
ISBN 0-521-44316-4
1. Structural adjustment (Economic policy) – Developing countries –
Computable general equilibrium models. 2. Petroleum products – Prices –
Developing countries – Computable general equilibrium models.
I. Mitra, Pradeep K.
HC59.7.A8218 1994
338.2′3282′091724–dc20   92-36214   CIP

ISBN 0 521 44316 4 hardback

VN

This book is dedicated to the memory of my parents

Contents

Foreword

The oil price shocks of 1973–4 and 1978–9 have by far exceeded all other terms-of-trade movements in the period since World War II. Together with the associated recessions in the industrial countries and the rapid increase in international interest rates between 1979 and 1981, they marked the beginning of a set of events that signaled the need for structural adjustment and economic reform in developing countries, a process that continues to this day. In this study, Pradeep Mitra and his associates analyze the nature and magnitude of those shocks, the adjustment polices of oil-importing developing countries and the effects of those events on economic growth, the sectoral composition of output and the distribution of income. Their work helps identify the patterns of successful and unsuccessful adjustment that can guide policy reform in the face of future terms-of-trade shocks. It also allows the authors to develop methods of comparative economic analysis which can be replicated in the study of similar episodes elsewhere.

The comparative method developed in this book is used to classify thirty three developing countries into groups according to the pattern of adjustment chosen to respond to external shocks and to explore the relationships among shocks, modes of adjustment and growth performance of those countries. The empirical framework used for this purpose is rich enough to incorporate simultaneous consideration of domestic and trade policies, but at the same time parsimonious enough to permit wide applicability to data-sparse developing countries. It is used to demonstrate the importance of public sector savings policies (revenue mobilization and public consumption restraint) as well as export-oriented trade policies in effecting successful adjustment.

The comparative analysis focusses on such issues as the association between external shocks, policy responses and economic growth; the role of public sector profligacy in aggravating the balance-of-payments impact of external shocks; the tendency to regard unfavorable shocks as temporary and favorable terms-of-trade movements as permanent; and the importance of a fiscal-cum-trade policy package in effecting growth-oriented adjustment. A number of the hypotheses suggested by these findings are explored in greater depth in studies of adjustment in four countries at different income levels and characterized by varying structures of trade and production. The common analytical structure used for this purpose is an applied general equilibrium model chosen to emphasize the links between external shocks and policy responses on the one hand and their macroeconomic, sectoral and distributional consequences on the other. The models are implemented separately on each of the countries and used to compare the results of policies actually followed against various alternative formulations of internal and external shocks as well as adjustment policies. The latter include different assumptions about exchange rate adjustment, the mix between domestic savings and foreign borrowing, resort to investment and growth-oriented policies, and the use of market signals to guide investment in different sectors of the economy. In doing so, the authors develop innovative extensions of existing methods of economywide modelling to track historical developments over an extended period, to analyze income distribution by size and function and to develop tractable shortcuts to explore the time-phasing of investment and foreign borrowing. Moreover, their presentation also draws attention to how the models might actually be implemented, in the expectation that readers may wish to use those techniques more widely in applied policy analysis.

The work of Mitra and his associates makes important contributions to two strands that have featured in the World Bank's research program: the development of the methodology of applied policy analysis and the use of a comparative case study method to examine leading issues in development economics. The conclusions reported in the following chapters of this book demonstrate the value of combining those two approaches in analyzing the adjustment experiences of oil-importing developing countries and in drawing appropriate lessons for the conduct of economic policy.

Lawrence H. Summers
Vice President, Development Economics
and Chief Economist
The World Bank

Preface

The work reported in this book was started in 1982, shortly after the World Bank had devoted the *World Development Report*, 1981 to an early assessment of developing-country adjustment to oil price-induced changes in their external environment in the 1970s and early 1980s. It was supported by the Bank's Research Committee. Work on the project was carried out intermittently since and completed in 1986. The last was a year when oil prices had plunged to a level as low as $10 a barrel, so that the study, on completion, seemed to refer only to an interesting, if somewhat distant, episode in economic history.

The near doubling of crude oil prices following Iraq's invasion of Kuwait in August 1990, the flight of thousands of workers from those two countries, and widespread discussion of the plight of the most seriously affected developing countries served notice that, with apologies to Mark Twain, rumors of an early demise of interest in this subject had proved to be vastly exaggerated. Although oil prices returned to pre-war levels in the second quarter of 1991, the crisis demonstrated the vulnerability of the oil market to supply disruptions and the consequent need for oil-importing developing countries, for most of whom this was a negative development, to be prepared to adjust to oil price shocks in the future. In that context, the lessons to be learned from the experience of the major oil price shocks of 1973/4 and 1979/80 are particularly helpful in shaping appropriate responses. It was therefore decided to bring together those lessons and the detailed supporting studies from which they had been derived both in their own interest and as a contribution to that discussion.

The book also serves another purpose. It extends existing methods of economy-wide modeling to answer a range of problems in development policy. These extensions will be seen to include, *inter alia*, the development of methods to track history, to analyze income distribution in detail, and to incorporate features of labor markets such as indexation, spillovers, and migration, where the advantages of general equilibrium methods over partial equilibrium approaches are decisive. It is hoped that the presentation will encourage readers to consult the basic model in its fully documented form, with a view to applying those techniques to similar issues elsewhere.

Many individuals have contributed to this study. That of my associates is acknowledged individually in the various chapters, but beyond that they have been a constant source of guidance and help. Gholam Azarbayejani, Jaber Ehdaie, and Derek McGreal provided helpful research assistance at various stages of the project. The late Tony Brooke, Arne Drud, and Alex Meeraus advised on all computational aspects of the work. Lans Bovenberg, Paul Fisher, Frank Lysy, Jeff Round, and Sweder van Wijnbergen gave us useful comments on different parts of the manuscript. Jeanne Rosen assisted with the editing of the country case studies. Among many colleagues at the World Bank who have been supportive of the study, I should particularly like to mention the late Bela Balassa, Hollis Chenery, Vinod Dubey, John Duloy, John Holsen, Graham Pyatt, T.N. Srinivasan, and Ardy Stoutjesdijk. Peggy Pender typed numerous versions of the manuscript with patience, skill, and a high degree of professionalism. Finally, my wife, Vijaya, put up cheerfully with the intrusion of this book into our home and offered encouragement that helped bring it to completion. I thank them all.

Pradeep Mitra
July 1992

Affiliation of authors

HENRIK DAHL   External associate professor, Copenhagen Business School Copenhagen

SHANTA DEVARAJAN   Principal economist, Policy Research Department, The World Bank

JEFFREY LEWIS   Economist, East Asia and Pacific Region, The World Bank

PRADEEP MITRA   Lead economist, South Asia Region, The World Bank

SHYAMALENDU PAL   Financial analyst, Risk Management and Financial Policy Department, The World Bank

ALAN ROE   Reader in economics, Warwick University

HECTOR SIERRA   Economist, Africa Region, The World Bank

SURESH TENDULKAR   Professor of economics, Delhi School of Economics

1 Introduction

The setting

The world witnessed two oil price shocks in the 1970s.

Petroleum prices more than quadrupled from under $3 to over $12 a
barrel in 1973–4 – a real increase of 150 percent – fell in real terms by a
sixth between 1974 and 1978, and then rose from $13 to $30 a barrel – a
real increase of 80 percent – between 1978 and 1980.

The industrial market economies went into a recession in 1974–5 and
thereafter recovered strongly before plunging into another recession in
1979–80, followed by a slow recovery. Stagflation was born in the
OECD countries with successive peaks of economic activity occurring
at ever higher levels of unemployment. The combination of recession
and inflation led, *inter alia*, to a fall in demand for exports from
developing countries and an increase in the price of manufactured
goods exported by the OECD to developing countries.

The end of the decade saw an "interest-rate shock" following the use of
restrictive monetary policies to combat inflation in the leading
industrial countries. To this must be added the fact that, in the early
1980s, the real prices of major primary products exported by
developing countries – adjusted for rising prices of imported manufactures – fell to their lowest levels since the Second World War.[1]

Some perspective on the magnitude of these convulsions may be
obtained from the following statistics. World trade in fuels increased from
$29 billion in 1970 to $535 billion in 1980. Paying for the 1970s fuel price
increases was equivalent to finding the money to buy all the exports of
another United States or (the then) West Germany.[2] The current-account
deficits of the oil-importing developing countries as a proportion of GNP
doubled from around 2.5 percent in 1973 to 5 percent in 1980. Debt-
servicing payments of all developing countries, deflated by their export unit

values, rose nearly threefold between 1972 and 1979; interest rates, deflated by export prices, rose from −10 percent in 1979 to 20 percent in 1981.

The theoretical literature on adjustment to import price shocks in a small open economy is large and, by now, standard.[3] It can and should influence thinking on appropriate policy responses to terms-of-trade shocks in the future. This book is not, however, a contribution to pure theory. That is summarily reviewed in chapter 2. The focus instead is on developing implementable frameworks of analysis that are informed by theory and on applying them to study the adjustment experience of the oil-importing developing countries to the two oil price shocks of the 1970s. In so doing, our intention is to identify successful and unsuccessful patterns of adjustment, to isolate policies that are appropriate in the light of country circumstances, and to elicit applicable lessons for adjustment to future external shocks.

Iraq's invasion of Kuwait in August 1990 resulted in a near doubling of the price of oil from around $16–17 to over $30 a barrel, a cessation of workers' remittances from Iraq and Kuwait for a number of developing countries, and a decline in tourism earnings for countries in the region affected by hostilities. Although oil prices returned to pre-crisis levels in the second quarter of 1991 following resolution of the crisis, the events of those critical months served as a clear reminder of the world's vulnerability to oil price shocks associated with increasing dependence on OPEC oil in general and, within OPEC, on a few countries – Saudi Arabia, Iran, the United Arab Emirates, Iraq, and Kuwait – in particular.

The world economy at the beginning of the decade of the 1990s is different in several important respects from that of the 1970s and early 1980s. First, the developing countries account for 28 percent of total world oil consumption compared to 18 percent in 1973, and are more dependent on oil than the OECD countries due to lack of fuel substitution capabilities, increasing motorization, and switching out of traditional fuels (firewood) to oil fuels in the household sector. Moreover, current projections suggest that the growth of their demand for oil over the decade of the 1990s will, at 57 percent, be well in excess of that of the rest of the world, 27 percent.[4] This is due to the transfer of the more energy-intensive industrial procedures to the developing countries, more rapid increases in economic growth in the newly industrialized countries, and higher population growth. Although developing countries as a whole are net exporters of oil, most of them are net oil importers. While net fuel imports as a share of their GDP averages 1.2 percent (see table 1.1) there are countries such as Guyana, Jordan, the Dominican Republic, and Tanzania where that figure exceeds 5 percent, so that the direct impact of an increase in oil prices on them could be significant (see table 1.1). Second, a number of countries with high shares of

Table 1.1 *Two indicators of external vulnerability in developing countries (in percent)[a]*

	Net fuel imports as a share of GDP[b]	Variable rate debt as a share of GDP
All developing countries	−0.5	14.7
Oil importers	1.2	12.1
Severely indebted		
Low income	1.9	3.3
Middle income	1.0	25.3
Moderately indebted		
Low income	3.0	2.1
Middle income	2.5	15.7
Others	0.8	4.4
Oil exporters[c]	−8.3	26.4

Notes:
[a] Figures are for 1988.
[b] A negative sign implies that the countries in the group are net exporters of oil in the aggregate.
[c] The definition of oil exporters is the same as that used in World Bank (1990). All other countries were placed in the oil importers category.
Source: World Bank data base.

variable rate debt to GDP (see table 1.1) would be particularly adversely affected by increases in real interest rates that are likely to be triggered by the macroeconomic policy responses of the industrial countries to oil price increases. Third, the withdrawal of commercial banks from lending for balance-of-payments purposes implies that the prospects of securing additional external financing to facilitate adjustment to future price shocks are much bleaker than at the time of the oil shocks of 1973–4 and 1979–80, particularly for the highly indebted countries such as Argentina, Costa Rica, Honduras, Madagascar, Sudan, and Tanzania.

This grim litany draws attention to two things. First, that a decade after the onset of the debt crisis and the collapse of primary product prices, many developing countries find themselves in very difficult circumstances. This is in stark contrast to 1973 which marked the culmination of nearly a quarter century of economic prosperity after the Second World War. Second, adjustment to future shocks will be difficult even if their magnitude is less than that of the oil price increases of the 1970s, as would be expected to be the case. In summary then, the smaller terms-of-trade shocks in the future must be set against more difficult initial conditions. How can the adjustment experience of oil-importing developing countries to the oil price shocks and the concomitant OECD recessions of 1973–4 and 1979–80 be used to guide adjustment to external shocks in the present decade?

Scope of the study

This book examines external shocks and modes of adjustment for oil-importing developing countries for the period 1973–4 to 1981–2 in considerable detail. The intention is both to understand an important episode in recent economic history and to draw applicable lessons for adjustment to similar events in the future.

Chapter 2 documents the severity of external shocks and studies adjustment to them in thirty-three developing countries, nine of which experienced favorable movements in external conditions. The countries examined are very diverse both with respect to initial conditions and adjustment experience. To help impose analytical order, we develop a methodology that derives from the basic theoretical framework of international economics and is empirically applicable even to countries lacking detailed data. The focus is at once comparative and issue-oriented. Can countries be classified into groups according to the broad contours of adjustment provided by our analytical framework? How does an individual country's experience compare with that of others in the same group? How important were external shocks compared to failures in economic management in aggravating adjustment problems? Do the policies actually adopted suggest that unfavorable shocks were regarded as temporary and favorable developments as permanent? Did more successful countries pursue a policy package that operated on many fronts rather than along any single dimension?

The method of analysis developed in chapter 2, though useful in identifying patterns of successful and unsuccessful adjustment that are examined in the rest of the book, does not lend itself to counterfactual analysis, i.e., the comparison of policies actually pursued with those that might instead have been followed. Might different policies have led to superior outcomes in terms of economic growth and income distribution? Did the second round of external shocks make unsustainable certain policies that a country was implementing in the aftermath of the first round of shocks? Given that countries, in addition to oil price shocks, faced other problems such as poor harvests arising from unfavorable weather conditions, were the particular policies chosen by them more suited to responding to one or the other type of shock?

Answers to these questions require considerably more information than may be processed by the method of chapter 2. It will be remembered that the latter was designed to be applicable to a large number of (possibly) data-sparse countries in order to help develop a comparative perspective. Further analysis, therefore, requires a more sophisticated framework implementable in practice in a handful of countries. This defines the agenda for the subsequent chapters which explore selected issues in adjustment policy in four countries in considerable detail.

Chapter 3 effects a transition toward more refined methods by first presenting a discussion of external shocks and modes of adjustment in one country (Kenya) using the analytical method of chapter 2 and then exploring in much further detail some of the ideas suggested by that discussion by resorting to partial equilibrium analysis. The latter method illuminates aspects of shocks and adjustment in Kenya, for example, the consequences of the 1976–7 boom in coffee and tea prices, the relative price shifts associated with higher oil prices, the resulting degree of import substitution, and the distributional implications of the pattern of output growth. However, at the same time, it points to its own limitations and emphasizes the need for a fully general equilibrium treatment of the underlying issues. This is offered for Kenya in chapter 8.

Chapter 4 develops the applied general equilibrium model that is imple-mented in each of four countries whose adjustment experience is analyzed in subsequent chapters of the book. The structure of the model is dictated by the need to study the macroeconomic, sectoral, and distributional consequences of actual and counterfactual policies. The chapter presents the common accounting structure underlying the models, including for example the number of sectors disaggregated on the production side, the categories of households identified for the distributional analysis, the working of factor markets, and the treatment of foreign trade and debt accumulation. It describes the technological and behavioral assumptions made (as well as some of the variations across the versions implemented for each of the countries), examines the role played by those assumptions in yielding the results found in the country studies, and indicates how the model may be used to set up experiments to analyze adjustment to external shocks. The presentation in the chapter also emphasizes implementability of the analytical framework in the expectation that others may replicate those techniques to investigate similar episodes elsewhere.

Chapter 5 presents the main economic characteristics of the four countries whose adjustment to the external shocks of 1973–4 and 1979–80 is subjected to detailed scrutiny in chapters 6 to 9. It discusses the kinds of questions that are asked in the policy simulations for each country, with a view to exploring the hypotheses put forward in chapter 2 in greater depth.

Chapter 6 examines the adjustment experience of India in the light of the perceptions shaped by twenty-five years of inward-looking industrialization. Could the stagnation of investment and growth in historical perspective be attributed to the external shocks and accommodating borrowing to which they gave rise? Or could they be explained by policy responses to exogenous weather-related shocks? How much contribution to economic growth and foreign indebtedness would have been made by a more investment-oriented adjustment, combined with supply-side anti-inflationary measures such as selective imports of wage goods and more vigorous nominal exchange-rate management?

Chapter 7 finds that Thailand grew rapidly during the period 1973–82 with little adjustment to changed world market conditions. Could this be attributed to the insulation of the economy from the adverse effects of external shocks by a series of fortuitous circumstances? Did those favorable temporary shocks obviate the need for adjustment to a more permanent change in the external environment? Or did Thailand simply postpone adjusting to the first oil shock by borrowing from abroad? Was the amount and the intertemporal phasing of investment and foreign borrowing appropriate in the light of the movement of international interest rates?

Chapter 8 asks what costs were imposed on the Kenyan economy in terms of consumption levels, the economy's growth potential, and the burden of external debt service as a result of the two oil price shocks of 1973 and 1979, as well as of the boom in coffee prices in 1975–7? To what extent was the volatility in some of the macroeconomic aggregates due to policy responses to terms-of-trade movements rather than to those movements themselves? What would have been the consequences of substituting domestic saving for external borrowing to finance historical levels of investment?

Chapter 9 studies policy responses to external shocks in Turkey. Could the strategy of growth without adjustment pursued in 1973–7 have been sustained in the absence of the second round of external shocks? How much difference would have been made to the macroeconomic aggregates if Turkey had adjusted through a combination of real exchange-rate devaluation, reduced public-sector spending, and higher private savings? To what extent could the high external borrowing requirements of the Turkish economy be attributed to oil price shocks and the concomitant slowdown in the OECD countries?

Chapter 10 synthesizes the findings from the comparative analysis of chapter 2 and the in-depth country studies of chapters 6 to 9. It ends with an answer to the question: how can the lessons of adjustment from the 1970s and early 1980s be adapted to fashion appropriate policy responses to future shocks emanating from the external environment facing oil-importing developing countries?

Notes

1 For an early assessment see Fried and Schultze (1975) and, subsequently, Cline (1981), Sachs (1981). A detailed analysis emphasizing the implications for developing-country adjustment is World Bank (1981a). The growing importance of oil in developing countries as a factor that would heighten their vulnerability to future oil price shocks was noted in Dunkerley (1979).
2 Thus, Gelb (1989) notes that the two oil price shocks "have dwarfed all other terms of trade movements in the postwar period."
3 See, for example, Marion and Svensson (1984), Svensson (1984). Analyses in models with quantity rationing are contained in Buffie (1986), Edwards and van Wijnbergen (1989).
4 See World Bank (1988a).

2 Shocks and adjustment: a comparative analysis

1 Introduction

Chapter 1 highlighted the main features of the world economy in the 1970s and early 1980s – oil price increases, stagflation in the OECD countries, and interest-rate increases.

This chapter studies the patterns of adjustment to those shocks in thirty-three developed countries over the period 1973–81. In doing so, it develops a common framework that imposes analytical order on the richness and diversity of individual country experience and that, by facilitating intercountry comparability, places individual country performance in comparative perspective. The analytical histories of shocks and adjustment so generated for individual countries and for groups of countries are used to draw general conclusions about patterns of adjustment to the external shocks of the 1970s and early 1980s. Those conclusions lay the groundwork for the investigations in subsequent chapters.

The approach taken in this chapter owes its stimulus to the pioneering studies of trade adjustment undertaken by Balassa (1981a, 1984). However, it generalizes that work in some important respects. Since this is best appreciated after a discussion of the approach developed here and the conclusions, the relationship of this chapter with Balassa's work is discussed in section 5 below.

2 The analytical framework

2.1 An open economy macroeconomic model

The framework used to measure external shocks and modes of adjustment is both consistent with open economy macroeconomic theory and simple enough to be empirically implementable in a large number of data-sparse developing countries. Proceeding heuristically,[1] define gross national income, inclusive of terms-of-trade changes as

$$Y = GNP + X\left(\frac{P_X}{eE} - 1\right) - M\left(\frac{P_M}{eE} - 1\right) \tag{2.1}$$

where

Y = gross national income
GNP = gross national product at market prices
X = exports of goods and non-factor services
M = imports of goods and non-factor services
P_X = export price index in local currency
P_M = import price index in local currency
e = exchange rate (units of local currency per dollar)
E = unit value index of manufactured exports fob from OECD countries (in dollars)

Hence

$$X_C = X\frac{P_X}{eE}$$

and

$$M_C = M\frac{P_M}{eE} \tag{2.2}$$

measure, respectively, the purchasing power of exports over manufactures exported by OECD countries and the purchasing cost of imports over manufactures exported by OECD countries. Thus (2.1) is a standard terms-of-trade correction, except that it is expressed in terms of an international numeraire to facilitate comparability across countries.

The national income identity may be written

$$C_p + C_g + I + X - M = GNP \tag{2.3}$$

where

C_p = private consumption
C_g = government consumption
I = investment

Substitute from (2.1) and (2.2) to get

$$C_p + C_g + I - Y = R \tag{2.4}$$

$$R = M_c - X_c \tag{2.5}$$

where R is the resource gap for a country, corrected for terms-of-trade changes.

The model developed here is demand driven[2] and moreover assumes that the country is unable to exert any influence over (1) its import and export prices, (2) growth in its principal trading partners, and (3) interest rates on external debt.

The determinants of the components of demand on the left-hand side of (2.3) are assumed to be as follows

$$C_p = \eta_p + c_p(Y - T) \tag{2.6}$$

$$C_g = \eta_g + c_g Y \tag{2.7}$$

$$T = \omega + t Y \tag{2.8}$$

$$M = \alpha + m Y \tag{2.9}$$

$$X = \beta + x Y^* \tag{2.10}$$

where

T = indirect taxes less subsidies
Y^* = GDP in trading partner countries

Equation (2.6) links private consumption to gross disposable income, while equations (2.7) to (2.9) link government consumption, taxes, and imports to gross national income. Equation (2.10) relates exports to income in partner countries.

Substitution of (2.6)–(2.8) in (2.4) yields

$$\eta_p + \eta_g - c_p\omega + I - sY = R \tag{2.11}$$

where $s = 1 - c_p(1 - t) - c_g$, the marginal propensity to save, while substitution of (2.2), (2.9), and (2.10) yields

$$R = \left[\alpha \frac{P_M}{eE} - (\beta + x Y^*) \frac{P_X}{eE} \right] + M \frac{P_M}{eE} Y \tag{2.12}$$

Equations (2.11) and (2.12) may, following the diagrammatic technique of Dornbusch (1980), be shown as in figure 2.1. Equation (2.11) is represented by the downward-sloping line with a (negative) slope of s. Since $C_p + C_g + I$ represents absorption, this schedule may be referred to as the excess absorption schedule. Equation (2.12) is represented by the upward-sloping line with a slope of $m \dfrac{P_M}{eE}$ and may be referred to as the resource gap schedule. Equilibrium is represented by the point A with income equaling Y_o and the resource gap equaling R_o, the two endogenous variables determined by the model. Variables exogenous to the model are

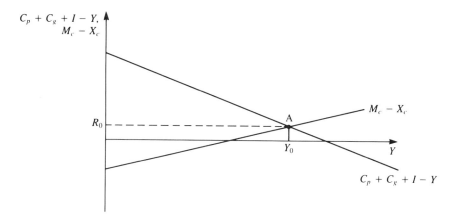

Figure 2.1 Equilibrium in the open economy

Import prices	$\dfrac{P_M}{eE}$
Export prices	$\dfrac{P_X}{eE}$
Trading partner income	Y^*
Export coefficients	(β, x)
Import coefficients	(α, m)
Private consumption coefficients	(η_p, c_p)
Public consumption coefficients	(η_g, c_g)
Tax coefficients	(ω, t)
Investment	I

Equations (2.11) and (2.12) and figure 2.1 can be used to deduce how the equilibrium of the open economy would change in response to a change in any of the exogenous variables. Thus, for example, an increase in $\dfrac{P_M}{eE}$, corresponding to a deterioration in the terms of trade, would cause the resource gap schedule both to shift up along the vertical axis and become steeper, while leaving the excess absorption schedule unchanged. This has the effect of lowering Y, the economy's income, and raising R, the resource gap, as figure 2.2 illustrates. Or, to take another example, a restraint in government consumption, captured by a fall in (η_g, c_g) would cause the excess absorption schedule to shift down along the vertical axis and become steeper (in absolute terms), while leaving the resource gap schedule unchanged, as shown in figure 2.3. This has the effect of lowering both Y and R.

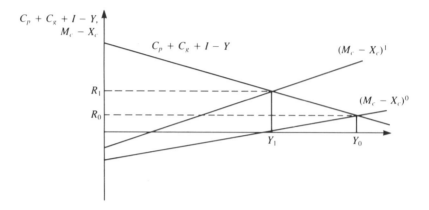

Figure 2.2 Effect of higher import prices

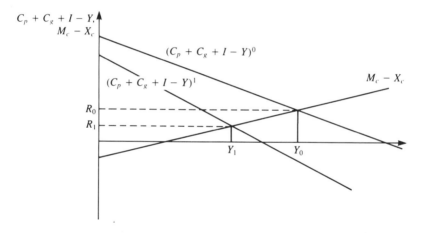

Figure 2.3 Effect of restraining government consumption

Table 2.1 summarizes the comparative statics results. The first eight rows of the table refer to movements in the resource gap schedule. These affect Y and R in opposite directions, with the effect on R (in absolute terms) being s times that on Y, where it will be recalled that s is the (absolute) slope of the excess absorption schedule which remains unchanged in the face of those movements. Rows 9–14 of table 2.1 refer to movements in the excess absorption schedule. These affect Y and R in the same direction, with the effect on R being $\bar{m} \left(= m \dfrac{P_M}{eE} \right)$ times that on Y, where $\bar{m}$ is the slope of the resource gap schedule.[3]

Table 2.1 *Comparative statics results*

	Exogenous variable (EV)	Effect on Y $\left[\dfrac{dY}{d(EV)}\right]$	Effect on R $\left[\dfrac{dR}{d(EV)}\right]$
1	$\dfrac{P_M}{eE}$	$-\dfrac{M}{s+\bar{m}}$	$\dfrac{sM}{s+\bar{m}}$
2	$\dfrac{P_x}{eE}$	$\dfrac{X}{s+\bar{m}}$	$-s\dfrac{X}{s+\bar{m}}$
3	Y^*	$\dfrac{\bar{x}}{s+\bar{m}}$	$-\dfrac{s\bar{x}}{s+\bar{m}}$
4	β	$\dfrac{(P_x/eE)}{s+\bar{m}}$	$-\dfrac{s(P_x/eE)}{s+\bar{m}}$
5	x	$\dfrac{(P_x/eE)Y^*}{s+\bar{m}}$	$-\dfrac{s(P_x/eE)Y^*}{s+\bar{m}}$
6	α	$-\dfrac{(P_M/eE)}{s+\bar{m}}$	$\dfrac{s(P_M/eE)}{s+\bar{m}}$
7	m	$-\dfrac{(P_M/eE)Y}{s+\bar{m}}$	$\dfrac{s(P_M/eE)Y}{s+\bar{m}}$
8	η_p	$\dfrac{1}{s+\bar{m}}$	$\dfrac{\bar{m}}{s+\bar{m}}$
9	C_p	$\dfrac{Y-T}{s+\bar{m}}$	$\dfrac{\bar{m}(Y-T)}{s+\bar{m}}$
10	η_g	$\dfrac{1}{s+\bar{m}}$	$\dfrac{\bar{m}}{s+\bar{m}}$
11	c_g	$\dfrac{Y}{s+\bar{m}}$	$\dfrac{\bar{m}Y}{s+\bar{m}}$
12	ω	$-\dfrac{c_pY}{s+\bar{m}}$	$\dfrac{\bar{m}c_pY}{s+\bar{m}}$
13	t	$-\dfrac{c_pY}{s+\bar{m}}$	$-\dfrac{\bar{m}c_pY}{s+\bar{m}}$
14	I	$\dfrac{1}{s+\bar{m}}$	$\dfrac{\bar{m}}{s+\bar{m}}$

Note: $\bar{m}=m\dfrac{P_M}{eE}$, $\bar{x}=x\dfrac{P_x}{eE}$.

2.2 *A shock-adjustment decomposition*

On using the results from the last column of table 2.1 the change in the resource gap consequent on small changes in the exogenous variables (EV) may be written

$$dR = \sum_i \frac{dR}{d(EV_i)} \cdot d(EV_i)$$

Application of this to the full list of exogenous variables together with some rearrangement of terms then yields

$$\overbrace{\left(\frac{sX}{s+\bar{m}}\right)\left[-d\left(\frac{P_X}{eE}\right)\right]}^{A} + \overbrace{\left(\frac{sM}{s+\bar{m}}\right)d\left(\frac{P_M}{eE}\right)}^{B} + \overbrace{\left(\frac{s\bar{x}}{s+\bar{m}}\right)(-dY^*)}^{C} =$$

$$\overbrace{\left[\frac{s(P_X/eE)}{s+\bar{m}}\right](d\beta + Y^*dx)}^{D} + \overbrace{\left[\frac{s(P_M/eE)}{s+\bar{m}}\right](-d\alpha - Ydm)}^{E} \tag{2.13}$$

$$+ \overbrace{\left(\frac{\bar{m}}{s+\bar{m}}\right)(-d\eta_p - (Y-T)dc_p)}^{F} + \overbrace{\left(\frac{\bar{m}}{s+\bar{m}}\right)(d\eta_g - Ydc_g)}^{G}$$

$$+ \overbrace{\left(\frac{\bar{m}c_p}{s+\bar{m}}\right)(d\omega + Ydt)}^{H} + \overbrace{\left(\frac{\bar{m}}{s+\bar{m}}\right)(-dI)}^{I} + \overbrace{dR}^{J}$$

where the various terms may be characterized as follows:

A   Export price effect
B   Import price effect   } External shocks
C   Recession-induced effect

D   Export expansion
E   Import substitution
F   Private resource mobilization
G   Public consumption restraint } Modes of adjustment
H   Tax intensification
I   Investment slowdown
J   Additional external financing

Equation (2.13) is a rearrangement of the determinants of changes in the resource gap into "external shocks" (A–C) and "modes of adjustment" (D–J). It may be noted that shifts in the intercept and slope parameters in equations (2.6) to (2.10) have been identified with modes of adjustment.

The macroeconomic model described here is estimated over the 1963–81 period for each country and the results used to generate a shock-adjustment decomposition analogous to equation (2.13). However, since (2.13) is valid only for small changes, the version implemented in empirical work and derived in appendix I to this chapter is an adaptation which is applicable to large changes as well. To that end, the actual equilibrium (Y,R) in the years 1974–81 is compared to a post-1973 counterfactual situation defined by postulating (1) that relative prices $\left(\dfrac{P_M}{eE}, \dfrac{P_X}{eE}\right)$ and real interest rates after 1973 would have stayed at their average level for the years 1971–3,[4] (2) that the investment income ratio $\dfrac{I}{Y}$ after 1973 would have stayed at its average value for the years 1971–3, and (3) the responsiveness of consumption, imports, exports, and taxes to income and the growth of income in the OECD trading partner countries (the coefficients $\eta_p, c_p, \eta_g, c_g, \omega, t, \alpha, m, \beta, x$) after 1973 would have stayed at the values historically estimated for them over the 1963–73 period. Thus, for example, in the large change analogue of equation (2.13) used in empirical implementation[5] $d\left(\dfrac{P_M}{eE}\right)$ refers to the difference between actual $\dfrac{P_M}{eE}$ and its average value for 1971–3, while dm refers to the difference between the m estimated for 1963–81 and that for 1963–73.

3 External shocks and modes of adjustment

3.1 *External shocks*

Equation (2.13) defines external shocks as comprising (1) international price effects, the sum of export price and import price effects (items A and B respectively), (2) recession-induced effects (item C), and (3) net interest-rate effects.[6]

International price effects

International price effects measure the balance-of-payments impact of changes in an economy's terms of trade relative to the counterfactual, and are the sum of the *export price effect* and the *import price effect*. The export price effect measures the net impact of a fall in the purchasing power of exports over manufactures exported by the OECD countries. The import price effect measures the net impact of a rise in the purchasing cost of imports in terms of manufactures exported by the OECD countries.

When measured against a 1971–3 base as a percentage of GNP,

international price effects averaged on an annual basis over the 1974–81 period ranged from an extremely unfavorable 7.5 percent in Chile and 5.9 percent in Uruguay through a somewhat less unfavorable 3.5 percent in Malawi, 2.9 percent in the Philippines, and 2.6 percent in Taiwan to a moderately favorable 3.5 percent in Malaysia and 3.7 percent in Tunisia to an extremely favorable 9.8 percent in Nigeria and 14.2 percent in Indonesia. While import price effects were particularly unfavorable in Kenya (5.1 percent), Nigeria (5 percent), Singapore (4.4 percent), Uruguay (3.4 percent), and Taiwan (3.1 percent), the magnitude of export price effects was extremely unfavorable in Chile (4.7 percent) and Uruguay (2.5 percent), on the one hand, and very favorable in Nigeria (-11.8 percent) and Indonesia (-13 percent), on the other.

Recession-induced effects

Recession-induced effects on the balance of payments occur due to the shortfall in an economy's exports as a result of a slowdown in the rate of growth in GNP in principal trading partners *vis-à-vis* historical trends. Recession-induced effects were generally positive, ranging as a percentage of GNP from 0.1 percent in Spain and Uruguay through 1.4 percent in Korea and 1.9 percent in Taiwan to 3.7 percent in Indonesia.

Net interest-rate effects

Net interest-rate effects are twofold. The payments effect measures the impact on the balance of payments of an increase in *real* interest rates (in terms of manufactures exported by OECD countries) payable on a country's debt. From this figure must be subtracted the receipts effect, that is, the impact on the balance of payments of an increase in *real* interest rates (in terms of manufactures exported by OECD countries) earned by a country's interest-bearing assets.

Net interest-rate effects, when measured *vis-à-vis* real interest rates prevailing in 1971–3, ranged as a percentage of GNP from -0.6 percent in Mali and -0.2 percent in Kenya to 1.8 percent in Jamaica, 2 percent in Korea, and 2.5 percent in Bolivia. Payments effects were particularly important in Bolivia, Korea, and Singapore; the payments effect on short-term debt was important in Singapore and, to a lesser extent, in Portugal.

3.2 *Modes of adjustment*

The theory that informs our interpretation of shocks and adjustment is briefly as follows.[7] A permanent increase in the price of imported intermediate goods such as fuel, a contraction in export markets, or an increase in the rate of interest on external debt, requires an importing country to reduce its absorption, i.e., consumption and investment, in relation to income. It will be recollected that the excess of imports over exports, i.e., the trade deficit, equals the excess of absorption over income. If no additional external financing were available, an assumption to which we return below, the gap between absorption and income would have to be reduced to no more than that prevailing before the price increase. This may be effected by reducing *present* consumption, i.e., promoting savings, or by reducing investment, which would normally have added to *future* consumption[8] and by doing so in both the private and public sectors. Such a policy, by restraining absorption, serves to restore external balance and is usually accomplished by tightening a country's monetary and fiscal stance.

An absorption policy is sufficient to pay for more expensive oil or for debt servicing. But by cutting demand for non-tradeables as well as tradeables it can cause a recession unless wages and prices are flexible downwards. If, however, the downward rigidity applies to nominal rather than real magnitudes, a potential recession may be averted and internal balance restored through a "switching policy" that diverts domestic resources into and domestic demands away from tradeables, namely, exportables and import substitutes, *vis-à-vis* non-tradeables. An exchange-rate devaluation is an example of such a policy that can bring about export expansion and import substitution, raising the prices of tradeables compared to non-tradeables. Adjustment therefore calls for a combination of absorption and, in general, switching policies. Moreover, since both sets of policies reduce the resource gap, the amount of disabsorption required of the absorption policy can be expected to be less than if a switching policy were not also called for.[9]

Additional external financing makes possible less restraint in consumption and investment today at the expense of more restraint in the future when the credit must be repaid. The extent to which it should be used therefore depends on the country's judgments regarding the value of more restraint in the future compared to the present, the terms on which the additional funds are available, and the uses to which they are put.[10]

This discussion suggests that countries unfavorably affected by external shocks could respond through (1) trade adjustment, which includes export expansion and import substitution, (2) domestic resource mobilization, which includes restraining private as well as public consumption, (3) investment slowdown, and (4) additional external financing. In what follows, we measure these modes of adjustment for each of the thirty-three countries. Some caveats may usefully be entered. *First*, as with external shocks, all modes of adjustment are measured as deviations from the same counterfactual as described above. This implies that the method does not formally distinguish between the effects of changes undertaken in response to external shocks from those arising due to actions that might have been undertaken in any case. *Second*, changes in imported input prices, in addition to their transfer implications, also require a country's structure of production to be adapted to the new relative factor prices. Since oil is an intermediate good, a rise in its price reduces aggregate output and increases the price level. This is a supply-side effect.[11] Its recessionary effects need to be taken into account in designing an absorption policy. So too must the fact that a devaluation-induced switching policy further raises the price of oil and the associated negative effect on aggregate output. Data limitations for most countries preclude the method developed in this chapter from incorporating a supply side capable of reflecting that set of considerations; this is however done in chapter 3 and in the country studies presented in chapters 6 to 9.[12] *Finally*, the method does not distinguish between permanent and temporary shocks. The latter usually call for borrowing to smooth consumption patterns as between present and future, rather than absorption and switching policies,[13] paying due attention as before to the costs and benefits of borrowing. It is necessary to bear the above remarks in mind in reviewing the experience of individual countries. Nevertheless, we shall see that this methodology, which empirically implements the basic ideas of international economics to look at adjustment in a simple macroeconomic framework in a large number of developing countries, yields a useful analytical history of developments in the 1970s and early 1980s. The examples provided below have been drawn from a list of the twenty-four out of thirty-three countries in the sample investigated that suffered rather than benefited from external shocks during the 1974–81 period. Parenthetical references in the ensuing discussion are to equation (2.13).

Trade adjustment
Trade adjustment is the sum of *export expansion* and *import substitution*.

Export expansion
Export expansion (item D) is the increase in the responsiveness of exports to changes in GNP growth in principal trading partners. Of the countries to which the analysis underlying this chapter has been applied, those in which export expansion played a prominent role, include Chile, Korea, and Taiwan.

Import substitution
Import substitution (item E) is the reduction in the responsiveness of the economy's import demand to income. Examples of adjustment through significant import substitution are Brazil, Jamaica, and Yugoslavia.

Resource mobilization

Domestic resource mobilization measures the balance-of-payments impact of improved savings performance as defined below. It may be broken down into its private and public components. *Private resource mobilization* (item F) is the reduction in the responsiveness of private consumption to income. This was important in Honduras, Morocco, Singapore, and Yugoslavia. *Public resource mobilization* has two parts: (1) *public consumption restraint* (item G), or the reduction in the responsiveness of public consumption to income, and (2) *tax intensification* (item H), or the increase in the responsiveness to income of indirect taxes less subsidies. This term therefore ignores any changes in the direct tax effort, an omission that may be justified on grounds of their relative unimportance in developing economies. El Salvador, Honduras, and Singapore were characterized by this mode of adjustment.

Investment slowdown

Investment slowdown (item I) measures the balance-of-payments impact of a reduction in the ratio of investment to income compared to that prevailing during the period 1971–3. This was a dominant mode of adjustment in Jamaica, Kenya, and Singapore.

Net additional external financing

Net additional external financing (item J) measures changes in gross additional external financing (defined as capital flows, reserves, and transfers and services net of interest payments,[14] deflated by a price index of manufactures exported by OECD countries) less changes in net interest payments resulting from changes in real net debt.[15] This measure played an important role in El Salvador, Honduras, Morocco, and Portugal.

4 Patterns of adjustment

The countries analyzed in this chapter and listed in table 2.2 span a broad range in terms of 1973 per capita GNP: from $70 in Mali to $1,830 in Spain. Fourteen of these, in italics in table 2.2, may be considered semi-industrial, with the share of manufacturing in GNP in 1973 being 20 percent or more in all but Turkey and the share of manufacturing in merchandise exports being 15 percent or more in all but Chile and the Philippines; the remaining countries may be considered less developed. While the above structural characteristics allowed the semi-industrial countries greater potential flexibility in adjustment compared to the less-developed countries, some of which had undiversified patterns of output and exports, it will be seen that the policies pursued in response to external shocks were important.

Table 2.2 *Composition of country groups*

Group 1	*Chile*, Costa Rica, *Korea, Philippines, Singapore, Taiwan*
Group 2	*Argentina, Brazil*, Guatemala, Honduras, India, Kenya, Malawi, Mali, Thailand, *Turkey, Uruguay*
Group 3	Jamaica, *Portugal, Yugoslavia*
Group 4	El Salvador, *Mexico*, Morocco, *Spain*
Group 5	Benin, Bolivia, *Colombia*, Indonesia, Ivory Coast, Malaysia, Niger, Nigeria, Tunisia

Note: The semi-industrial countries are italicized in the table.

Twenty-four of the thirty-three countries considered here suffered adverse external shocks during the period 1974–81. Responses to those shocks varied considerably, a feature that is worth bearing in mind in the following discussion. To impose a measure of analytical order on the richness and diversity of experience, however, it was decided to subject the quantitative profiles of adjustment to statistical analysis. The results are as follows.

First, there is no statistically significant relationship, as measured by the Spearman coefficient of rank correlation, between external shocks expressed as a proportion of GNP and the rate of growth of GNP over the 1973–81 period. This does not imply that external shocks were not important for oil-importing developing countries. Growth rates in 1973–81 were on average lower than in 1963–73; indeed, the studies in chapters 6 to 9 will show that an absence of external shocks would have left affected countries better off in terms of GNP and other macroeconomic indicators. What the present finding suggests is that differences in growth performance across adversely affected countries must be sought not in the magnitude of external shocks but more in the conduct of economic management.

Second, this presumption regarding the association of economic policies with performance is supported by a Spearman coefficient of rank correlation of 0.43, significant at the 5 percent level, between export expansion expressed as a proportion of total adjustment and economic growth in 1973–81. This result is due to the comparatively strong growth performance and relative reliance on export expansion in Singapore, Taiwan, and Korea, and, to a lesser extent, Thailand and the Philippines, and also to the comparatively weak growth and export performance of countries such as Jamaica and Portugal. This result, though derived from a broader analytical framework, supports the findings of Balassa (1981a, 1985) on the positive consequences of export-expanding adjustment on economic growth. No significant relationship was however found between growth performance and any other mode of adjustment.

Third, turning to relationships between modes of adjustment, the rank correlation coefficient between export expansion and public resource mobilization, where both are expressed as a proportion of total adjustment, is 0.56, which is significant at the 1 percent level. This may be explained by the export expansion and public resource mobilization performance of Singapore, Korea, Taiwan, the Philippines, Costa Rica, and, to a somewhat lesser extent, Chile.[16] It is also due to weakness in export expansion and public resource mobilization in Jamaica, Portugal, and Yugoslavia, as well as in Morocco and Spain.

Fourth, a Spearman coefficient of rank correlation of -0.53, also significant at the 1 percent level, obtains between import substitution and additional real external financing, where both variables are again expressed as a proportion of total adjustment. There are two reasons for this result. The first is the import booms which were underwritten by external borrowing in Mexico, Morocco, and El Salvador, as well as Mali, and the second arises because of tightened quantitative import restrictions in countries such as Yugoslavia, where additional external financing was modest, and Jamaica, where additional external financing proved increasingly unavailable, as well as, to a somewhat lesser extent, Brazil and Malawi. This aspect of import substitution as practiced in a number of the countries under consideration, i.e. increased resort to quantitative restrictions as opposed to prices and exchange rates, tended to limit imports to essential material inputs and machinery for which domestically produced substitutes were generally unavailable, thereby making import substitutes virtually non-tradeable. Such a policy response, to the extent it sacrificed flexibility in favor of immediate balance-of-payments adjustment, helps explain the lack of association between import substitution in response to external shocks and economic growth, notwithstanding the theoretical finding of section 2 that import substitution, like export expansion, boosts income while reducing the resource gap.

Fifth, the Spearman coefficient between public resource mobilization and investment slowdown, where both are expressed as a proportion of total adjustment, is -0.46, which is significant at the 5 percent level. Once again, there are two patterns of responses that help explain this result. Countries such as Mali and Jamaica and, to a lesser extent, Portugal and Spain saw negative public resource mobilization aggravate the balance-of-payments effect of external shocks and resorted to a slowdown in investment as a prominent form of adjustment. In contrast, Costa Rica, Honduras, Mexico, and El Salvador witnessed improvements in public resource mobilization performance and a rise in their investment-to-income ratios.

Finally, the Spearman coefficient of rank correlation assumes a value of

−0.46, significant at the 5 percent level, between private resource mobilization and investment slowdown, with both variables being expressed as a proportion of total adjustment. In this case, Jamaica and Yugoslavia offer examples of an investment slowdown together with negative private resource mobilization, while, as before, Costa Rica, Honduras, Mexico, and Morocco were able to boost their investment ratios and exhibit positive private resource mobilization.

The empirical regularities uncovered by the cross-country analysis suggest that the twenty-four unfavorably affected countries may be divided into four groups depending on the characteristics of their adjustment. The remaining nine countries that experienced favorable external shocks comprise a fifth group. The countries belonging to each group are listed in table 2.2. The shock-adjustment profiles for the groups are shown in table 2.3 and those of the unfavorably affected individual countries in tables 2.4–2.7.

Group 1 (Chile, Costa Rica, Korea, Philippines, Singapore, and Taiwan) adjusted principally through *export expansion and public resource mobilization*. Group 2 (Argentina, Brazil, Guatemala, Honduras, India, Kenya, Malawi, Mali, Thailand, Turkey, and Uruguay) relied on either *export expansion or public resource mobilization*, whereas Group 3 (Jamaica, Portugal, and Yugoslavia) was characterized by *import substitution and negative public resource mobilization*. Group 4 (El Salvador, Mexico, Morocco, and Spain) resorted to *financing without domestic adjustment*. Finally, Group 5 (Benin, Bolivia, Colombia, Indonesia, Ivory Coast, Malaysia, Niger, Nigeria, and Tunisia) experienced *favorable external shocks*. The (unweighted) average shock adjustment figures for the 1974–81 period are shown for the five groups in table 2.3.

Group 1 Export expansion and public resource mobilization
The average shock was highest for Group 1 at 3.97 percent of GNP, with Chile, Korea, Taiwan, and the Philippines among the four most unfavorably affected within the entire sample of thirty-three countries. International price effects accounted for roughly 60 percent of total shocks, with the recession-induced and net interest-rate effects contributing equally to the remainder. All economies of the group resorted heavily to export expansion, which exceeded external shocks by more than one-third, and to public resource mobilization, of which the principal component was tax intensification. Together, export expansion and public resource mobilization accounted for 154 percent of external shocks. Import substitution was significantly negative everywhere except in Costa Rica, especially during the later years of the period. Whereas Chile, the Philippines, and Taiwan relied on substantial additional external financing and stepped up their

ratio of investment to GNP, Korea sustained an investment boom with comparatively limited recourse to additional external resources. In contrast, Singapore adopted a somewhat contractionary package, with a cut in the share of investment and real repayment of borrowed funds, the latter being true in Costa Rica as well. The ratio of external financing to external shocks was higher in 1974–81 as compared to 1974–8, but was nevertheless very modest in relation to the other country groups. The highest growth rates among the twenty-four unfavorably affected countries were recorded by Taiwan, Korea, and Singapore, with the Philippines being the sixth most rapidly growing country in the 1973–81 period.

Group 2 Export expansion or public resource mobilization
International price effects accounted for roughly 80 percent of external shocks for Group 2. This group occupies a position somewhat intermediate between Groups 1 and 3 in terms of adjustment characteristics. Three broad patterns of adjustment may be distinguished. *First*, Argentina, Guatemala, India, Mali, and Uruguay resorted to export expansion while exhibiting negative import substitution and negative public resource mobilization, which was significantly worse in the years 1979–81 compared to 1974–8. *Second*, and somewhat contrastingly, Honduras and Kenya adjusted through a combination of import substitution and public resource mobilization, with export expansion turning negative. *Third*, the remaining countries – Brazil, Malawi, Thailand, and Turkey – relied on a combination of export expansion and import substitution, with negative public resource mobilization aggravating the balance-of-payments impact of disturbances from the international environment. For the group as a whole, negative public resource mobilization added 40 percent to external shocks. There was significant additional external financing, especially in countries such as Honduras, Mali, Guatemala, Turkey, Kenya, and Thailand, with this mode of adjustment exceeding external shocks by over 20 percent for the group as a whole. There was some increase in the share of investment in GNP in all countries except Kenya, Malawi, and Mali.

Group 3 Import substitution and negative public resource mobilization
Although the shocks experienced by Group 3 were less unfavorable than those affecting Groups 1 and 2, their composition was rather different. International price effects accounted for less than 30 percent of external shocks, whereas net interest-rate effects exceeded 55 percent of shocks, largely because of their relative importance in Jamaica. The adverse balance-of-payments impact of negative public resource mobilization was

Table 2.3 *Balance-of-payments effects of external shocks and modes of adjustment, 1974–8 and 1974–81 averages (percentage of local currency GNP)*

	Group 1		Group 2		Group 3		Group 4		Group 5	
	1974–8	1974–81	1974–8	1974–81	1974–8	1974–81	1974–8	1974–81	1974–8	1974–81
I *External shocks*										
1 *International price effects*										
a Export price effect	0.41	0.18	−0.27	−0.08	−0.99	−0.89	−1.41	−1.25	−4.66	−5.69
b Import price effect	1.27	2.25	1.72	2.00	1.34	1.51	1.00	0.75	1.13	1.17
Sum (=1a+1b)	1.68	2.43	1.45	1.91	0.35	0.61	−0.41	−0.50	−3.53	−4.52
2 *Recession-induced effect*	0.70	0.76	0.30	0.30	0.34	0.39	0.57	0.66	0.65	0.93
3 *Net interest-rate effect*										
a Payments effect										
i Medium and long term	0.11	0.68	−0.09	0.18	0.05	0.72	0.06	0.45	0.10	0.75
ii Short term	−0.01	0.87	−0.01	0.16	0.00	0.40	−0.03	0.22	−0.01	0.15
Sum (=i+ii)	0.10	1.54	−0.10	0.34	0.04	1.12	0.03	0.68	0.09	0.90
b Receipts effect	0.01	0.76	−0.01	0.09	−0.10	−0.15	0.00	0.06	0.00	0.28
Difference (=3a−3b)	0.10	0.78	−0.09	0.25	0.14	1.27	0.04	0.62	0.09	0.63
Total shock (=1+2+3)	2.48	3.97	1.66	2.47	0.83	2.28	0.20	0.77	−2.79	−2.96

II Modes of adjustment

1 Trade adjustment										
a Export expansion	3.70	5.45	0.57	1.11	−2.19	−2.08	0.31	0.15	0.89	0.83
b Import substitution	−0.48	−1.61	0.50	0.48	1.31	1.30	−1.77	−2.00	−3.71	−4.68
Sum (=1a+1b)	3.22	3.84	1.07	1.59	−0.88	−0.78	−1.46	−1.86	−2.82	−3.85
2 Resource mobilization										
a Private	1.08	0.54	−0.61	−0.44	−1.53	−0.96	0.72	0.65	0.98	1.27
b Public										
i Public consump. restraint	−0.09	0.19	−0.69	−0.88	−2.93	−4.04	−0.61	−0.87	−0.25	0.16
ii Tax intensification	0.49	0.49	−0.10	−0.12	0.28	0.39	−0.25	−0.24	−0.86	−1.14
Sum (=i+ii)	0.40	0.68	−0.79	−1.00	−2.65	−3.64	−0.86	−1.11	−0.61	−0.98
Sum (=2a+2b)	1.48	1.22	−1.39	−1.44	−4.18	−4.61	−0.14	−0.46	0.37	0.29
3 Investment slowdown	−1.13	−1.91	−0.46	−0.69	2.48	2.78	−1.60	−0.84	−1.31	−1.74
4 Net additional ext. financing	−1.09	0.83	2.45	3.01	3.41	4.88	3.39	3.93	0.97	2.34
Total (=1+2+3+4)	2.48	3.97	1.66	2.47	0.83	2.28	0.20	0.77	−2.79	−2.96

Note: The adjustment characteristics of the groups are described in the text.
The countries included in each group are listed in table 2.2.
Subtotals in each column may not add due to rounding.

Table 2.4 *External shocks and modes of adjustment, 1974–8 and 1974–81 averages: Group 1 countries*

		(1) Export price effect	(2) Import price effect	(3) International price effect (1)+(2)	(4) Recession induced effect	(5) Interest rate effect	(6) External shocks (3)+(4)+(5)	(7) Export expansion	(8) Import substitution	(9) Private resource mobilization	(10) Public resource mobilization	(11) Investment slow-down	(12) Additional external financing
		As a percentage of GNP						As a proportion of external shocks					
Korea	74 78	0.47	0.70	1.17	1.14	-0.17	2.14	3.60	-1.01	0.79	0.04	-1.39	-1.03
	74 81	0.32	1.31	1.63	1.35	2.01	4.99	1.59	-0.63	0.37	0.07	-0.91	0.52
Taiwan	74 78	0.17	1.72	1.89	1.76	0.21	3.86	1.66	-0.33	-0.17	0.11	-0.62	0.35
	74 81	-0.46	3.06	2.60	1.90	0.32	4.82	1.63	-0.57	-0.23	0.11	-0.56	0.62
Singapore	74 78	-1.48	1.60	0.12	0.14	0.14	0.40	4.53	2.00	10.35	3.00	7.98	-26.88
	74 81	-4.08	4.41	0.33	0.31	-0.03	0.61	3.67	-1.74	2.93	3.39	4.41	-17.87
Chile	74 78	3.42	1.63	5.05	0.15	0.44	5.64	0.76	-0.02	0.08	0.06	-0.18	0.30
	74 81	4.66	2.85	7.51	0.21	1.28	9.00	0.81	-0.17	-0.10	0.06	-0.28	0.68
Philippines	74 78	-0.45	2.72	2.27	0.54	-0.08	2.73	0.61	-0.26	-0.10	0.01	-0.78	1.52
	74 81	0.16	2.76	2.92	0.48	0.97	4.37	0.77	-0.36	-0.08	0.03	-0.54	1.17
Costa Rica	74 78	0.33	-0.75	-0.42	0.47	0.04	0.09	3.89	5.89	13.22	3.67	-16.56	-9.33
	74 81	0.46	-0.87	-0.41	0.33	0.15	0.07	2.63	5.13	25.13	5.13	-25.00	-12.13
Group 1	74 78	0.41	1.27	1.68	0.70	0.10	2.48	1.49	-0.19	0.44	0.16	-0.46	-0.44
	74 81	0.18	2.25	2.43	0.76	0.78	3.97	1.37	-0.40	0.14	0.17	-0.48	0.21

Table 2.5 External shocks and modes of adjustment, 1974–8 and 1974–81 averages: Group 2 countries

		(1) Export price effect	(2) Import price effect	(3) International price effect (1)+(2)	(4) Recession-induced effect	(5) Interest-rate effect	(6) External shocks (3)+(4)+(5)	(7) Export expansion	(8) Import substitution	(9) Private resource mobilization	(10) Public resource mobilization	(11) Investment slow-down	(12) Additional external financing
		As a percentage of GNP						As a proportion of external shocks					
Argentina	74 78	0.86	0.55	1.41	0.22	-0.02	1.61	0.96	0.30	0.71	-0.57	0.05	-0.45
	74 81	0.82	0.77	1.59	0.12	0.56	2.27	1.14	-0.04	0.47	-0.47	-0.07	-0.04
Uruguay	74 78	2.65	2.50	5.15	0.04	0.10	5.29	0.73	-0.05	-0.20	-0.26	-0.36	1.16
	74 81	2.51	3.43	5.94	0.05	0.55	6.54	0.75	-0.11	0.07	-0.31	-0.48	1.19
Brazil	74 78	-0.47	0.73	0.26	0.09	0.06	0.41	0.46	1.39	1.15	-1.83	-1.34	1.17
	74 81	-0.53	0.79	0.26	0.07	0.18	0.51	0.08	2.18	0.16	-1.65	-0.24	0.45
Turkey	74 78	-0.11	1.90	1.79	0.26	0.00	2.05	-0.01	-0.35	-0.03	-0.12	-0.76	2.27
	74 81	-0.32	2.44	2.12	0.24	0.41	2.77	0.03	0.16	0.21	-0.32	-0.65	1.58
Guatemala	74 78	-0.90	1.58	0.68	0.41	-0.12	0.97	0.81	-1.48	0.20	0.51	-1.81	2.77
	74 81	-0.77	2.09	1.32	0.49	0.09	1.90	0.35	-0.65	0.29	-0.35	-0.63	1.98
Honduras	74 78	-1.37	0.46	-0.91	0.47	0.04	-0.40	4.10	0.02	-0.37	0.56	6.85	-10.15
	74 81	-0.72	0.04	-0.68	0.23	1.35	0.90	-0.91	0.03	2.89	0.29	-4.92	3.62
India	74 78	0.35	1.34	1.69	0.17	-0.15	1.71	0.96	-0.17	0.02	-0.02	-0.01	0.22
	74 81	0.72	1.45	2.17	0.18	-0.04	2.31	0.93	-0.50	0.01	-0.07	-0.01	0.60
Kenya	74 78	-3.05	4.85	1.80	0.18	-0.19	1.79	-0.45	1.03	-1.63	-0.05	1.10	0.98
	74 81	-2.75	5.10	2.35	0.24	-0.24	2.35	-0.51	0.83	-1.45	0.02	1.03	1.09
Malawi	74 78	0.07	2.09	2.16	0.56	-0.22	2.50	0.09	1.61	-1.14	-0.12	0.48	0.28
	74 81	0.93	2.55	3.48	0.49	-0.13	3.84	0.25	1.05	-1.01	-0.01	0.23	0.47
Mali	74 78	0	0.76	0.76	0.16	-0.49	0.43	-0.05	-0.56	-0.65	-11.98	2.86	11.37
	74 81	-0.04	0.63	0.59	0.22	-0.55	0.26	0.73	-0.77	-1.30	-20.92	4.62	18.69
Thailand	74 78	-0.96	2.17	1.21	0.70	-0.01	1.90	0.51	0.85	-0.78	-0.04	-0.49	0.95
	74 81	-0.75	2.67	1.92	0.98	0.57	3.47	0.78	0.30	-0.52	-0.12	-0.37	0.94
Group 2	74 78	-0.27	1.72	1.45	0.30	-0.09	1.66	0.34	0.30	0.37	-0.48	-0.28	1.48
	74 81	-0.08	2.00	1.92	0.30	0.25	2.47	0.45	0.19	-0.18	-0.40	-0.28	1.22

Table 2.6 *External shocks and modes of adjustment, 1974–8 and 1974–81 averages: Group 3 countries*

		(1) Export price effect	(2) Import price effect	(3) International price effect (1)+(2)	(4) Recession-induced effect	(5) Interest-rate effect	(6) External shocks (3)+(4)+(5)	(7) Export expansion	(8) Import substitution	(9) Private resource mobilization	(10) Public resource mobilization	(11) Investment slow-down	(12) Additional external financing
		As a percentage of GNP						As a proportion of external shocks					
Portugal	74 78	0.01	1.88	1.89	0.35	-0.10	2.14	-1.44	0.50	-3.07	-1.49	0.58	5.93
	74 81	0.30	2.06	2.36	0.39	1.58	4.33	-0.54	0.26	-1.33	-0.95	0.29	3.27
Yugoslavia	74 78	-0.57	1.06	0.49	0.40	0.03	0.92	-0.14	1.13	1.57	-0.26	-1.18	-0.10
	74 81	-0.95	1.55	0.60	0.45	0.39	1.44	-0.13	0.86	1.42	-0.49	-0.73	0.06
Jamaica	74 78	-2.41	1.09	-1.32	0.26	0.49	-0.57	5.88	-3.18	-0.98	7.93	-12.81	4.16
	74 81	-2.04	0.91	-1.13	0.33	1.82	1.02	-3.60	1.49	0.78	-5.92	8.07	0.34
Group 3	74 78	-0.99	1.34	0.35	0.34	0.14	0.83	-2.64	1.58	-1.84	-3.19	2.99	4.11
	74 81	-0.89	1.51	0.62	0.39	1.27	2.28	-0.92	0.57	-0.42	-1.60	1.22	2.15

Table 2.7 *External shocks and modes of adjustment, 1974–8 and 1974–81 averages: Group 4 countries*

		(1) Export price effect	(2) Import price effect	(3) International price effect (1)+(2)	(4) Recession-induced effect	(5) Interest-rate effect	(6) External shocks (3)+(4)+(5)	(7) Export expansion	(8) Import substitution	(9) Private resource mobilization	(10) Public resource mobilization	(11) Investment slow-down	(12) Additional external financing
		As a percentage of GNP						As a proportion of external shocks					
Mexico	74 78	0.05	-0.42	-0.37	0.41	0.04	0.08	11.37	-3.88	9.88	-1.25	-6.63	-8.50
	74 81	-1.29	-0.30	-1.59	0.41	1.28	0.10	14.45	-34.63	2.00	0.73	-4.64	23.09
Spain	74 78	-0.16	1.22	1.06	0.11	0.39	1.56	-0.08	-0.16	-0.29	-0.69	0.00	2.22
	74 81	-0.32	1.45	1.13	0.05	0.41	1.59	-0.03	-0.25	-0.32	-0.82	0.28	2.14
El Salvador	74 78	-3.44	0.95	-2.49	1.33	-0.06	-1.22	-0.81	2.12	0.25	-1.78	2.61	-1.39
	74 81	-1.65	-0.50	-2.15	2.00	0.67	0.52	-0.10	-3.29	-1.56	3.06	-1.73	4.60
Morocco	74 78	-1.89	2.22	0.33	0.11	-0.13	0.31	-3.09	-7.19	12.22	-14.22	-9.81	23.13
	74 81	-1.74	2.33	0.59	0.17	0.11	0.87	-1.03	-2.41	4.24	-5.55	-2.77	8.52
Group 4	74 78	1.41	1.00	0.41	0.57	0.03	0.19	1.63	-9.32	3.79	-4.53	-8.42	17.48
	74 81	-1.25	0.75	-0.50	0.66	0.61	0.77	0.19	-2.60	0.84	-1.44	-1.09	5.10

more than one-and-a-half times as large as that of external shocks in this group with this effect being extremely strong in Jamaica and, to a lesser extent, in Portugal. Import substitution played a dominant role in all of the countries in Group 3 with Jamaica and Yugoslavia being among the five countries which made the heaviest use of this mode of adjustment. As previously noted, this involved increased reliance on quantitative import restrictions in Jamaica and Portugal. Export expansion was significantly negative in all three countries. External financing was much more important than in Groups 1 and 2 but much less so in the later years of the period. The average, however, conceals marked intercountry differences: although external financing played a prominent role in Portugal, it was much less important in Jamaica and quite modest in Yugoslavia. Jamaica and Portugal were among the five slowest growing countries within the twenty-four adversely affected by external shocks.

Group 4 Financing without domestic adjustment
External shocks averaged 0.77 percent of GNP for Group 4 countries. Recession-induced and net interest-rate effects accounted for one and two-thirds times this figure, principally because of their overwhelming importance relative to external shocks in El Salvador and Mexico. Additional net external financing was more than five times as important as external shocks for the group as a whole, with the four constituent countries being among the seven where additional external financing was the most dominant mode of adjustment among the twenty-four countries unfavorably affected by external shocks. Table 2.2 clearly indicates the virtual lack of domestic adjustment across the board. Export expansion was negative except in Mexico (because of petroleum) and especially in Morocco and El Salvador. A major import and investment boom was underway in Morocco, and, in relation to external shocks, in El Salvador. Public resource mobilization was positive in El Salvador but was more than offset by worsening performance in the other countries, expecially Morocco and Spain.

Group 5 Favorably affected countries
The countries of Group 5 experienced favorable shocks usually because they had been exporters of petroleum or of other primary commodities, so that the boom in prices in the mid 1970s allowed them to benefit over the period as a whole. International price effects alone exceeded total shocks by more than one-half in absolute terms. Export price effects, as a proportion of shocks, were extremely favorable in the non-fuel primary producers (the Ivory Coast, Bolivia, Tunisia, and Malaysia) followed by petroleum exporters (Nigeria and Indonesia), which

were in turn succeeded by Colombia. Import price effects, though significant in the Ivory Coast, were distinctly less important. Differences in the relative price movements of primary commodities during the 1970s accounted for variations in the pattern and timing of adjustment among members of the group. On average, however, adjustment to favorable shocks took the form of an import boom which intensified in 1979–81 as compared to 1974–8, a stepping up of the share of investment in GNP, a slackening of public resource mobilization efforts, and substantial additional external financing at the end of the period under review. Turning to individual countries, there was an import boom in Bolivia, Colombia, Malaysia, and Tunisia, and, to a somewhat lesser extent, in Indonesia and Nigeria. It was accompanied by an investment boom, which was particularly marked in the Ivory Coast and Benin. There was a slackening of public resource mobilization efforts in the Ivory Coast and less so in Malaysia and Tunisia. Net real additional financing was important in Tunisia, Colombia, and Bolivia, was negligible in Indonesia and Nigeria, and was negative in Malaysia and the Ivory Coast.

Notwithstanding the diversity of experience of the thirty-three developing countries under investigation, the application of the analytical method of this chapter to individual countries and the resulting classification into groups based on characteristics of adjustment suggest the following observations.

First, Group 1 countries that resorted heavily to export-expanding adjustment with comparatively limited recourse to additional external financing were able to grow more rapidly than the other unfavorably affected countries, notwithstanding the fact that greater openness to world trade increased their vulnerability to external shocks. The lack of statistical association between external shocks and economic growth was noted before; the reason countries such as those in Group 1 – the so-called "outward-oriented" countries – were able to turn closer integration with the world economy to their advantage is authoritatively documented in Balassa (1984). By way of example, a brief discussion of Korea's adjustment experience appears in chapter 10.

Second, while many developing countries were subject to external shocks over which they had virtually no control, a significant number experienced equally important internal shocks in the form of public-sector profligacy.[17] Thus, as noted above for Group 3 countries, the balance-of-payments impact of negative public resource mobilization was one-and-a-half times as large as that of external shocks. The evidence from individual countries shows that attempts to adjust to external shocks were seriously compromised in most of the cases where public resource mobilization was substantially negative. Two examples follow.

In *Jamaica*, the government which came to power in 1972, was committed to (1) expanding the role of the public sector in creating an economy less dependent on bauxite, (2) creating increased employment opportunities for the large numbers of urban unemployed, and (3) redistributing income. Expansionary policies caused the central government deficit to increase from 4 percent of GDP in 1972 to almost 20 percent in 1976, notwithstanding a near quadrupling of government revenue from a levy on bauxite that, however, also contributed to a sharp fall in Jamaica's share of world trade in bauxite and alumina. Large wage increases were granted and consumption increased from 78 percent of GDP in 1972 to 90 percent in 1976. Notwithstanding some efforts to control expenditures and raise revenues in 1977–9, the balance-of-payments effect of negative public resource mobilization equaled 5.28 percent of GNP over the period 1974–81 or nearly six times the magnitude of external shocks.

In *Portugal*, resource mobilization deteriorated until 1977. There was a rapid increase in money wages after the Revolution and the institution of minimum wages and ceilings on salaries. Real wages increased by 23 percent in 1973–6 before falling by 9 percent in 1977. The consequence of redistribution from profits to wages during those years led to poor private resource mobilization. There was a massive increase in real public consumption after 1973. Subsidies were granted to public-sector enterprises and on food and there was an expansion in employment. These policies were not to change until 1978 when Portugal adopted a stabilization program.

Third, and related to the above, a very notable example of inconsistency between the objectives of internal and external balance targets is provided by attempts in the countries of the Southern Cone of Latin America to use exchange-rate policy to counter inflationary pressures generated by inappropriate monetary and fiscal policies. The examples are taken from Group 2 countries – Argentina and Uruguay – where there was export expansion and negative public resource mobilization which was significantly worse in the years 1979–81 compared to 1974–8.[18]

In *Argentina*, inflation proved difficult to control and, in December 1978, the authorities began to use a preannounced devaluation schedule as an anti-inflationary device. With an open capital account, this inevitably pushed domestic nominal interest rates down toward the sum of international interest rates and expected devaluation. With the price of non-tradeables responding more slowly than nominal interest rates, real interest rates became negative, leading to a step-up in investment which more than offset its slowdown in earlier years. The slowdown in the rate of nominal devaluation and the sluggish response of prices of non-tradeables began to squeeze the tradeable sectors. In addition, an increase in the public-sector deficit to 4 percent of GDP in 1980, financed by monetary emission, was inconsistent with a slowdown in the rate of preannounced devaluation. Furthermore, the authorities were unwilling to provide official exchange-rate insurance at the levels announced, leading to a substantial premium developing between domestic interest rates and exchange-rate-corrected international interest rates. There was a flight of private capital and the system was abandoned in March 1981.

In *Uruguay*, in 1978, the authorities switched to a system of preannounced exchange-rate devaluation to control inflation. For reasons similar to those in Argentina, this led to an appreciation in the real exchange rate. Uruguay enjoyed a boom in 1979 and 1980 due to overvaluation of the Argentinean peso and a consequent increased demand for goods and services generated by that country. This came to an end in 1981 because of the deterioration in the Argentinean economy and the concomitant massive devaluations of the Argentinean peso. The Uruguayan authorities were unable to control the fiscal deficit and negative public resource modification aggravated external shocks by 30.7 percent over the period as a whole. There was a drying up of capital inflows and the preannounced exchange-rate system had to be abandoned in 1982.

Fourth, many of the less developed countries among the sample considered here experienced peaks and troughs in terms of trade, mainly caused by fluctuations in primary commodity prices. This made it difficult to formulate and maintain a coherent set of adjustment policies. Thus, the need to adjust trade policies and factor prices to the first oil price shock was masked for two reasons. First, there was a perception (shared in a number of developed countries) that the oil price rise was temporary and could therefore be appropriately met through borrowing. Second, the oil shock was followed by a surplus of foreign exchange arising from a boom in a number of primary commodities such as cocoa, coffee, phosphate, and uranium in the mid 1970s which, due to imperfect sterilization and attendant real exchange-rate appreciation, removed any incentive for undertaking policies for adjustment. Indeed, the superimposition of a favorable shock of possibly shorter duration with an unfavorable shock of longer duration made consistent policy-making in practice hard to implement, a theme that is analyzed in detail in the context of Kenya in chapters 3 and 8. This was further aggravated by a tendency in a number of countries to underestimate the transitory nature of a primary commodity boom. When, as was typically the case, the boom occurred in a sector with which the government either had direct fiscal ties or which was a source of export tax revenue, it led to increased government expenditure–cum–investment programs, from which retrenchment was subsequently difficult.[19] The expansion of such programs was often financed by eagerly offered "pro-cyclical" external borrowing. The second oil price increase of the late 1970s, the subsequent collapse of oil prices in the 1980s, and the interest-rate shock of the late 1970s then found many countries with undiversified export structures, an inappropriate pattern of energy prices *vis-à-vis* other factor prices, and large government deficits. The country examples refer to two non-fuel primary producers Ivory Coast and Bolivia, drawn from Group 5. However, it may be noted that Morocco, for example, which belongs to Group 4, also underwent a similar experience with regard to the phosphate price boom in 1974.

The *Ivory Coast* had negative GDP growth for the first time in 1982 after more than a decade of continuous and sustained growth (7.5 percent over the 1965–75 period). The causes may be found in its pattern of adjustment to the 1975–7 primary commodity boom when the prices of coffee and cocoa, which accounted for 33 percent of export revenue, rose by 360 percent. The government launched an extremely ambitious investment program and the share of public investment rose from 15 percent to over 25 percent of GDP between 1976 and 1978. This was however accompanied by a sharp decline in the quality of projects and it is estimated that earnings foregone as a result of relaxing investment selection criteria used earlier amounted to 5 percent of GDP in the early 1980s. The subsequent sharp drop in coffee and cocoa prices in 1978, as well as rising oil prices and real interest rates did not lead to a corresponding cut in public investment which was maintained at 20 percent of GDP. In 1981, the country began to implement a wide-ranging program of adjustment.

In common with other countries that enjoyed primary commodity booms, *Bolivia*, faced with increases in energy and metal prices especially in the early part of the decade, embarked on a program of stepping up public investment. This was financed partly by increased public revenues from the rise in primary commodity prices and partly by substantial borrowing from foreign banks, and the current-account deficit as a percentage of GNP, which was negligible prior to 1975, rose to 8 percent in 1978. Real imports doubled between 1972 and 1979, not only because of the capital goods requirements of the investment program, but also because imports of consumer goods were stimulated by a 35 percent appreciation in the real exchange rate till late 1978. However, foreign lenders began to reassess their exposure to Bolivia in 1979 as the country's exportable surpluses began to be eroded. This was due to (1) a marked rise in real wages in terms of tin prices, leading to a decline in tin exports in 1978–80 *vis-à-vis* 1970–2; and (2) subsidized fuel prices which, between 1974 and 1980, caused domestic consumption of petroleum to rise by 31 percent at a time when its domestic production fell by 18 percent. Furthermore, the country's petroleum resources did not turn out to be as large as expected.

Finally, where developments like the above were compounded by other exogenous shocks such as political instability, as was the case in a number of the Central American countries, or a devastating succession of droughts, as was the case in the Sahelian countries, the implementation of a consistent set of macroeconomic adjustment policies would have been virtually impossible. Examples used to illustrate this phenomenon are El Salvador and Guatemala.

External shocks were favorable in *El Salvador* over the period 1974–8, due to the boom in coffee and cotton prices in the mid 1970s. Aided by public consumption restraint and increased revenues from the primary commodity boom, the period before 1977–8 was characterized by a tight budgetary policy and the investment–GNP ratio stood at 23 percent in 1976–8. The situation however changed in the later half of the period, when internal political shocks dominated developments in El Salvador, a situation which was further aggravated by deteriorating terms-of-trade and trade difficulties in the Central American Common Market. The overall fiscal deficit changed from 0.7 percent of GDP in 1979 to 6.4 percent in 1981 because of a significant reduction in tax revenues and expansion in expenditure following a major land reform in 1980. Real public investment fell by 69 percent between 1978 and 1981. Primary commodity exports declined sharply toward the end of the period because of production problems, the impact of agrarian reform, and guerilla warfare, and manufactured exports encountered difficulties in 1979–81 owing to financial difficulties in Costa Rica and Nicaragua as well as lack of credit.

Although rising oil prices were an important factor in *Guatemala*, their overall impact on the balance of payments up to 1978 was cushioned in part by favorable developments in the international coffee market, with the export tax on coffee bringing in a substantial amount of revenue to the government, as well as by an expansion of exports brought about through a resurgence of trade within the Central American Common Market. However, the country also experienced a major internal shock in the form of severe earthquakes in 1976. Additional external financing allowed a step up in public investment, admittedly from strikingly low levels, and the country was able to undertake the goals of the 1970–5 development plan as well as reconstruction activity following the earthquakes. The broad contours of adjustment were to change after 1978. While terms-of-trade movements continued to be adverse, there were, in addition, a weakening of demand for traditional exports, contraction in the Central American Common Market, and a decline in tourism following political uncertainty in the region. The failure to enact new fiscal legislation pertaining to both external and internal sectors led to a steady decline in the proportion of tax revenue to GDP and the size of the public deficit doubled between 1971 and 1980 to 5.4 percent of GDP and to 6.8 percent in 1981. Political uncertainty also led to capital flight, a slowdown in private investment, and a decline in the role of additional external financing compared to the earlier years of the period.

5 Relationship with other work

Many readers of this chapter will be familiar with the analysis of external shocks and policy responses due to Balassa (1981a, 1985). While sharing many similarities, the treatment of this chapter differs from the above-mentioned approach in two important respects.

First, the focus of Balassa's approach was on trade adjustment to external shocks. The modes of adjustment identified in his analysis were: (1) trade adjustment (including export expansion and import substitution), (2) additional external financing, and (3) a slowdown in economic growth. In contrast, the present analysis offers a unified treatment of trade adjustment as well as other policy measures, such as improved resource mobilization, both public and private, and changes in investment. The importance of implementing both switching and absorption restraining policies is basic in international economics; indeed, as argued earlier, trade adjustment cannot be effected without restraining domestic absorption. Its theoretical significance is further confirmed by one of the main empirical findings of this chapter, namely that, for many countries, the adverse balance-of-payments effects of public-sector profligacy were at least as important as those of external shocks. An analytical framework that includes resource mobilization and changes in investment as important components, therefore, offers a theoretically as well as empirically more complete account of policy responses to external shocks.[20]

Second, the analysis of shock and adjustment is based on a decomposition of the resource gap into changes in the parameters and exogenous variables of an explicitly formulated macroeconomic model. The latter is separately estimated for each country over the period 1963 to 1978 and 1963 to 1981 for the first and second round of external shocks, respectively.[21] The model, while not explicitly incorporating policy variables, goes beyond the purely accounting-based approach which characterized earlier work.[22] It will, however, be seen to be an important intermediate step in the development of policy-focused models of adjustment that are used in subsequent chapters of this book.

Appendix I   The methodology

I   An appropriate concept of income

The national income identity in local currency is

$$P_{c_p}C_p = P_{c_g}C_g + P_I I + P_X X - P_M M + F = P_N GNP \qquad \text{(A.1)}$$

where

C_p = private consumption
C_g = public consumption
I = investment
M = imports of goods and non-factor services
X = exports of goods and non-factor services
F = net factor service income from abroad
GNP = gross national product at market prices and the P's denote respective deflators

Two corrections have been applied in moving from GNP thus defined to an appropriate concept of income. *First*, capital gains arising from inflationary erosion of the country's net debt need to be taken into account. *Second*, national income must reflect the effects of terms-of-trade changes.

Correction for inflation
Toward the first objective, the term F is broken down into

F = net interest receipts + other net factor service income

$$= (\Delta_n A - r_n D - \Delta_n S) + \text{other net factor service income} \qquad (A.2)$$

where

D = outstanding and disbursed medium- and long-term debt (in dollars)
S = outstanding short-term debt (in dollars)
A = reserves (in dollars)
r_n = nominal interest rate payable on medium- and long-term debt
Δ_n = nominal interest rate payable on short-term debt and receivable on reserves

To isolate real interest payments and receipts it is necessary to subtract international inflation from the nominal rates.
Let

$$r = r_n - \hat{E}'$$
$$\Delta = \Delta_n - \hat{E}' \qquad (A.3)$$

where

E' = The unit value index of manufactured exports fob from OECD countries (in dollars) and "$\hat{\ }$" denotes a proportional year-to-year change

Thus

$$\Delta A - rD - \Delta S = [\Delta_n A - r_n D - \Delta_n S] + \hat{E}'(D + S - A) \qquad (A.4)$$

or

(real interest receipts) = (nominal interest receipts)
+ (inflationary erosion of net debt)

where

$D + S - A$ = net debt

Thus, factor service income, corrected for inflation may be defined as

$$F_c = F + e'\hat{E}'(D + S - A) \tag{A.5}$$

where e' = exchange rate (units of local currency per dollar). Equations (A.1) and (A.5) imply that

$$P_{c_p}C_p + P_{c_g}C_g + P_I I + P_X X - P_M M + F_c = P_N GNP + e'\hat{E}'(D + S - A) \tag{A.6}$$

The right-hand side of (A.6) is nominal GNP augmented by capital gains due to inflationary erosion of net debt. To convert this into constant prices, the right-hand side of (A.6) is deflated by P_N, the GNP deflator, while the first five terms on the left-hand side are deflated by their respective deflators. This generates an implicit deflator for F_c and yields

$$C_p + C_g + I + X - M + RF_c = GNP + \frac{e'\hat{E}'(D + S - A)}{P_N} \tag{A.7}$$

where RF_c balances the two sides of (A.7). The right-hand side of (A.7) is *real GNP corrected for capital gains and losses on net debt.*

Correction for terms-of-trade changes
To account for the effects of changes in import and export prices on income, it is necessary to revalue exports and imports. To preserve consistency with the earlier correction for inflation, the numeraire chosen for this purpose is a basket of manufactures exported by OECD countries. Define

$$X_c = X \frac{P_X}{eE} \tag{A.8}$$

$$M_c = M \frac{P_M}{eE} \tag{A.9}$$

where $eE = \dfrac{e'E'}{e_o E_o}$ and $e_o E_o$ is the value of $e'E'$ in the base year in which the country's national accounts at constant prices are expressed.

X_c therefore measures the purchasing power of exports over manufactures exported by OECD countries. Similarly, M_c measures the purchasing cost of imports in terms of the same numeraire. Write

$$C_p + C_g + I + X_c - M_c + RF_c = GNY + \frac{e\hat{E}(D + S - A)}{P_N} \qquad (A.10)$$

where GNY, gross national income, is defined by (A.10), so that

$$GNY = GNP + X\left(\frac{P_X}{eE} - 1\right) - M\left(\frac{P_M}{eE} - 1\right) \qquad (A.11)$$

which is *a standard terms-of-trade correction, except that it is expressed in terms of an international numeraire.*
    Finally, define

$$Y = GNY + \frac{e\hat{E}(D + S - A)}{P_N} \qquad (A.12)$$

Thus Y is *gross national income corrected both for capital gains and losses on net debt as well as for terms-of-trade changes.*

II The model

For each of the thirty-three countries that form the basis of the analysis in this chapter, the following system of equations is estimated over the period 1963 to 1981.

$$C_p = \eta_p + \delta_p Z + (c_p + \phi_p Z) Y_f \qquad (A.13)$$

$$C_g = \eta_g + \delta_g Z + (c_g + \phi_g Z) Y \qquad (A.14)$$

$$T = \omega + \delta_t Z + (t + \phi_t Z) Y \qquad (A.15)$$

$$M = \alpha + \delta_m Z + (m + \phi_m Z) Y \qquad (A.16)$$

$$X = \beta + \delta_x Z + (x + \phi_x Z) Y^* \qquad (A.17)$$

where

  Y^*: the export trade-weighted average of GDP in the three most important trading partner countries

  $Z =$ dummy variable assuming the values
        0 for 1963 to 1973
        1 for 1974 to 1981
  $T =$ indirect taxes less subsidies

$$Y_f = Y - T \qquad (A.18)$$

Thus, Y_f may be thought of as gross value added at factor cost. All variables are measured in constant prices. Substitution of definitions (A.8) and (A.9) and relations (A.13)–(A.18) into the national income identity derived from (A.10) and (A.12), i.e.

$$C_p + C_g + I + X_c - M_c + RF_c = Y \tag{A.19}$$

allows the latter to be solved for Y.
Introduce the notation

$$\eta_p^0 = \eta_p, \eta_p^1 = \eta_p + \delta_p Z$$
$$c_p^0 = c_p, c_p^1 = c_p + \phi_p Z$$

for the variables in equation (A.13) and analogously for those in equations (A.14) to (A.17). Then, manipulations standard in a Keynesian open economy model allow the solution to (A.19) to be written

$$Y = \frac{\eta_p^1 + \eta_g^1 + \beta^1 \dfrac{P_X}{eE} - c_p^1 \omega^1 - \alpha^1 \dfrac{P_M}{eE} + I + RF_c + x^1 \dfrac{P_X}{eE} Y^*}{[1 - c_p^1(1 - t^1) - c_g^1] + m^1 \dfrac{P_M}{eE}} \tag{A.20}$$

The system (A.13)–(A.17) is estimated using non-linear two-stage least squares, where the first stage is applied to equation (A.20) with $\dfrac{P_X}{eE}, \dfrac{P_M}{eE}, I$, RF_c, and Y^* assumed exogenous. The values of

$$\frac{P_X}{eE}, \frac{P_M}{eE}, I \text{ and } RF_c$$

are taken directly from the data. The values of Y^* are estimated from the following equation over the period 1963–81

$$Y^* = \gamma + \delta_h Z + (g + \phi_h Z)t \tag{A.21}$$

where

$t = $ time
$Z = $ dummy variable defined as above

The reason for estimating Y^* will become clear in the next subsection.

III Shock-adjustment methodology

The macroeconomic model described above can be put to a number of uses. In this section, its output is summarized in measures of shock and adjustment which are defined in relation to certain counterfactual developments. The counterfactual chosen here assumes that relative prices and real interest rates would have stayed at their 1971–3 levels and that the responsiveness of consumption, imports, exports, and taxes to incomes and the growth of incomes in the OECD trading partner countries would have stayed at the values historically estimates for them over the 1963–73 period. Specifically the following assumptions characterize the counterfactual:

(1) *On structural parameters*: all δ and ϕ coefficients on the dummy variable Z in (A.13)–(A.17) are zero, i.e., no change in structural parameters which prevailed during 1963–73.

(2) *On exogenous variables*: (a) the δ and ϕ coefficients on the dummy variable Z in (A.21) are zero, i.e., the growth of Y^* continues at the rate attained in 1963–73; (b) $\dfrac{P_M}{eE}$ and $\dfrac{P_X}{eE}$ are assumed to stay at their 1971–3 values; (c) r and Δ are assumed to stay at their 1971–3 values; (d) the $\dfrac{I}{Y}$ ratio is assumed to stay at its value for 1971–3.

(3) RF_c on the counterfactual is taken to equal the actual value of RF_c every year.[23]

Denote values of variables on the counterfactual by the superscript "T". Then Y^T may be written, following (A.20) as

$$Y^T = \frac{\eta_p^0 + \eta_g^0 + \beta^0 \left(\dfrac{P_X}{eE}\right)^T - c_p^0 \omega^0 - \alpha^0 \left(\dfrac{P_M}{eE}\right)^T + I^T + RF_c^T + x^0 \left(\dfrac{P_X}{eE}\right)^T Y^{*T}}{[1 - c_p^0(1 - t^0) - c_g^0] + m^0 \left(\dfrac{P_M}{eE}\right)^T} \tag{A.22}$$

The resource gap for a country, corrected for terms-of-trade changes and augmented by real interest transactions, may be written

$$\frac{R}{eE} = \frac{P_M}{eE} M - \frac{P_X}{eE} X + \left[\frac{rD + \Delta S}{E} - \frac{\Delta A}{E}\right] e_0 \tag{A.23}$$

where e_0 is the exchange rate in the base year in which the country's national accounts at constant prices are expressed.

The corresponding equation for the counterfactual is

$$\left(\frac{R}{eE}\right)^T = \left(\frac{P_M}{eE}\right)^T M^T - \left(\frac{P_X}{eE}\right)^T X^T + \left[\frac{r^T D^T + \Delta^T S^T}{E^T} - \frac{\Delta^T A^T}{E^T}\right] e_0^T \tag{A.24}$$

Subtract (A.24) from (A.23) to get

$$\left[\left(\frac{R}{eE}\right) - \left(\frac{R}{eE}\right)^T\right] = \left[\frac{P_M}{eE} - \left(\frac{P_M}{eE}\right)^T\right] M + \left[\left(\frac{P_X}{eE}\right)^T - \frac{P_X}{eE}\right] X$$

$$+ (r - r^T)\frac{De_0}{E} + (\Delta - \Delta^T)\frac{Se_0}{E} - (\Delta - \Delta^T)\frac{Ae_0}{E} \qquad (A.25)$$

$$- \left(\frac{P_M}{eE}\right)^T [M^T - M] - \left(\frac{P_X}{eE}\right)^T [X - X^T]$$

$$- \left(\frac{D^T e_0^T}{E^T} - \frac{De_0}{E}\right) r^T - \left(\frac{S^T e_0^T}{E^T} - \frac{Se_0}{E}\right)\Delta^T - \left(\frac{Ae_0}{E} - \frac{A^T e_0^T}{E^T}\right)\Delta^T$$

The next step is to substitute the value of Y from (A.20) into (A.16) to solve for M. A similar exercise has to be done for the counterfactual, this time substituting from (A.22) into (A.16), remembering that all δ and ϕ coefficients are zero. Some rearrangement of terms in (A.25) then yields the following decomposition

$$\overbrace{\left[\left(\frac{P_X}{eE}\right)^T - \left(\frac{P_X}{eE}\right)\right]\left(1 - \frac{\bar{m}^0}{s^0 + \bar{m}^0}\right) X}^{A} + \overbrace{\left[\frac{P_M}{eE} - \left(\frac{P_{MT}}{eE}\right)\right]\left(1 - \frac{\bar{m}^0}{s^0 + \bar{m}^0}\right) M}^{B}$$

$$+ \overbrace{\left(1 - \frac{\bar{m}^0}{s^0 + \bar{m}^0}\right)\bar{x}^0(Y^{*T} - Y^*)}^{C} + \overbrace{(r - r^T)\frac{De_0}{E} + (\Delta - \Delta^T)\frac{Se_0}{E}}^{D} \overbrace{- (\Delta - \Delta^T)\frac{Ae_0}{E}}^{E} =$$

$$\overbrace{\left(\frac{P_X}{eE}\right) T\left(1 - \frac{\bar{m}^0}{s^0 + \bar{m}^0}\right)(\delta_x Z + \theta_x Z Y^*)}^{F} + \overbrace{\left(\frac{P_M}{eE}\right) T\left(1 - \frac{\bar{m}^0}{s^0 + \bar{m}^0}\right)(-\delta_m Z - \theta_m Z Y)}^{G}$$

$$+ \overbrace{\frac{\bar{m}^0}{s^0 + \bar{m}^0}[-\delta_p Z - \theta_p Z(1 - t^1)Y - \omega^1]}^{H} + \overbrace{\frac{\bar{m}^0}{s^0 + \bar{m}^0}[-\delta_g Z - \theta_g Z Y]}^{I}$$

$$+ \overbrace{\frac{\bar{m}^0 c_p^0}{s^0 + \bar{m}^0}[\delta_t Z + \theta_t Z Y]}^{J} + \frac{\bar{m}^0}{s^0 + \bar{m}^0}(I^T - I) +$$

$$\overbrace{\left(\frac{D^T e_0^T}{E^T} - \frac{De_0}{E}\right) r^T + \left(\frac{S^T e_0^T}{E^T} - \frac{Se_0}{E}\right)\Delta^T + \left(\frac{Ae_0}{E} - \frac{A^T e_0^T}{E^T}\right)\Delta^T + \left[\frac{R}{eE} - \left(\frac{R}{eE}\right)^T\right]}^{L}$$

$$(A.26)$$

where $s^0 = 1 - c_p^0(1 - t^0) - c_g^0$ (savings propensity on the counterfactual).

42 Shocks and adjustment

$$\bar{m}^0 = \left(\frac{P_M}{eE}\right)^T m^0 \text{ (import propensity on the counterfactual revalued in terms}$$

of a basket of manufactures exported by OECD countries).

$$\bar{x}^0 = \left(\frac{P_X}{eE}\right)^T x^0 \text{ (export propensity on the counterfactual revalued in terms}$$

of a basket of manufactures exported by OECD countries), and

A Export price effect
B Import price effect
C Recession-induced effect $\left.\right\}$ External shocks
D Interest payments effect
E Interest receipts effect

F Export expansion
G Import substitution
H Private resource mobilization
I Public consumption restraint $\left.\right\}$ Modes of adjustment
J Tax intensification
K Investment slowdown
L Net real additional external financing

$(D + E)$ equals net interest-rate effect with the two components of D corresponding to (a) medium- and long-term debt payments and (b) short-term debt payments.

$(I + J)$ equals public resource mobilization.

The decomposition provided by equation (A.26) measures the effects on the balance of payments of external shocks and modes of adjustment. The results are printed out as 1974–81 averages.

To derive the 1974–8 averages, the equations (A.13) to (A.17) are estimated over the period 1963 to 1978. The rest of the procedure is identical.[24]

Appendix II Data

Data on national accounts, price deflators, and exchange rates are taken from the World Bank's *World Tables*. The index of international inflation, E, is the unit value index of manufactured exports fob from developed countries and is taken from various issues of the *UN Monthly Bulletin of Statistics*. Export and import trade weights are taken from the IMF's *Direction of Trade Statistics*.

The calculations distinguish public and publicly guaranteed medium- and long-term debt from short-term debt. The latter has a maturity of less than one year. Outstanding medium- and long-term disbursed debt belongs to different vintages and carries different interest rates. Data on interest payments therefore reflect such terms and conditions. In the absence of a detailed breakdown, the nominal interest rate, r_n, on medium- and long-term debt has been calculated as

$$r_n = \frac{\text{interest payments}}{\text{outstanding and disbursed debt}}$$

Both numerator and denominator are taken from the World Bank's *Debtor Reporting System* (DRS), which, however, only reports public and publicly guaranteed medium- and long-term debt.

It is assumed that Δ_n, the rate payable on short-term debt as well as that earned by the country's interest-bearing assets, equals LIBOR. This has been taken to be that corresponding to six months' maturity (source: Salomon Brothers up to 1978 and the *International Financial Statistics* (IFS) of the IMF thereafter). Short-term debt data are derived from the Bank for International Settlements' *Maturity Distribution of International Bank Lending*. Interest-bearing assets, S, are defined as follows: [total reserves minus gold (line 1Δ.a in the IFS) less use of Fund credit (line 2 e.s. in the IFS), expressed in dollars].[25]

Notes

1 The model is developed fully, including details omitted here for expositional simplicity, in appendix 1 to this chapter.
2 This aspect is discussed in section 3.2 on "Modes of adjustment."
3 $\bar{m} = m\frac{P_M}{eE}$ is an import propensity revalued in terms of a basket of manufactures exported by OECD countries. Similarly $\bar{x} = x\frac{P_x}{eE}$ is an export propensity (corresponding to increases in Y) revalued in terms of the same basket.
4 Although the period 1971–3 did witness a world boom, the terms of trade of developing countries during this period were somewhat less favorable than in the 1960s if fuel, the price of which started rising in 1973, is excluded.
5 For details see appendix I to this chapter.
6 The inclusion of interest-rate effects was not shown in the heuristic development of section 2 for expositional simplicity but forms part of the empirical implementation.
7 For an excellent textbook exposition, see Corden (1985).
8 It will be seen that a number of countries undertook unproductive investments in times of plenty. Reduction in such investments would actually increase future benefits.

9 Corden (1985) points out that, strictly speaking, no single policy may be uniquely associated with either external or internal balance. Thus, tightening of the monetary-fiscal stance may have some switching effects just as a devaluation might bring about some disabsorption. This complication is ignored here for expositional simplicity but is taken into account in the empirical implementation of these ideas in later chapters.

10 A detailed analysis is contained in Martin and Selowsky (1984).

11 van Wijnbergen (1984) lays out a theoretical model that distinguishes the demand- and supply-side effects of an oil price shock. See also Bruno (1982) and the application of these ideas to stagflation in industrial countries in Bruno and Sachs (1985).

12 It has been argued (see van Wijnbergen, 1985) that the demand-deflationary effects of a rise in the price of imported oil has dominated its supply-reducing effects for LDCs because oil is relatively more important in imports and relatively less important in their production than is the case in industrial countries. This lends some perspective to the exclusion of the supply side in the empirical analysis of this chapter.

13 For an exposition of the theory, see Svenson (1984), Edwards (1989).

14 The measure of external financing used in this chapter includes transfers, such as workers' remittances, which may carry no repayment obligation.

15 See equation (A.26) in appendix I for an algebraic statement.

16 Adjustment in Mexico also featured public resource mobilization and export expansion but the latter was due to petroleum.

17 Khan and Knight (1983) also attempt to isolate the role of external versus domestic factors in the deterioration of the current-account positions of non-oil developing countries by pooling data from thirty-two countries. The treatment here, in contrast, develops a framework of analysis that is separately implemented for each country.

18 See Corbo and de Melo (1987).

19 See also the analysis in Chu (1987a,b) on the relationship between fiscal and trade cycles.

20 Thus Sachs (1981) was among the earliest to emphasize the need to see current-account developments in terms of the difference between investment and saving.

21 For details, see appendix I.

22 In addition to Balassa (1981a, 1985), see Balassa and McCarthy (1984) and, more recently, McCarthy and Dhareshwar (1992).

23 This assumption is made for simplicity only. It clearly introduces a bias in cases where significant movements in items such as workers' remittances could be related to external shocks.

24 It may be noted that the export and import price effects and additional external financing are measured vis-à-vis E, the unit value index of manufactured exports fob for OECD countries.

25 Gold has not been included as part of reserves.

3 Toward policy-based analysis

1 Introduction

The previous chapter developed a simple framework which, while grounded in theory, made sufficiently modest demands on data so as to be empirically implementable in a large number of developing countries. In so doing, it provided analytical histories of individual countries, helped construct comparators that can place individual country performance in perspective, and yielded conclusions on patterns of adjustment. However, the effectiveness of particular policy responses is often most usefully judged *vis-à-vis* the consequences of other policies that a country might have pursued in response to external shocks. For example, would a more aggressive expansion of investment in high priority sectors underwritten by additional external financing and, hence, higher external debt have been more appropriate in terms of economic growth and income distribution? By how much could the economy's growth potential have been increased by more careful phasing of investment and foreign borrowing? Even if total investment were not increased, to what extent could the adverse effects of external shocks have been offset by a sectoral reallocation of investment in line with sectoral profitability? Would more timely exchange-rate policy in response to the first oil price shock of 1973–4 have placed the economy in a better position to weather the effects of the second round of shocks in 1979–80?

Answers to these and related questions require a more policy-based framework that describes links between instruments – such as exchange rates, tariffs, subsidies, and quantitative restrictions – and outcomes – such as imports and exports. The formal apparatus of chapter 2, however, makes no explicit reference to incentives. Thus, for example, a fall in the responsiveness of imports to GDP in Kenya is identified with import substitution. These shifts are proxies for changes in incentives that are brought about through changes in policy instruments not included in the

45

framework. That omission is due not to any conceptual difficulties, but to the following two limitations of data. First, time series on a number of policy variables are not available for many countries. Second, the level of aggregation at which comparative analysis must necessarily be conducted to make it implementable in a large number of countries is not well suited, for example, to exploring the effects of policy instruments on outcomes.

In this chapter we use Kenya as an example to motivate the search for policy-based models. To that end, we begin by presenting the results of using the method of chapter 2 to Kenya. Some of the salient features of Kenya's adjustment uncovered by that description are explored in further detail using partial equilibrium methods of analysis in section 3. While that mode of analysis illuminates various aspects of external shocks and adjustment, it has certain limitations which can only be overcome using general equilibrium analysis. Those methods are set out in some detail in chapter 4 and applied to four countries (of which Kenya is one) in subsequent chapters of the book, with a view to examining the conclusions of chapter 2 in greater depth.

2 Kenya: a shock adjustment analysis

External shocks in Kenya equaled 2.35 percent of GNP, a figure exceeded for the nineteen less-developed countries in the sample by Malawi (3.84 percent) and Thailand (3.47 percent) (see table 3.1). International price effects equaled this figure, with unfavorable import price effects arising from petroleum price increases in 1973–4 and 1979–80 more than offsetting the favorable effects of the coffee boom in 1976–7. Recession-induced effects on the balance of payments arising from the slowdown in the UK, West Germany, and the USA were only 0.24 percent of GNP, mainly a consequence of Kenya's relatively limited dependence on manufactured exports. In this respect, Kenya's experience contrasts sharply with that of the more export oriented of the semi-industrial countries such as Korea and Taiwan, where the recessionary effects accounted for an average equivalent to almost 2 percent of GNP. However, it was very similar to the experience of more "typical" middle-income countries such as Chile, Turkey and Colombia where the recession-induced effects were 0.2 percent of GNP.

The sign and timing of shocks suggest that it would probably have been difficult for the authorities to sustain a coherent program of adjustment to the first oil shock when the foreign exchange situation turned much easier during the 1976–8 period. The dominant mode of trade adjustment to foreign exchange tightening was import substitution (83 percent of total adjustment) which was effected principally through the use of quantitative restrictions. Partly as a consequence of this, export expansion was

Table 3.1 *Balance-of-payments effects of external shocks and modes of adjustment, 1974–8 and 1974–80 averages (percentage of local currency GNP): Kenya*

	1974–8	1974–80
I *External shocks*		
1 *International price effects*		
a Export price effect	−3.05	−2.75
b Import price effect	4.85	5.10
Sum (=1a+1b)	1.80	2.35
2 *Recession-induced effect*	0.18	0.24
3 *Net interest-rate effect*		
a Payments effect		
i Medium and long term	−0.17	−0.21
ii Short term	0	0.04
Sum (=i+ii)	−0.17	−0.17
b Receipts effect	0.02	0.07
Difference (3a−3b)	−0.19	−0.24
Total shock (=1+2+3)	1.79	2.35
II *Modes of adjustment*		
1 *Trade adjustment*		
a Export expansion	−0.80	−1.21
b Import substitution	1.85	1.95
Sum (=1a+1b)	1.06	0.74
2 *Resource mobilization*		
a Private	−2.91	−3.40
b Public		
i Public consump. restraint	−0.60	−0.81
Tax intensification	0.52	0.85
Sum (i+ii)	−0.09	0.05
Sum (2a+2b)	−2.99	−3.35
3 *Investment slowdown*	1.97	2.41
4 *Net additional ext. financing*	1.76	2.56
Total (=1+2+3+4)	1.79	2.35

Source: Chapter 2 and appendix II to chapter 2.

consistently negative, with the situation being made even more difficult by the breakup of the East African Community and the political situation in Uganda. Moreover, table 3.2 shows that the export-weighted real exchange rate appreciated not only during the coffee boom years, but over the period as a whole.

Table 3.2 *Kenya: index of export-weighted real exhange rate,*
1974–80 (1971–3 = 1.00)

Year	1974	1975	1976	1977	1978	1979	1980
Export-weighted real exchange rate*	0.92	0.94	0.82	0.68	0.83	0.89	0.90

Note:
*Using relative export weights to the three main partner countries for Kenya's exports: UK, 50.3%; Germany, 33.5%; USA, 16.27%.
Source: IMF, Direction of Trade Statistics.
    IMF, International Financial Statistics

Resource mobilization made a negative contribution to adjustment, but the performance of the public sector was somewhat positive. Of this, public consumption restraint was negative, being fueled by large budgetary outlays associated with the establishment of independent Kenyan corporations following the disintegration of the East African Community in 1977, by a rapid growth of educational as well as defense expenditure and by the costs of general public administration. However, public resource mobilization was helped by a series of discretionary tax adjustments which injected considerable buoyancy into tax revenues. In the private sector, however, the increase in consumption relative to income resulted in a decline in available resources to finance investment, equivalent to 3.4 percent of GNP on average. Indeed, Kenya was the second poorest performer with respect to private resource mobilization among countries unfavorably affected by external shocks.

The negative overall resource mobilization effort was accompanied by substantial external borrowing, notwithstanding a significant fall in the investment–GNP ratio from its levels of the early 1970s. There was an extremely rapid buildup of debt in 1980 and 1981, and overall net additional external financing exceeded external shocks by 9 percent. This gave rise to increased future debt-servicing obligations at the same time as lower investment was reducing the growth potential to meet these obligations. In a number of countries, for example, those in Groups 4 and 5 in chapter 2, external borrowing was generally used at least in part to avert an investment slowdown. In Kenya, in most years, this was not the case: among the unfavorably affected less-developed countries only Mali and Jamaica relied more heavily than Kenya on investment slowdown (as a proportion of total adjustment).

Finally, there is nothing in the Kenyan pattern which suggests a "natural" time-phasing of adjustment – heavy external borrowing in the early phases of adjustment helping to sustain an increased share of investment in GDP followed, at a later stage, by increased reliance on trade adjustment and improved domestic resource mobilization. On the contrary, the buildup of borrowing in Kenya occurred most obviously at the end of the 1970s, investment fell sharply in the early stages of the "adjustment" process, and the efforts at resource mobilization in the public sector remained at least as inadequate during the latter stages of the process as they were early on. Until the end of the 1970s, at any rate, there is evidence of the problems arising from external shocks being exacerbated rather than resolved by the policy response. Because of Kenya's low initial level of debt and the good fortune of the coffee/tea boom, the inadequacy of policy was not critically important. But, because of the greater magnitude of the 1980s shocks and the far less favorable starting conditions, a more soundly based adjustment policy would have been required in the decade of the 1980s.

3 Kenya: a partial equilibrium analysis

This discussion of Kenya's experience during the 1970s and early 1980s highlights, among other things, (1) the considerable difficulty of sustaining coherent adjustment to the first oil price shock in the light of the easy foreign exchange situation prevailing as a result of the commodity price boom of the mid 1970s; and (2) the importance of import substitution in adjustment to periods of shortage of foreign exchange.

The above issues may be more adequately treated using a general equilibrium approach that, *inter alia*, models the links between policies, relative prices, and outcomes. Such a model is indeed used in chapters 6–9 to conduct a detailed investigation of policy responses to external shocks, including for Kenya in chapter 8. Before doing so, however, it proves instructive to first use the disaggregated data base[1] assembled for that study, namely, a Social Accounting Matrix (SAM) for Kenya for 1976,[2] to explore changes in the structure of the economy that took place during this period. Those structural shifts in the economy are identified by comparing actual changes in certain aggregates with counterfactuals constructed using fixed coefficients in various sections of the SAM. This procedure has similarities with that used to generate the earlier shock/adjustment decomposition figures of chapter 2. However, since the disaggregated data base contains more information than the national accounts, it allows an examination of a richer set of hypotheses than was previously possible. Such preliminary analysis exploits the full data consistency of the SAM and provides useful raw material with which to inform the eventual specification of the fuller general equilibrium model used in chapter 8 to study adjustment in Kenya. The rest of this section reports four separate pieces of analysis aimed at assessing, in addition to the two themes raised at the beginning of section 2, namely, (1) the 1976–7 coffee/tea boom; (2) the degree of import substitution, two other themes on which data are available; (3) the relative price shifts associated with higher oil prices; and (4) the distributional consequences of the actual pattern of output growth. The Social Accounting Matrix for Kenya distinguishes seven factors of production, fourteen institutional categories, and twenty-eight production sectors: a list of the titles appears in table 3.4 in rows 1–7,[3] 9–22, and 23–50 respectively.

3.1 The impact of the 1976–7 coffee and tea price boom

Mainly as a consequence of a severe frost in Brazil in July 1975, there was an increase, between 1975 and 1976, of 103 percent in the price which Kenya was able to obtain for her coffee exports. In the subsequent year there was a further 82 percent increase in price (as well as spillover effects which resulted in a near doubling of the tea price), before the price slumped by some 28 percent in 1978 to find a level which remained relatively stable until 1981. Since merchandise exports in 1975 totaled $635 million of which coffee accounted for about 15 percent, the price rise in coffee between 1975 and 1977 (270 percent), by itself was enough to add more than 40 percent to the 1975 value of exports in dollar terms. The rise in the price of tea added a further 5 percent or more to this.

Rough calculations suggest that in the 1976 base year of the SAM which also happens to be in the middle of the coffee/tea price boom, coffee and tea exports accounted for approximately 85 percent of total exports from the agricultural sector. In order to assess the economy-wide impact of the commodity boom, we have recalculated the value of agricultural-sector exports for both 1975 and 1977 using the 1976 value of such exports as the base and adjusting this for the price changes 1975–6 and 1976–7, respectively (i.e., the volume changes during these two periods are ignored). The results of this calculation which assumes no price changes for agricultural sector commodities other than tea and coffee are presented in the first two lines of table 3.3.

The next stage of our calculation involves an assumption about the nature of the incomes generated by the commodity price increases. Since we are considering a pure price effect, none of the extra revenue shown in row 2 of table 3.3 will have been used to purchase additional intermediate goods. In the first round of income generation at least, it will go entirely into value added. Furthermore, if we assume an initial equilibrium in labor markets, there need be no quantity changes in either the demand for, or supply of labor and therefore no adjustment in wages. In this case, the whole of the

Table 3.3 *Some effects of the 1975–7 commodity boom*
(*sh. million*)

	1975	1976	1977
Agriculture sector exports	99.1	151.6	263.6
Changes due to price effects			
(compared with 1976 base)	− 52.5	0	+ 112.0
of which Operating surplus	− 34.7	0	+ 74.0
Self-employment inc.	− 17.8	0	+ 38.0
Induced effects (relative to 1976)			
Imports	− 18.3	0	+ 38.9
Private consumption	− 68.2	0	+ 145.8
Public consumption	− 13.4	0	+ 28.5

additional revenue in the first round will go to operating surplus or to self-employment income (with a small amount to indirect taxes). For simplicity we have assumed that the split of additional revenues as between these two categories of value added is proportional to the values shown in the 1976 SAM, i.e., sh. 254.8 million (self-employment income) to sh. 130.4 million (operating surplus in agriculture). Thus, for example, comparing 1977 with 1976, the first round effect of the windfall coming from the commodity boom which totals sh. 112 million is assumed to be split as sh.

74 million $\left(= \dfrac{254.8}{254.8 + 130.4} \times \text{sh. } 112 \text{ million} \right)$ of additional operating

surplus and sh. 38 million $\left(= \dfrac{130.4}{254.8 + 130.4} \times \text{sh. } 112 \text{ million} \right)$ of additional

self-employment income.

An order of magnitude for the effects of each of the second and subsequent rounds was calculated using equation (3.1) below. This allows the first round increments to income, which we have just described, to generate both income multipliers (i.e., higher income generates higher consumption and so higher output and incomes elsewhere, and so on) as well as input–output multipliers (i.e., higher consumption generates higher intermediate demands and so higher output and incomes elsewhere).

$$\begin{bmatrix} Y_f \\ Y_i \\ g \end{bmatrix} = I - \left(\begin{bmatrix} O & O & F \\ I_n & T_r & O \\ O & C & A \end{bmatrix} \right)^{-1} \begin{bmatrix} ab \\ oth \\ f \end{bmatrix} \qquad (3.1)$$

where

Y_f = an eight element vector of factor incomes including indirect taxes
Y_i = a fourteen element vector of institutional incomes

g = a twenty-eight element vector of gross outputs

F = an 8×28 coefficient matrix showing factor payments by production sectors

I_n = a 14×7 coefficient matrix showing institutional incomes paid by each factor

T_r = a 14×14 coefficient matrix of transfers between institutions

C = a 28×14 coefficient matrix of consumption by institutions of the products of the production sectors

A = a 28×28 input–output coefficient matrix

ab = an eight element vector of factor incomes from abroad and not elsewhere captured in the accounting

oth = a fourteen element vector of exogenous institutional incomes

f = a twenty-eight element vector of exogenous final demands (exports and investment in this case)

Our use of equation (3.1) involves adjusting two of the elements of the ab vector by the first round changes in incomes already described and then computing the resulting changes in Y_f, Y_i, and g on the assumption that all the coefficients of the five submatrices shown in that equation, are constant.

The results of this exercise in terms of the changes in the Y_f, Y_i, and g vectors are shown in figure 3.1 and table 3.4. All the results in the figure and the table are presented as percentage changes from the 1976 base. The results suggest a number of interesting conclusions. First, the effects on incomes and outputs are quantitatively large in both time periods. Income effects average about 7 percent in 1975–6 and 17 percent in 1976–7 while output effects average about 4 percent in 1975–6 and almost 9 percent in 1976–7. To the extent that these results are derived on the assumption of constant factor prices they are biased upwards.[4] Second, the boost to incomes associated with the commodity price changes seems to be reasonably even across both factors and institutions excepting, of course, the larger than average rise in profits (factor category, 6) which is implicit in our earlier assumption about the first round effects. Lower-income urban households, however, fare significantly worse than high-income urban households and all categories of rural households (figure 3.1b). The boost to central government revenues (institutional income category, 13) is 5.5 percent in 1975–6 and 11.8 percent in 1976–7. In total this represents about 40 percent of the actual increase in revenues which the government was able to mobilize during that period. The balance was obtained from discretionary tax changes and from the revenue effects of general inflation. However, the commodity boom alone was evidently a permissive factor of major importance lying behind the major increase in government expenditure which took place during that period.

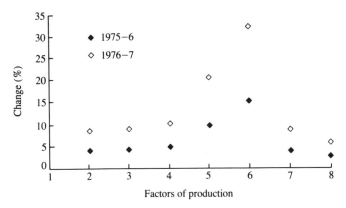

Figure 3.1a Income changes of factors (percent)

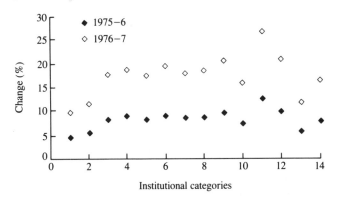

Figure 3.1b Income changes of institutional categories (percent)

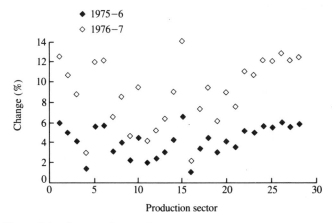

Figure 3.1c Output changes by sector (percent)

Table 3.4 *Income and output effects of increased commodity prices (relative to 1976 values)*

Row	1975–6	1976–7
1 Unskilled and semi-skilled workers	4.5	9.6
2 Skilled workers	4.0	8.4
3 Officer workers and semi-professionals	4.1	8.8
4 Professional workers	4.7	10.1
5 Self-employed and family workers	9.6	20.5
6 Operating surplus	15.2	32.4
7 Consumption of fixed capital	4.0	8.6
8 Indirect taxes	2.8	5.9
9 Urban households <6,000 sh.	4.4	9.5
10 „ „ 6,000–20,000 sh.	5.3	11.4
11 „ „ >20,000 sh.	8.2	17.6
12 Rural households <0.5 ha	8.8	18.8
13 „ „ 0.5 ha+add. incomes	8.2	17.5
14 „ „ 0.5 ha–1.0 ha	9.1	19.5
15 „ „ 0.5 ha–1.0 ha+add. incomes	8.4	17.8
16 „ „ 1.0 ha–8.0 ha	8.7	18.6
17 „ „ >8.0 ha	9.6	20.5
18 Other rural	7.4	15.9
19 Private enterprises	12.6	26.9
20 Public enterprises	9.7	20.8
21 Central government	5.5	11.8
22 Local government	7.7	16.4
23 Traditional economy	5.9	12.5
24 Agriculture	5.0	10.6
25 Forestry and fishing	4.1	8.7
26 Mining and quarrying	1.4	3.0
27 Food and beverages	5.6	11.9
28 Textiles and clothing	5.7	12.1
29 Wood, wood products	3.1	6.6
30 Paper and printing	4.0	8.5
31 Petroleum refining	2.2	4.7
32 Other chemicals	4.4	9.4
33 Non-metallic minerals	2.0	4.2
34 Metal products	2.4	5.2
35 Other manufacturing	3.0	6.3
36 Electricity	4.2	9.0
37 Water	6.6	14.0
38 Building and construction	1.1	2.2
39 Wholesale and retail trade	3.4	7.3
40 Hotels and restaurants	4.4	9.4

Table 3.4 (*cont.*)

Row	1975–6	1976–7
41 Transport services	3.0	6.2
42 Communication	4.1	8.9
43 Finance and business services	3.6	7.6
44 Ownership of dwellings	5.2	11.0
45 Other services	5.0	10.7
46 Public administration and defense	5.7	12.1
47 Education	5.6	12.0
48 Health	6.0	12.8
49 Agricultural services	5.6	12.1
50 Other services	5.8	12.2

Note: Rows 1–8 denoted Y_f; rows 9–22 denoted Y_i; rows 23–50 denoted g.
ha = hectares.

Third, there is considerable variability in the output effects of the boom (see figure 3.1c). Relatively large increases are suggested for sectors such as water (sector 15), food (sector 5), textiles (sector 6), and agriculture itself (sectors 1 and 2). All service-sector outputs also receive a considerable boost. Relatively smaller output increases, however, are suggested for most manufacturing sectors other than the two already mentioned.

Finally in order to complete our picture of the indirect effects of the boom, we have calculated the levels of imports and consumption associated with the outcome shown in table 3.4. For this purpose we have relied on the assumption of fixed coefficients for both imports (relative to sectoral production for intermediate imports) and consumption (relative to institutional incomes). The results are shown in the lower part of table 3.3. Taking the two-year period as a whole, the percentage changes which these numbers suggest relative to 1975 levels are approximately 25 percent in the case of private consumption, 19 percent in the case of public consumption, and 14 percent in the case of imports. The last of these numbers would certainly be increased in a model in which a more realistic assumption was made about the economy's supply constraints. But, even within our framework, the enormity of the disturbance to aggregate demand in the economy associated with the boom is clear enough. In the face of this disturbance, it would have been extremely difficult for the economy to have maintained a coherent pattern of response to the earlier disturbances in oil prices.

3.2 *Assessing the extent of import substitution*

The fixed coefficients of the SAM obviously prevent a full analysis of the degree of substitution achieved by the economy in any given period. However, the use of the fixed coefficient assumption as a counterfactual which can be compared with actual outcomes does provide a basis for assessing the order of magnitude of substitution in certain aspects of production. In this subsection we consider the substitution of imports in domestic production.

The approach used takes the actual values of four exogenous elements of final demand, namely private consumption, public consumption, exports of goods, and non-factor services and investment (including stock changes), in four selected years namely 1973, 1976 (the base year), 1978, and 1980. Those years should be fairly representative of the various major developments which have affected the economy. The final demand elements were used to produce an estimate of imports in each of the three "projection" years using the counterfactual assumptions that (i) input–output coefficients, (ii) the ratios of intermediate imports to gross output in each sector, and (iii) the ratios of final imports to the corresponding final demand aggregates, all remained constant. This permits us to implement the following equation.

$$m_t = m_b(I - A)^{-1}(f_t) + m_c C + m_I In \qquad (3.2)$$

where $m_t =$ the import values in the projection year t, $m_c =$ the import coefficient of consumption (C), $m_I =$ the import coefficient of investment (In), $f_t =$ a vector of exogenous final demands in projection year t and base year prices.

It may be noted that to the extent that the projected values m_t diverge from actual measured values of imports in the same year (also 1976 base prices) a combination of two things have happened. First, there may have been technical substitution causing changes in the physical requirement of certain inputs including imports relative to production. Second, the import prices which are implicitly incorporated in the m_b coefficients for 1976 may *not* be appropriate to that projection year. Our procedure was to attempt to isolate the first of these two factors by putting the import coefficients m_b on to a projection year basis using the actual price indices for oil imports, other imports, and the exchange rate which are discussed more fully later in this section (see table 3.10). The calculation indicated in equation (3.2) was then carried out with this *price corrected* set of import coefficients substituting for the base year coefficients. The exogenous data as well as the results of this exercise are shown in table 3.5.

The first part of the table reports information on exogenous final

Table 3.5 *A calculation of import substitution, 1973–8*

	1973	1976 (base year)	1978	1980
Final demands (relative to 1976 levels)				
Private consumption	0.92	1.0	1.21	1.33
Public consumption	0.77	1.0	1.30	1.31
Export of goods and NFS	0.96	1.0	1.05	1.05
Investment ^{a}	1.1	1.0	1.40	1.17
Projections of imports (i) using the m_b coeffs.				
(i.e., non-price adjusted)	461.4	461.6	577.7	575.1
(ii) using m_{bt} coeffs.				
(i.e., price adjusted)	213.6	461.6	676.7	1,079.6
Actual imports	527.7	461.6	695.8	620.0
Projection error (using price adjusted coeffs.)	−314.1	0	−19.1	+459.6

Note: ^{a}In addition, stock-building of the following absolute amounts were added to the final demand vector, 1973, 83.0; 1978, 84.1; 1980, 92.2.

demands. Fixed capital formation fell sharply between 1973 and 1976, then rose extremely strongly till 1978 only to decline thereafter. Public consumption, by contrast, grew rapidly both between 1973 and 1976 and then again between 1976 and 1978. In the two years thereafter it levelled off in real terms but did not fall. Private consumption also grew fast in the 1973 to 1978 period but somewhat less rapidly than public consumption; it was, however, a more dominant growth factor in demand in the 1978–80 period. Finally exports rose relatively sluggishly in real terms in both the two subperiods to 1978 and leveled off thereafter. Ideally, the changes in each of the four categories of final demand ought to be allocated to the twenty-eight production sectors which are identified in the SAM on the basis of shifts in the structure of that demand. Unfortunately, the data available to us do not permit this and we have fallen back on the assumption of proportional change across the twenty-eight sectors for each of the four final demand categories considered separately (i.e., the changes are proportional to the 1976 base values for each relevant entry). The results of this exercise are summarized in table 3.6.

Turning to the second part of table 3.5 (summarized in table 3.7), the results are quite striking. For the 1976 to 1978 calculation (column 3), the fixed coefficient projections for imports are extremely close to the actual

Table 3.6 *Aggregate final demands, 1973–80 (in 1976 prices)*

Sector	1973	1978	1980
1 Traditional economy	78.9	78.2	102.2
2 Agriculture	392.0	398.7	477.8
3 Forestry and fishing	7.2	7.4	9.0
4 Mining and quarrying	3.5	3.3	4.0
5 Food and beverages	190.8	193.7	240.5
6 Textiles and clothing	57.2	59.0	73.0
7 Wood, wood products	13.4	13.0	16.3
8 Paper and printing	6.7	5.2	7.2
9 Petroleum refining	54.1	52.4	60.0
10 Other chemicals	50.5	52.3	60.9
11 Non-metallic minerals	11.8	11.5	13.4
12 Metal products	57.6	52.9	71.4
13 Other manufacturing	23.6	21.7	29.2
14 Electricity	4.0	3.6	5.0
15 Water	−0.1	0.2	−0.2
16 Building and construction	130.6	114.4	165.0
17 Wholesale and retail trade	108.6	108.0	129.2
18 Hotels and restaurants	59.5	61.3	73.2
19 Transport services	107.7	107.6	124.7
20 Communication	6.3	6.0	7.8
21 Finance and business services	16.2	15.0	19.0
22 Ownership of dwellings	58.3	61.4	75.9
23 Other services	43.9	45.4	54.9
24 Public administration and defense	74.7	93.2	123.5
25 Education	79.6	98.8	130.6
26 Health	21.7	26.3	34.5
27 Agricultural services	15.7	19.6	26.0
28 Other services	25.0	31.0	41.0

outcome (probably within the margin of error of the methodology: 676.7 as against 695.8). This suggests that, in that period, the economy was operating in a manner whereby foreign exchange constraints on importing were not changing significantly. The pressures coming from the extremely rapid increases in final demand could be accommodated without contravention of the fixed technical coefficients of the A matrix and the m_{bt} vector. This conclusion is consistent with the evidence presented later and summarized in table 3.11 that the relative price changes of the 1976–8 period were modest and less likely (than in our other subperiods) to be signaling the need for significant resource reallocation. To the extent that

Table 3.7 *Import coefficients, 1973–80*

Sector	1973	1978	1980
1 Traditional economy	0.01	0.01	0.01
2 Agriculture	0.04	0.03	0.03
3 Forestry and fishing	0.03	0.02	0.02
4 Mining and quarrying	0.11	0.08	0.07
5 Food and beverages	0.10	0.07	0.07
6 Textiles and clothing	0.41	0.31	0.28
7 Wood, wood products	0.20	0.15	0.14
8 Paper and printing	0.25	0.19	0.17
9 Petroleum refining	0.47	0.90	1.57
10 Other chemicals	0.32	0.25	0.22
11 Non-metallic minerals	0.18	0.13	0.12
12 Metal products	0.47	0.36	0.32
13 Other manufacturing	0.34	0.26	0.23
14 Electricity	0.10	0.08	0.07
15 Water	0.05	0.04	0.03
16 Building and construction	0.12	0.01	0.08
17 Wholesale and retail trade	0.04	0.03	0.03
18 Hotels and restaurants	0.04	0.03	0.02
19 Transport services	0.10	0.08	0.07
20 Communication	0.25	0.19	0.17
21 Finance and business services	0.11	0.09	0.08
22 Ownership of dwellings	0.00	0.00	0.00
23 Other services	0.08	0.06	0.05
24 Public administration and defense	0.03	0.03	0.02
25 Education	0.01	0.01	0.01
26 Health	0.06	0.04	0.04
27 Agricultural services	0.07	0.05	0.04
28 Other services	0.07	0.05	0.05

Note: The coefficients shown above are those which are implicit in the counterfactual experiments described in section 3.2.

the subperiod nonetheless saw rapid growth and a sharp rise in import demand, this could be accommodated without major coefficient changes because of the foreign exchange windfalls associated with the coffee boom as well as with additional external borrowing. This result is also consistent with the conclusion from the World Bank, 1982a.

The situation in the other two subperiods is radically different from this. The backward "projection" from the 1976 base to 1973 results in a serious underprojection of imports (213.6 as against 527.7). This, in turn, suggests

Table 3.8 *Distribution of oil*
input coefficients by sector
(1976)[a]

Size of coefficients	Frequency
0–1	10
1–5	11
5–10	3
10+	4

Note:
[a] The figures shown are the
standard input–output
coefficients × 100.

that the technical (physical) coefficients incorporated in the m_{bt} vector were significantly higher in 1973 than in 1976. In other words, that period saw a sharp reduction in either the demand for imports or in their availability or both. Similarly, the forward projection from 1976 to 1980 results in a sharp overprojection of imports (1,079.6 as against 620.0). This again suggests that some mechanism was operating in that period to restrain imports relative to the levels suggested by the 1976[5] relationships and the growth of imports to 1978. The mechanism through which the significant restraint on imports was achieved between 1973 and 1976 and again between 1978 and 1980 is obviously not identified by our approach. The presumption is that quantitative restrictions would have exerted the main effect but rationing by price cannot yet be ruled out as a significant force. This is a matter which we consider more formally in the general equilibrium analysis of chapter 8.

3.3 *Relative price effects of oil price changes*

In this subsection we use the production structure of the 1976 SAM to calculate the orders of magnitude of the relative price changes arising from the 1973–4 and 1980–1 adjustments of the dollar price of oil. The results are again assessed for a selection of time periods which are representative of the range of experiences for the period 1973–81. The years chosen are 1973, 1976 (the base year), 1978, 1980, and 1981. We initially apply the assumption of zero substitution of the oil input in oil-using sectors. Since in most of Kenya's productive sectors the oil input coefficient is small, this will normally be a trivial assumption having little consequence for our results (see tables 3.8 and 3.9 for evidence on this).

The four sectors having an oil input greater than 10 percent of gross output are: mining, non-metallic minerals, electricity (easily the largest

Table 3.9 *The oil input coefficient in Kenyan production (1976)*

Sector	Coefficient (%)
1 Traditional economy	0.0
2 Agriculture	0.75
3 Forestry and fishing	4.04
4 Mining and quarrying	11.48
5 Food and beverages	0.39
6 Textiles and clothing	1.13
7 Wood, wood products	8.33
8 Paper and printing	0.75
9 Petroleum refining	0.08
10 Other chemicals	1.41
11 Non-metallic minerals	13.83
12 Metal products	1.77
13 Other manufacturing	3.20
14 Electricity	17.49
15 Water	3.92
16 Building and construction	8.17
17 Wholesale and retail trade	2.74
18 Hotels and restaurants	0.81
19 Transport services	11.79
20 Communication	0
21 Finance and business services	1.04
22 Ownership of dwellings	0
23 Other services	4.21
24 Public admininstration and defense	2.47
25 Education	0.81
26 Health	1.14
27 Agricultural services	8.04
28 Other services	0.65

coefficient), and transport. Obviously for these sectors and also for the sectors having coefficients greater than 5 percent (namely wood products, construction, and government agricultural services), the assumption of no substitutability should result in some overstatement of the relative price effects of more expensive oil. The significant increase in the share of electricity production coming from hydroelectric sources after 1976 (72 percent of supply came from this source in 1979), is the most obvious example to which attention needs to be directed.[6] Our approach is to apply the following pricing equation to each of the elements of the import vector of the 1976 SAM

$$pm_i = pw_i \cdot ER \qquad (3.3)$$

where pm_i is the local currency price of imports of type, i; pw_i is the corresponding foreign currency world price and ER is the exchange rate.

Ideally, this equation should be applied separately to each imported commodity making up the import bill of each import-using sector. However, this requires an import matrix which is not available in the Kenyan SAM. Thus, we are forced to rely on the assumption of the homogeneous price behavior of each of the commodities making up the import bill of each sector. Fortunately, in the case of oil imports, this is not too serious a problem since all crude and refined product imports are attributable to one sector of the SAM namely petroleum refining and this sector is likely to import only small amounts of goods other than oil. The analysis is normalized around an assumption of prices of unity for all import prices in the base year of 1976. The analysis is conducted using the standard input–output pricing equation

$$pg = (I - A')^{-1}(v + m) \qquad (3.4)$$

where pg is a vector of gross output prices, v is a vector of total value added outlays in each sector (including for our present purposes, all indirect taxes) expressed as a proportion of gross output, m is a vector of the imports into each sector expressed as a proportion of gross output. The imports, in turn, are measured in domestic prices for each sector.

By changing the vector pm_i by reference only to the actual changes in pw_i and ER from the 1976 base year, it is possible to construct a value for pg for each of the years we are considering. Relative prices are then constructed by comparing each element in the pg vector in any year by the (gross-output) weighted prices of the same year. It can be noted that wage rates and other prices incorporated in v are held constant for this purpose. Indeed this is crucial to ensure that relative prices do change. We have used 1976 gross output weights in every case.

In recalculating the values of the vector pm_i for each of our four years, emphasis is directed at the change of the oil price and in the exchange rate (see table 3.10). All non-oil elements of pm_i are assumed to move at the general rate of price change on non-oil imports. The underlying elements for the calculation are as follows. We have calculated the movement of domestic relative prices using equation (3.4) and two different sets of assumptions, namely:

(a) assuming that only oil prices change;
(b) assuming that both oil prices and the exchange rate change.

This two level approach permits us to obtain some idea of the relative importance of the two factors in causing relative price shifts.

The results are shown in figure 3.2 and table 3.11 and they reveal some

Table 3.10 *Import price and exchange-rate movements ($) 1973–81*

	1973	1976	1978	1980	1981
Index of oil prices ($)	0.253	1.0	1.19	3.33	3.35
Index of exch. rate ($)	0.830	1.0	0.891	0.911	1.238
so price of one 1976 dollar of oil in local currency	0.210	1.0	1.06	3.03	4.09
Index of other import prices	0.642	1.0	1.189	1.571	2.348
so price of one 1976 dollar of other imports in local currency	0.533	1.0	1.189	1.571	2.348

Source: Table 3.7 of World Bank (1982a) for all years to 1980 and tentative guesses based on generalized estimates for 1981.

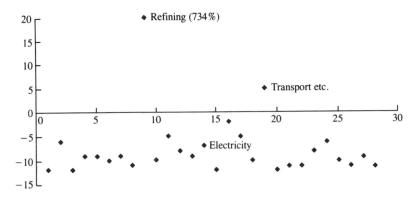

Figure 3.2a Relative price changes, 1973–81

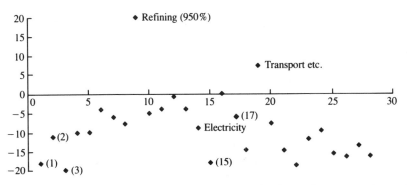

Figure 3.2b Relative price changes, 1973–81 (allowing for exchange-rate changes)

Table 3.11a *Relative prices, 1973–81 allowing only for oil price ($)*
changes

Sector	1973	1978	1980	1981	Proportional change 1973–81
1 Traditional economy	0.79	0.76	0.70	0.70	−0.12
2 Agriculture	0.78	0.77	0.74	0.74	−0.06
3 Forestry and fishing	0.51	0.49	0.45	0.45	−0.12
4 Mining and quarrying	0.64	0.62	0.58	0.58	−0.09
5 Food and beverages	1.66	1.61	1.51	1.51	−0.09
6 Textiles and clothing	0.75	0.73	0.67	0.67	−0.10
7 Wood, wood products	0.76	0.74	0.70	0.70	−0.09
8 Paper and printing	0.86	0.83	0.77	0.77	−0.09
9 Petroleum refining	0.17	0.57	1.38	1.38	+7.34
10 Other chemicals	0.75	0.72	0.68	0.68	−0.10
11 Non-metallic minerals	0.70	0.69	0.67	0.67	−0.05
12 Metal products	0.84	0.82	0.77	0.77	−0.08
13 Other manufacturing	0.72	0.70	0.66	0.66	−0.09
14 Electricity	0.59	0.58	0.55	0.55	−0.07
15 Water	0.64	0.62	0.57	0.57	−0.12
16 Building and construction	1.94	1.93	1.91	1.91	−0.02
17 Wholesale and retail trade	1.09	1.07	1.03	1.03	−0.05
18 Hotels and restaurants	0.77	0.74	0.69	0.69	−0.10
19 Transport services	1.61	1.64	1.69	1.69	+0.05
20 Communication	0.73	0.70	0.64	0.64	−0.12
21 Finance and business services	0.70	0.67	0.62	0.62	−0.11
22 Ownership of dwellings	0.56	0.54	0.50	0.50	−0.11
23 Other services	0.74	0.72	0.68	0.68	−0.08
24 Public administr. and defense	0.89	0.87	0.83	0.83	−0.06
25 Education	0.67	0.64	0.60	0.60	−0.10
26 Health	0.57	0.55	0.51	0.51	−0.11
27 Agricultural services	0.56	0.54	0.51	0.51	−0.09
28 Other services	0.60	0.58	0.54	0.54	−0.11

interesting patterns. Only two of the twenty-eight gross output prices show a rise after 1973 relative to the weighted average of prices when oil price changes alone are considered. These are petroleum refining where the rise between 1973 and 1981 is over 700 percent and transport and related services where the rise is 5 percent. Somewhat counter-intuitively the price of electricity (sector 14) falls by almost 7 percent (relative to the weighted average), during this period. This can be explained by the fact that apart from its large oil input coefficient, electricity also has a large reliance on

Table 3.11b *Relative prices, 1973–81 allowing only for oil price ($)
changes and exchange-rate changes*

Sector	1974	1976	1978	1980	1981	Proportional change 1973–81
1 Traditional economy	0.81	0.76	0.77	0.71	0.66	−0.18
2 Agriculture	0.80	0.77	0.78	0.75	0.71	−0.11
3 Forestry and fishing	0.53	0.50	0.50	0.46	0.43	−0.20
4 Mining and quarrying	0.64	0.63	0.62	0.58	0.57	−0.10
5 Food and beverages	1.65	1.62	1.61	1.52	1.49	−0.10
6 Textiles and clothing	0.72	0.73	0.71	0.67	0.69	−0.04
7 Wood, wood products	0.75	0.74	0.73	0.69	0.70	−0.06
8 Paper and printing	0.84	0.84	0.82	0.76	0.78	−0.08
9 Petroleum refining	0.15	0.49	0.53	1.30	1.59	+9.50
10 Other chemicals	0.73	0.73	0.71	0.67	0.69	−0.05
11 Non-metallic minerals	0.70	0.69	0.68	0.67	0.67	−0.04
12 Metal products	0.81	0.82	0.80	0.76	0.80	−0.01
13 Other manufacturing	0.70	0.71	0.69	0.65	0.67	−0.04
14 Electricity	0.60	0.58	0.58	0.56	0.54	−0.09
15 Water	0.66	0.62	0.63	0.58	0.54	−0.18
16 Building and construction	1.92	1.93	1.92	1.90	1.93	−0.00
17 Wholesale and retail trade	1.10	1.07	1.08	1.04	1.01	−0.08
18 Hotels and restaurants	0.78	0.74	0.75	0.70	0.66	−0.15
19 Transport services	1.60	1.63	1.63	1.68	1.71	+0.07
20 Communication	0.71	0.70	0.69	0.64	0.65	−0.08
21 Finance and business services	0.71	0.68	0.68	0.63	0.60	−0.15
22 Ownership of dwellings	0.58	0.55	0.56	0.51	0.47	−0.19
23 Other services	0.75	0.72	0.72	0.68	0.66	−0.12
24 Public administr. and defense	0.90	0.87	0.88	0.84	0.81	−0.10
25 Education	0.68	0.65	0.65	0.61	0.57	−0.16
26 Health	0.58	0.55	0.56	0.52	0.48	−0.17
27 Agricultural services	0.57	0.54	0.55	0.51	0.49	−0.14
28 Other services	0.62	0.59	0.59	0.55	0.51	−0.17

inputs from services (non-traded), sectors whose own cost structures are little affected by the particular cost changes we are considering here.

When account is also taken of changes in the exchange rate (part b of the figure), the percentage changes in relative prices rise to over 900 percent in the case of petroleum refining and almost 7 percent in the case of transport. In addition, a small relative price increase is shown for building and construction (sector 16). It can also be noted that the appreciation of the exchange rate between 1976 and 1978 results in temporary increases in the

Table 3.12 *Distribution of relative price movements, 1973–81*

	Allowing for oil price changes	Allowing for oil price and exchange-rate changes
0–5 percent	4	6
5–9 percent	10	6
9–12 percent	13	6
12 percent +	1	11

relative prices of some outputs in that period even though the 1973–81 trend is downward. This is true of both agricultural sectors (1) and forestry (3), electricity (14), water (15), trade (17), and several other service sectors. In other words, the movement of the exchange rate somewhat dampened the price signals which would otherwise have emerged from the oil price disturbance.

Aside from the few obvious cases we have highlighted, there is a considerable concentration of the price movements which our calculations generate. This is evident from table 3.12. In the case of the experiment involving oil price changes alone, twenty-three of the relative price shifts are clustered within the range 5–12 percent (all but one of these being negative). Allowance for exchange rate changes sharply increases the dispersion. The more dramatic relative price falls in this case include traditional agriculture, forestry, water, and a number of the service sectors. In general, in spite of large absolute price changes, the close concentration of these gives rise to surprisingly few cases where relative price changes were in any sense dramatic. This might in turn suggest a limited need for resource reallocation even in price-responsive sectors.

3.4 *The distributional consequences of output expansion*

In this final subsection, we use the distributional data of the SAM to examine the *actual* changes in the structure of production in the economy between 1973 and 1980 and try to assess the consequences for both the factorial and the institutional distribution of income. For this purpose no attempt is made to explain the interaction of supply and demand forces which caused the changes in production structure: these are taken as given and we merely examine their likely distributional consequences. The pattern of production movements as revealed by data on GDP by industrial origin is shown, in constant 1976 prices, in table 3.13. The table reveals considerable variation in growth both over time and as between

Table 3.13 *Growth rates of GDP, 1973–80*
(*constant 1976 prices, percent*)

	1973–6	1976–8	1978–80
Traditional economy	9.4	7.6	6.9
Agriculture	6.6	14.4	−2.1
Forestry and fishing	11.5	12.7	4.5
Mining and quarrying	4.4	21.4	−2.2
Manufacturing	5.9	30.5	12.0
Building and construction	−13.3	22.2	8.4
Electricity and water	19.7	25.5	19.0
Trade, restaurants, and hotels	−0.8	17.6	8.0
Transport and communications	5.9	17.7	14.8
Finance, Insurance Etc.	36.3	14.1	8.6
Ownership and dwellings	10.1	7.6	14.5
Other services	19.8	17.0	22.5
Government services	21.9	11.8	12.8
Total GDP at factor cost	1.8	16.0	6.7
Equivalent annual rate	2.5	7.7	3.3

Source: World Bank (1982a), table 2.2.

sectors. The slow overall growth of 1973–6 was largely attributable to slow growth in manufacturing and construction but utility and service sectors including government services grew extremely rapidly in that period. The accelerated overall growth between 1976 and 1978 was largely attributable to the strong recovery of manufacturing and construction output and the continued rapid growth of the main utilities. At the same time, the growth rate slowed down considerably both in the traditional economy and in government services. Finally, in the 1978–80 period when overall growth slowed sharply, the reduction was widely based but with the primary producing sectors and especially agriculture sustaining the largest falls.

In order to examine the distributional consequences of these variations of output growth, we first allocate the thirteen sectors shown in table 3.13 to the twenty-eight production sectors of the SAM. More specifically, where the classification of table 3.13 involves some aggregation relative to that of the SAM, we assumed identical growth rates in the two or more SAM categories making up the single aggregated category shown in the table.[7] It was further assumed that the ratios of gross outputs to value added remained constant during the period under consideration so that the value-added growth rates shown in table 3.13 were also indicative of the growth rates of gross output. On this basis new gross output vectors, were constructed for 1973, 1978, and 1980. The factorial and institutional distribution consequences of output change were then generated using the following two calculations

$$fy_t = (CFINC)g_t \tag{3.5}$$

and

$$hy_t = (CINSINC)fy_t \tag{3.6}$$

where g_t is a vector of gross output in time period t, fy_t is a vector of factor incomes in time period t, hy_t is a vector of household incomes in time period t, where $t = 1973$, 1976, 1978, and 1980.

$CFINC$ is a 7×28 submatrix of the SAM showing (in coefficient form) the proportion of output of each sector paid to each of seven factors.

$CINSINC$ is a 14×7 submatrix of the SAM, showing (again in coefficient form) the proportion of factor income of each type paid to each of fourteen institutional categories.

The results of this calculation expressed in terms of income shares are shown in tables 3.14 and 3.15.

As far as factor incomes are concerned, the results show a modest but clear tendency for wage incomes to rise relative to the incomes of the self employed and family workers. The production sectors stand apart as a source of self-employment incomes: the traditional sector where 98 percent of 1976 value added was distributed in this way and agriculture where the corresponding percentage was 55 percent.[8] The growth of these two sectors together has fallen behind the average growth rate by a significant margin since 1976 and this largely accounts for the simulated decrease in the factorial share of the self employed and family workers shown in table 3.14.

A less marked but nonetheless important result is the increase in the share of value added going to professional labor and, to a lesser extent, office workers. The two most intensive users of professional labor are education and health services (87 percent and 36 percent of sectoral value added, respectively), followed by finance, real estate, etc. (28 percent). The first of these sectors has quite clearly grown much faster than the economy-wide average in the 1973–80 period. Although education and health are not separately distinguished in the government services figure of table 3.13, that aggregate has also grown much faster than the overall economy average.

Obviously all these results depend upon the assumption of fixed coefficients in the $CFINC$ submatrix and the preponderance of demand influences as a cause of distributional changes. However, the restrictions on formal-sector wage settlements throughout most of the period and the effects of this on actual numbers employed may invalidate this assumption.

Table 3.14 *Movements of factor income shares, 1973–80*

Factors	1973	1976	1978	1980
Unskilled and semi-skilled workers	0.13	0.13	0.13	0.13
Skilled workers	0.07	0.07	0.07	0.08
Office workers and semi-professionals	0.08	0.09	0.09	0.09
Professional workers	0.11	0.11	0.11	0.12
Self-employed and family workers	0.30	0.29	0.28	0.27
Operating surplus	0.24	0.24	0.24	0.24
Consumption of fixed capital	0.07	0.07	0.07	0.07

Source: World Bank (1982a), table 2.2.

Table 3.15 *Movements of institutional income shares, 1973–80*

Institutional group	1973		1978		1980	
1 Urban <6,000 sh.	0.07		0.08		0.08	
2 Urban 6,000–20,000 sh.	0.13	0.28	0.13	0.30	0.13	0.30
3 Urban >20,000 sh.	0.08		0.09		0.09	
4 Rural <0.5 ha.	0.01		0.01		0.01	
5 Rural 0.5 ha + add. incomes	0.02		0.02		0.02	
6 Rural 0.5 ha–1.0 ha	0.03		0.03		0.02	
7 Rural 0.5 ha–1.0 ha + add. incomes	0.02	0.4	0.02	0.41	0.02	0.39
8 Rural 1.0–8.0 ha	0.21		0.21		0.20	
9 Rural >8.0 ha	0.01		0.01		0.01	
10 Other rural	0.10		0.11		0.11	
11 Private enterprise	0.20		0.20		0.20	
12 Public enterprise	0.03		0.03		0.03	
13 Central government	0.01		0.01		0.01	
14 Local government	0.01		0.01		0.01	

The results in table 3.14 also fail to capture the effects on profits and so the income from capital associated with the wide variation in the availability of import licenses during the period. As we shall see later, in the general equilibrium analysis of chapter 8, these have the potential of introducing variations in the income from capital relative to labor.

Similar remarks apply *pari passu* to our results on institutional incomes (table 3.15). Here, there is a modest tendency for urban income shares to rise relative to rural shares. The aggregated urban share of value added rises from 28.8 percent in 1973 to 29.4 percent in 1978 and then to 30.2 percent by

Table 3.16 *The importance of transfer incomes for different households*

Institutional group	(1) Factor incomes	(2) Transfer incomes	(3) = (2)/(1)
Urban <6,000 sh.	97.0	4.0	0.041
Urban 6,000–20,000 sh.	172.0	21.1	0.123
Urban >20,000 sh.	111.8	56.9	0.509
Rural <0.5 ha	18.8	1.7	0.09
Rural 0.5 ha + add. incomes	21.1	5.1	0.242
Rural 0.5 ha–1.0 ha	34.1	3.9	0.114
Rural 0.5 ha–1.0 ha + add. incomes	23.3	5.4	0.232
Rural 1.0 ha–8.0 ha	273.8	28.9	0.106
Rural >8.0 ha	15.7	5.2	0.331
Other rural	137.5	57.1	0.415

Source: Allen and Hayden (1980).

1980. If anything, the middle-income urban groups seem to have done disproportionately well from this development.

In the rural sector, households are differentiated both by size of land holding and according to whether they receive additional non-farm income. Here there is a clear indication that those rural households with little additional income other than that from farming, have fared slightly worse than those having similar land holdings but some access to non-farm incomes.[9] For example, amongst households with land holdings of up to 1.0 hectare but little additional income (categories 4 and 6 in the table), the results suggest a fall in their value-added share from 4.1 percent in 1973 to 3.8 percent in 1980. The corresponding figures for those in the same land-owning categories having access to non-farm incomes (categories 5 and 7 in the table) are from 3.4 percent in 1973 to 3.3 percent in 1980. Furthermore, these results would be accentuated if explicit account were to be taken of transfer incomes (and especially profits distributed from private enterprises) since these add proportionately more to the incomes of rural households having significant off-farm incomes than to other incomes (see table 3.16).

4 Conclusions

The approach developed in this chapter has allowed us to probe more extensively into aspects of Kenya's adjustment to external shocks un-covered by the analytical method of chapter 2. As in that chapter, the analysis compared actual outcomes with a counterfactual defined by fixity of underlying coefficients to arrive at a deeper understanding of the nature of Kenyan policy responses to external shocks. Since the social accounting matrix for Kenya contains, as is customary for such a data base, detailed information not only on disaggregated production sectors but also on institutional categories as well as factors of production, it proved possible to examine a range of hypotheses that exploited the richness of that structure. The conclusions emerging from that analysis are as follows.

First, the 1976–7 coffee and tea price boom had a quantitatively large impact on outputs in agriculture, water, food, textiles, and the service sectors, on incomes across the entire range of factors and institutions with lower-income urban households, however, benefiting less than high-income urban households and all categories of rural households, and on public and private consumption and imports. It also boosted central government expenditure. The enormity of this disturbance and its economy-wide effects made it virtually impossible to maintain a coherent pattern of policy response to the first round of oil price increases.

Second, the analysis of import substitution shows that while the sharp rise in imports induced by the coffee/tea price boom in 1976–8 was financed by the associated foreign exchange windfall, there was a significant restraint on imports between 1973 and 1976 and again between 1978 and 1980. The mechanisms – presumably a combination of price and non-price restrictions – which made this possible are left unspecified and will be formally treated by the general equilibrium analysis of Kenya's adjustment in chapter 8.

Third, in spite of large absolute price movements, relative price changes arising from the 1973–4 and 1980–1 adjustments of the dollar price of oil, allied to exchange-rate changes, affected a surprisingly small number of sectors, suggesting a limited need for resource reallocation even in price responsive sectors.

Fourth, the changes in the structure of production between 1973 and 1980 led to a rise in wage incomes relative to the incomes of the self employed and family workers and to an increase in the share of value added going to professional labor and, to a lesser extent, office workers. Urban income shares rose relative to rural shares, with middle-income urban groups having benefited particularly from this change, while rural households with little additional non-farm income fared somewhat worse than those with similar land holdings but with access to various sources of non-farm incomes. These results, however, do not take into account restrictions on formal-sector wage settlements operating in the labor market. Nor do they account for the effects on profit and income of capital associated with premia enjoyed on import licenses during the period of the analysis. The analysis of chapter 8 addresses both questions.

It is characteristic of the partial equilibrium method employed in this chapter that value-added prices are taken to be constant and that supply constraints are assumed away.[10] In contrast, the general equilibrium policy analysis pays detailed attention to the modeling of factor markets. Thus, depending on the country being analyzed, particular segments of the labor market may not clear because of formal or informal wage indexation mechanisms. Those unable to find wage employment then swell the ranks of the self employed, where flexible wages help clear the market. Moreover, sectoral wage-rate differentials might characterize the same type of labor. Turning to capital markets, the general equilibrium analysis, which tracks historical developments as well as alternative policy sequences over ten years as opposed to a single period, allows the sectoral pattern of investment to respond to differences in rates of return earned in different sectors. This makes it possible, for example, to ask whether the gains from following such a market-oriented reallocation of investment, with the total volume of the latter held at the same level as that actually implemented, would have offset losses from adverse terms-of-trade disturbances.

To help develop this agenda, we turn next to a general equilibrium-based policy analysis of shocks and adjustment in four countries. As in chapter 2, a common analytical structure is used to study the experiences of those countries. Describing that structure is the task of the next chapter.

Notes

1 See Allen and Hayden (1980).
2 Chapter 4 contains a brief account of the properties of social-accounting matrices.
3 Row 8 which is also included in the "factors-of-production block" refers to indirect taxes.
4 For a discussion of this point, see chapter 4, Section 3.6.3.
5 All of this analysis assumes that it is the import coefficients rather than the input–output coefficients which have changed. While this assumption might raise some objections, it does conform with the normal practice in CGE approaches where substitutability between foreign and domestic traded goods is normally incorporated while substitutability between different categories of domestically supplied intermediate goods normally is not. Certainly, this is the assumption embodied in the computable general equilibrium model as described later in chapter 4.
6 See, World Bank (1982a).
7 This was done purely for computational convenience. The alternative of aggregating the twenty-eight production sectors of the SAM into fourteen should produce identical results but involves much more manipulation of data.

8 The next largest coefficient is 27 percent in the case of wholesale and retail trade. After that there are only three of the SAM sectors where the coefficient exceeds 10 percent: hotels and restaurants, textiles, and wood products.

9 It should be noted that the SAM classifies rural households according to two criteria: the size of land holdings (in ha) and whether the household derives income additional to that from its own farming activity.

10 For a detailed discussion, see chapter 4.

4 The structure of the country models

1 Introduction

This chapter describes the structure and working of the general equilibrium models used to analyze country adjustment to external shocks in chapters 6 through 9.[1] This is done in the following steps. Section 2, following this introduction, presents an accounting framework which describes the flows of payments and receipts in the models. Section 3 turns to a more formal description of technological and behavioral assumptions underlying the analysis. This focuses on general features rather than elaborating on the specific assumptions made. It also provides some intuition that helps explain why results come out the way they do. Section 4 addresses the dynamic aspects of the analysis and reviews how the sequence of static equilibria obtained by solving the model are linked together. This section also describes how the models are made to track various historical economic indicators. Section 5 looks at ways in which the four country models differ from each other. It also indicates how the specific assumptions can be expected to affect the results of the country analysis undertaken in chapters 6 to 9. Section 6 demonstrates how the model may be used to set up policy experiments to analyze adjustment to external shocks. Section 7 concludes. Readers interested in following the workings of the model and the policy simulations, with a view to replicating such analysis, are referred to Brooke, Kendrick, and Meeraus (1988) which contains the relevant software and full model documentation.[2]

2 An accounting framework for the models

All the models employed in chapters 6–9 are based on comprehensive accounting for payments made. Whereas in certain partial models, such as the one in chapter 3, it is not very important to account for all income, general equilibrium models rest explicitly on the fact that a payment made from one agent to another will affect the budget of the recipient, who then spends the additional income according to some behavioral rule.

To enable consistent accounting of all flows in the economy, the models are based on a social accounting matrix (SAM).[3] This is nothing more than a convenient way to represent all the double entries of bookkeeping. In a SAM, an entry in cell (i, j) indicates a flow of services from account i to account j, and correspondingly a payment from account j to account i. Just as in traditional bookkeeping, all accounts must balance. In a SAM, this means that the sum of entries in a particular column must equal the sum of entries in the corresponding row. Or, using economic language, all services must be paid for, and all income must be spent. Note that the fact that all income must be spent does not imply that all household income must be consumed. Instead, it means that whatever is not consumed must be saved (which is a payment to a savings account). Similarly, what is saved, must be invested. This, of course, is the familiar investment–savings balance.

2.1 Uses of the SAM

2.1.1 Establishing a consistent data base

In the context of general equilibrium modeling, a SAM serves several useful purposes. One is the above accounting function. Using a SAM to establish a data base for a general equilibrium model ensures consistency of the data used. Typically, data come from many different sources and at different levels of aggregation. In raw form, they may not be consistent. Thus, different figures for current-account surplus or deficit may result from using national accounts statistics, trade statistics, or revenue statistics. Such discrepancies are easily isolated and corrected when using the SAM framework.

Consequently, all the models in this study use data which generate a balanced SAM.

2.1.2 An overview of the economy

Another use of the SAM is to give a quick overview of the economy in question. More than a matrix of numbers, a SAM is also usefully regarded as a statement of economic structure. Instead of describing in detail the SAM for each model, the discussion here focuses on the more general structural features shared by them. Table 4.1 below shows the structural SAM that underlies the models used in this study.

This SAM is seen to have nine accounts. The first one is production. This describes the flows of services and payments in domestic production. Although we represent production as one account in the SAM, it really consists of six sector-specific accounts in the country-specific models

Table 4.1 Structural SAM

	Production	Composite commodity	Labor	Land and capital	Infrastructure	Households	Government	Rest of the world	Consolidated capital	Total
Production		Domestic production								Domestic production
Composite commodity	Domestic intermediates + trade margins					Private consumption	Government consumption	Exports	Investment	Aggregate demand
Labor	Labor factor income									Gross labor income
Land and capital	Capital factor income									Gross capital income
Infrastructure	Infrastructure rents									Infrastructure revenue
Households		Import license premia	Labor income	Capital income	Infrastructure rents	Household transfers	Government transfers	World transfers		Private income
Government	Taxes and tariffs on intermediates	Final import tariffs and sales taxes	Labor taxes	Capital taxes	Infrastructure rents	Consumption and income taxes		Export taxes	Commodity taxes	Government revenue
Rest of the world	Intermediate imports at world prices	Final imports at world prices					Government imports		Imported capital goods	World "revenue"
Consolidated capital						Private savings	Government savings	Foreign savings		Total savings
Total	Domestic production	Aggregate supply of goods and services	Gross labor income	Gross capital income	Infrastructure rents	Total private income	Government revenue	World "revenue"	Total investment	

(except in the case of Turkey, where seven sectors are distinguished) (see section 5.1). Reading down the column, it is seen that each production sector uses inputs of so-called composite commodities. The precise definition of composite commodities differs across the models, but fundamentally they are just domestically produced goods at market prices. The production sectors also pay for trade and transportation services in the form of trade margins.

Next, the production sectors use labor in various forms, land and capital services, and infrastructural inputs. Corresponding payments are factor remunerations. Production also requires that payments be made to particular households for rents in the form of premia on import licenses (when imports are restricted), and to the government in the form of indirect taxes and tariffs. Finally, in addition to the domestic inputs, production uses imported intermediates.

Reading across the row for the production account, it is seen that all domestic output is used to "produce" the composite commodity. In the models of this study there are exactly as many composite commodities as production sectors. Each production sector produces a specific commodity which may be used both as an intermediate in the production of the commodity itself and other commodities, as well as for final demands.

The column for composite commodities shows that, in addition to domestically produced goods (which, it will be recollected, use *intermediate* imports) it takes final imports (specifically imported *capital goods*) to produce composites (see also figure 4.1 on the structure of production). These imports generate rents to households and tariffs to the government. Also, the gross output may be subject to sales taxes.

On the usage side (the row for composite commodities) the gross output may be used either as intermediates, or for final demands. The models cover private consumption, government consumption, exports, and investment (including stock changes) as final demand categories.

Turning to the factor accounts, i.e., the labor, land, and capital, and infrastructure accounts, it is seen that the factor incomes are allocated to households, net of taxes and possible rents accruing to the government.

The row for households shows the composition of household income. Again, although the SAM presented here only shows a single household account, the country-specific models cover different household types, thus enabling an analysis of income distribution (for details see section 5.2.1). Beyond the sources of income mentioned already (import license premia and factor income and rents) households receive transfers from one another, government transfers, and transfers from the rest of the world, typically in the form of workers' remittances.

Household income net of direct taxes is spent on private consumption of

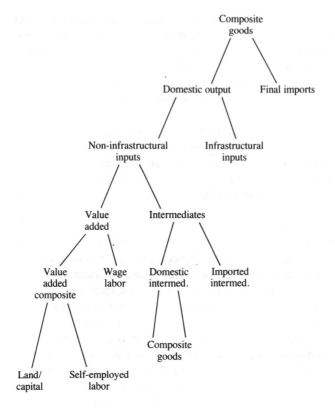

Figure 4.1 The structure of production

the various composite commodities, on which the government may have levied consumption taxes, and for interhousehold transfers. The rest is saved.

Similarly, government revenue consists of taxes on intermediates, import tariffs, factor taxes, infrastructural rents, consumption and income taxes, as well as export taxes (typically negative: export subsidies), and taxes on capital goods. The revenue is spent on government consumption of the various composite commodities, on government transfers to the households, and on direct government imports (oil), while the budget surplus (deficit) is saved (dissaved). Transactions with the rest of the world include various types of imports (intermediates, final goods, and capital goods), and exports including subsidies or taxes, as well as international transfers. The difference between imports and exports and world transfers is foreign savings.

The last account in the SAM covers savings and investment. As mentioned above, total savings consist of private savings, government savings, and foreign savings. These are the funds available for investment, consisting of demands for domestic and imported investment goods, on both of which the government may levy taxes.

Summarizing, although the country models use a simplified representation of the actual economies, they do cover many interactions. These include (1) production sectors that demand various factors and primary inputs and supply commodities; and (2) institutions, such as (i) different households that supply factors, demand consumption goods, and save, (ii) a government that collects taxes, makes transfers, consumes, and saves, and (iii) the rest of the world that supplies imports and demands exports. Moreover, the models are built to handle all these interactions in a consistent manner, with full accounting for receipts and payments.

It should be mentioned that the SAM in table 4.1 is not an exact replica of the structure of all the different models. This is because not all the flows shown in table 4.1 occur in every model. Thus, in some cases, all infrastructure rents are assumed to accrue to households alone. In other cases, income taxes have not been explicitly modeled. The SAM presented here is, however, only meant to offer a rough overview of the structure of the models, rather than telling the whole story. In fact, it is a bit more general than any of the SAMs used for the country models, thus accommodating the particular cases when some of the flows in table 4.1 turn out to be zero.

2.1.3 Helping ensure equilibrium

A third use of the SAM is more directly linked with modeling and has to do with the definition of the equilibrium used. The economies modeled are said to be in equilibrium when all transactions planned by economic agents can be carried out. It is supposed that, if certain plans cannot be executed, agents will adjust their behavior and modify those plans. This adjustment continues until all plans are made mutually consistent, i.e., can be simultaneously carried out. In this situation no agent feels the need to adjust behavior, and the economy will be in an equilibrium. In the context of a SAM, this means that all *ex-ante* transactions must generate a balanced SAM. In order to guarantee this relationship, the model must be formulated in a way that recognizes all the balancing requirements implied by the SAM.

For that reason, a large part of all the models are simply transcriptions of the SAM. For instance, the balance condition for households is given by forcing the household row sums to equal the household column sums.

For each household:

Income =
  labor income
  + capital income
  + infrastructure rents
  + transfers from other households to this household
  + government transfers
  + world transfers
Income =
  the total value of goods consumed
  + transfers from this household
  + total taxes paid for consumption
  + total income taxes paid
  + savings

Similarly, these row-sum-equals-column-sum conditions are stated explicitly or sometimes implicitly for all other accounts. The SAM establishes what the correct income and expenditure measures are. In addition it helps in understanding why one balancing condition may be left out from the models: if $n-1$ of the n column sums are equal to the sums of the corresponding $n-1$ rows, the last column sum must equal the last row sum.[4] Therefore, that last account must be balanced if all other accounts are balanced. This is the relationship known as Walras' law which says that if $n-1$ of n markets are in equilibrium, then the n'th market is also in equilibrium. From a modeling point of view, this means that we can choose to drop any market- or account-balancing constraint from the model: it will automatically be satisfied if all other balancing constraints are satisfied. Thus, for example, the country models do not spell out the savings investment balance explicitly. However it is still satisfied by all of them.

3 The static core model

The discussion so far has noted which kinds of transactions are covered by the country-specific models. We now go a step further and specify the core model fully. We focus here on what is common to the country models. In section 5 we describe the dissimilarities.

The model used is multiperiod in nature. It is solved as a sequence of static models, where investment this year affects the capital stock next year. This section describes the single period, or static, model. In the next section, we turn to the dynamic aspects of the model.

The description that follows includes (1) a general overview, (2) production technology and producers' behavior, (3) income generation and distribution, (4) the institutions of the economy (households, government, rest of the world), (5) equilibrium in the markets for commodities and factors, and (6) the workings of the model as a whole.

3.1 *Overview of the model*

The outline of the SAM has already shown that the model covers the interactions of producers, households, the government, and the rest of the world.

Producers in each sector produce domestic outputs. In doing so, they have access to a technology that allows for various degrees of substitution among factors. These factors include intermediates and primary factors (capital, land, infrastructural inputs, as well as different types of labor). Producers act as profit maximizers in perfectly competitive markets, i.e., they take factor and output prices (inclusive of any taxes) as given and express demands for factors so as to minimize unit costs of output. The precise description of production technology and the factor demands that result from producers' profit maximization is worked out in section 3.2 below.

Households supply factors inelastically to production (initial endowments are fixed), and demand commodities for consumption based on utility maximization given income and market prices. Also, households save and may pay taxes to the government. We provide a detailed description of household income generation in section 3.3.1, and consumption and savings behavior in section 3.4.1 below. We return to these topics again with a discussion of the specific behavioral assumptions employed in the country models in sections 5.2.1 and 5.3.1.

The government is not assumed to be an optimizing agent. Instead, government consumption, transfers, tax rates, etc. are exogenous policy instruments. Total government revenue generation is described in section 3.3.2 and spending patterns are described in section 3.4.2.

The rest of the world supplies goods to the economy which are imperfect substitutes for domestic output, makes transfer payments, and demands exports. Imports are combined with domestic goods, according to the cost-minimizing behavior of domestic agents, to produce composite outputs for each sector, which are then traded in the commodity markets. The country is assumed to be a price-taker in import markets, i.e., world prices are exogenously given. A similar structure for the rest of the world is implicit in the model: exports from the economy are imperfect substitutes for foreign goods. Given prices, the rest of the world minimizes unit costs of their composite commodities, which gives rise to a downward-sloping export demand curve. The difference between rest-of-the-world incomes (from imports) and expenditure (transfers and exports) is saved. A more precise description of the transactions with the rest of the world is given in sections 3.3.3 and 3.4.3.

In most experiments with the model, investment is assumed to be exogenous. However, in some cases the level of investment may change to accommodate specific foreign borrowing targets. In addition, the sectoral allocation is mostly exogenous, although in some experiments, the sectoral allocation is allowed to vary according to market signals. The layout of such an experiment is discussed in section 6.3.

It is the task of the model to ensure that all plans for production, factor demands, factor supplies, consumption, etc., as derived from the optimizing behavior of the different agents, can be simultaneously carried out, i.e., that supplies are equal to demands in all markets. These market-clearing conditions are given in section 3.5. To establish this general equilibrium, the model solver finds a set of relative prices that leads to plans that are mutually consistent. The model solution is thus a set of market-clearing relative prices and quantities and will of course be a function of exogenous variables (government consumption, tax rates, oil prices, etc.), and the assumptions made in the model.

Perhaps the most important simplification in the models is that they focus exclusively on flows of commodities and services. Thus, the models cover only the "real" and not the monetary aspects of the economies being studied. This means that issues such as the impact of oil price shocks on inflation, or the effects of government financing decisions cannot be highlighted by the models. In contrast, however, they are well suited for analyzing structural effects of external shocks and fiscal responses to them. This is due to the comprehensive modeling of intersectoral and interinstitutional linkages.

Since (almost) all agents are rational, the model is founded solidly in economic theory. It is not a pure standard textbook general equilibrium model, however, because of the presence of distortionary taxes, various wage indexation schemes allowing the emergence of unemployment, and the like (see sections 3.5.2 and 5.4.2 for a discussion of the workings of factor markets). It is the combination of the general equilibrium framework and the inclusion of institutional features particular to the economy being analyzed that makes the model well suited for the analysis of adjustment to external shocks.

The general equilibrium framework allows a comprehensive coverage of all the direct and indirect effects of external shocks. Thus, an oil price shock affects intermediate commodity prices, leading to input substitutions by way of the cost-minimizing response of producers to changes in relative prices. This changes demands for all factors as well as output prices for all sectors. The changes in factor demands affect prices of factors and thus household incomes. Since both household incomes and relative prices change, consumption demands will also change. Export demands will be affected too. This leads to a round of adjustment of production and prices to clear commodity markets. But, as a result of this, new factor demands result. To clear factor markets, a new set of factor prices is required, affecting household income, and so on. This process of simultaneous quantity and price adjustment in all markets continues until a new general equilibrium is reached. In addition, since the models are multisectoral and cover multiple factors and households, they can be used to analyze changes in economic structure and income.

The emphasis on particular institutional structures and rigidities allows the model to mimic the workings of the economy of a particular country. Thus, although the models used in the study of adjustment in India, Kenya, Turkey, and Thailand, are all structurally similar (they are all general equilibrium models of the above type), they include different institutional descriptions and are of course based on different data. In particular, as described in section 4.2 of this chapter, each one is calibrated to track the historical evolution of various macroeconomic indicators for the country in question. This allows the model to be used in simulating counterfactual experiments: what would have happened if there had been oil price shocks and if particular policies had reduced rigidities or inefficiencies in the economy?

As can be seen, there are many building blocks in the model. In what follows, we shall describe each of these in more detail.

3.2 Production

In this section, we shall describe production in the model. We first discuss technology and producers' behavior, and next spell out the mathematical details of the implementation of production in the model.

3.2.1 Technology
Overview
In all the models, the production technology features constant returns to scale. Thus, doubling all inputs will double the output. To produce a commodity, several inputs are used. These include domestic and imported intermediates and primary factors. The primary factors cover different types of labor (for example skilled, unskilled, and agricultural labor), land, and capital, and infrastructural inputs. In all the models, land, capital, and infrastructure are sector specific. In contrast, labour may move between sectors. This means that, although the technology has constant returns to scale, it also contains fixed factors, so that there are decreasing returns to scale in the variable factors.

In order to accommodate various degrees of substitution among the factors, the models implement the technology as a tree structure. The tree is outlined in figure 4.1 above.

At the highest level, domestic output is combined with particular final imports (typically capital goods, or in some models nothing) to form composite commodities, which are the goods sold for final uses. Domestic output is produced by a combination of infrastructural and non-infrastructural inputs, the latter consisting of value added and intermediates. Value added is produced by some combination of capital and land and various types of labor. In the figure, we use two labor types (wage labor and self-employed labor), although in some of the models the labor types are different. Intermediates, on the other hand, comprise domestic and imported intermediates, where the domestic intermediate good is made up of composites.

At all levels of this tree, particular assumptions can be made as to the degree of substitutability of inputs entering that level. The models use an assumption of constant elasticity of substitution (CES) to represent technology. This is a rather general form, which allows for imperfect substitution but also includes as special cases perfect substitution (when the elasticity of substitution is infinite), Cobb–Douglas technology (when the elasticity of substitution is 1), and fixed coefficients, or Leontief, technology (when the elasticity of substitution is 0). The choice of substitution elasticity affects the functional distribution of income. If production is Cobb–Douglas the factor income shares are constant. If, on the other hand, the elasticity of substitution is between 0 and 1, for example, between capital and labor, this implies that a wage increase will increase the share of labor income. If the elasticity of substitution is higher than 1, the factor income share decreases when the factor remuneration rate increases.

Also, it may be noted that, if the elasticity of substitution is the same at two consecutive levels of the tree, these two levels may be collapsed to only one level with three inputs instead of two levels with two inputs at each level. Therefore, since the structure can accommodate mixtures of these assumptions at various levels of the tree, it is very flexible, provided the assumption of constant returns to scale is found acceptable. Although the partial elasticity of substitution may be high at one level of the tree, the general equilibrium elasticity may be high or low, depending on the rest of the tree.

Note, however, that the substitution elasticities are partial, i.e., only valid under the *ceteris paribus* assumption. Once the above production technology is embedded in the full general equilibrium model that assumption clearly does not hold true. For instance, assume that the wage rate for self-employed labor increases. A partial argument based on a low elasticity of substitution between self-employed and wage labor would indicate that the share of self-employed labor in income would increase markedly. However, in the general equilibrium setting, the labor substitution implies that the demand for wage labor would increase, thus increasing the wage rate of that labor type as well. The overall effect could be that the relative wage rate does not change very much, and consequently that the income distribution would not vary a great deal. A similar effect would occur if the partial elasticity of substitution were high. Thus, in general it appears that the implied general equilibrium elasticity of substitution is closer to 1 than the partial elasticity of substitution. This is worth bearing in mind, since it may in part account for some of the findings in our study that the income distribution remains rather stable under various scenarios.

Each production sector in the models is represented using the above tree. However, the particular elasticities of substitution may differ from sector to sector. Furthermore, some inputs may be zero in particular sectors, in which case the output from that level in the tree is equal to the other (non-zero) input.

Mathematical formulation

We shall now formulate the production technology more formally. For each level of the tree (save the composition of domestic intermediates) the production structure has the following form

$$X - f(F, G, a, d, s) \qquad (1)$$

where

$X =$ the output at that level
$F =$ the input of the first factor
$G =$ the input of the second factor
$a =$ the total factor productivity
$d =$ the distribution parameter
$s =$ the elasticity of substitution

Specifically, under the CES assumption, the production function for a given level of the tree in a given sector is given by

$$X - a(dF^{-r} + (1-d)G^{-r})^{-1/r} \qquad (1')$$

Here, r is related to the elasticity of substitution by

$$s = 1/(1+r)$$

In some cases, particular inputs are fixed. This, for instance, is the case for infrastructural inputs and land/capital. Otherwise, the factors are variable.

At the lowest level of the tree, in the production of domestic and imported intermediates, the elasticity of substitution is zero in all models, i.e., fixed quantity coefficients are maintained among the individual commodities making up the intermediate good. In this case, letting

N_i denote the intermediate input to sector i,

A_{ji} denote the fixed quantity coefficient of sector j commodities in the production of sector i intermediates, and

X_j denote the quantity of the sector j commodity, we have that

$$N_i = \Sigma_j A_{ji} X_j \tag{2}$$

The fixed quantity coefficients assumption implies that the relative usage of intermediates is price insensitive. This may seem to be an extreme assumption. However, in support of the assumption two observations may be made. First, although the quantity composition of a bundle of intermediates remains fixed, the overall level of intermediates usage in production is price responsive, since intermediates substitute imperfectly for value added. Secondly, the availability of data on intermediates use is limited. Typically, it is published in the form of an input–output matrix and is available for only a single year. For these reasons, the assumption of fixed quantity coefficients may be regarded as the neutral one for the countries considered in this study.

3.2.2 Producers' behavior

Producers are assumed to behave as profit maximizers. In addition, every producer is assumed to be small, so that he can take market prices of inputs and outputs as given. Also, since the model describes a competitive general equilibrium, the producer may correctly assume that any demand for a factor can be satisfied at the going price, and that there will be no quantity rationing.

Under these assumptions, the producer's problem is to maximize the net value of output, subject to the production possibilities as described above. Of course, since production has constant returns to scale, the profits will be zero, implying that the product is completely exhausted.

Under the nested CES tree above, the profit-maximization or cost-minimization problem is separable. This means that if inputs are optimally chosen at every level of the tree, without reference to any other level, the overall input composition will be efficient. Therefore, the easiest way to view the producer's behavior is to assume that he minimizes the cost or maximizes the profits of producing each of the composites entering the CES tree.

This leads to a sequence of optimization problems of the following form. For every level of the tree, choose a combination of the two inputs, which maximizes profits subject to the technological possibilities, and subject to prices being fixed and no quantity rationing:

Let P_X denote the price of the output created at the given level of the tree in the given sector,
P_F denote the factor price of the first factor,
P_G denote the factor price of the second factor.

Then, mathematically, the problem is to

Maximize $P_X X - P_F F - P_G G$
subject to $X = f(F, G, a, d, s)$

The solution is to demand inputs to the level where the marginal factor productivity equals the real product wage rate. Under the specific assumption of a CES function, the solution turns out to yield a relative factor composition of

$$F/G = (dP_G/(1-d)P_F)^s \qquad (3)$$

along with product exhaustion

$$P_X X = P_F F + P_G G \qquad (4)$$

or, expressed relative to output

$$F = X a^{(s-1)}(dP_X/P_F)^s \qquad (3')$$

$$G = X a^{(s-1)}((1-d)P_X/P_G)^s \qquad (3'')$$

(3') and (3'') imply (3) and (4) and vice versa.

It may be verified that the partial factor demand curves are downward sloping in the factor price, with a constant elasticity of s. However, as was mentioned above, partial arguments may be misleading in a general equilibrium setting. For instance since the output price will normally be affected if a factor price increases, the general equilibrium response to a factor price change will typically be smaller than indicated in (3') and (3'') above.

Another point worth mentioning is that one must be careful in interpreting (3') and (3'') as determining factor demands. Strictly speaking, they only state that, in equilibrium, those simultaneous relationships must be satisfied. In some cases, notably for capital and infrastructural inputs, factor supplies to a sector are fixed. Therefore, (3') will not determine factor usage, but rather determine factor price.

Similarly, for the levels of the tree where fixed quantity coefficients are used, we have that the price of the bundle of intermediates is just the weighted average price of the individual intermediates entering the bundle, where the weights are the quantity shares of each intermediate in the bundle. Mathematically, this gives the following pricing relation

$$P_{Ni} = \Sigma_j A_{ji} P_j \qquad (5)$$

where

P_{Ni} = the price of the intermediates bundle in sector i
P_j = the (tax inclusive) market price of the sector j commodity

3.2.3 The full production structure

It may now be appropriate to write out the full production structure of the models. We omit the sector subscript to ease notation. However, every sector of the economy has the same production structure with only the values of coefficients and parameters varying.

Starting from the top of the tree and moving downwards, we have a sequence of expressions, each in the format of (1') (production function), (4) (product exhaustion), and (3) (relative factor demands) above. For the top level of the tree, we have that

$$Q = a_Q(d_Q X^{-rQ} + (1 - d_Q)M^{-rQ)(-1/rQ)} \tag{6}$$

$$P_Q Q = P_X X + P_M M \tag{7}$$

$$X/M = (d_Q P_M/(1 - d_Q)P_X)^{SQ} \tag{8}$$

where Q is composite output, X is domestic output, and M is final import. The same are used as subscripts to indicate to what prices (P) refer.

Next, domestic output is described by

$$X = a_X(d_X Z^{-rx} + (1 - d_X)G^{-rx})^{(-1/rx)} \tag{9}$$

$$P_X X = P_Z Z + P_G G \tag{10}$$

$$Z/G = (d_X P_G/(1 - d_X)P_Z)^S X \tag{11}$$

where Z is non-infrastructural inputs, and G is inputs of infrastructure services. To describe the generation of non-infrastructural inputs, we have

$$Z = a_Z(d_Z V^{-rz} + (1 - d_Z)N^{-rz})^{(-1/rz)} \tag{12}$$

$$P_Z Z = P_V V + P_N N \tag{13}$$

$$V/N = (d_Z P_N/(1 - d_Z)P_V)^S Z \tag{14}$$

Here, V is value added, and N is intermediates. We now first describe the value-added branch of the tree. Value added is described by

$$V = a_V(d_V S^{-rv} + (1 - d_V)LW^{-rv})^{(-1/rv)} \tag{15}$$

$$P_V V = P_S S + WLW \tag{16}$$

$$S/LW = (d_V W/(1 - d_V)P_S)^S V \tag{17}$$

Here, S is a composite of capital and self-employed labor (or skilled labor in the Turkey model), and LW is wage labor (unskilled labor in the Turkey model). W denotes the wage rate.

The capital/self-employed labor composite is described by

$$S = a_S(d_S K^{-rs} + (1 - d_S)LS^{-rs})^{(-1/rs)} \tag{18}$$

$$P_S S = P_K K + P_{LS} LS \tag{19}$$

$$K/LS = (d_S P_{LS}/(1 - dS)P_K)^{Ss} \tag{20}$$

where K is the capital stock, and LS is the input of self-employed labor.

We turn next to the intermediates branch. Intermediates are a composite of domestic and imported intermediates

$$N = a_N(d_N ND^{-rN} + (1 - d_N)NM^{-rN})^{(-1/rN)} \tag{21}$$

$$P_N N = P_{ND} ND + P_{NM} NM \tag{22}$$

$$ND/NM = (d_N P_{NM}/(1 - d_N)P_{ND})^{S_N} \tag{23}$$

Here, ND and NM signify domestic and imported intermediates respectively.

The prices of domestic and imported intermediates are given by the fixed coefficients assumption in (5) above. Taxes and trade margins are treated as follows. Let

A_{ij} denote the input–output coefficients for domestic intermediates (scaled to sum to 1 over i),

AM_{ij} denote the input–output coefficients for non-competitive imported intermediates (scaled to sum to 1 over i),

t_{NDi} denote the *ad valorem* tax rate on domestic intermediates from sector i,

t_{NMi} denote the *ad valorem* tax rate on imported intermediates from sector i

t_{mi} denote the *ad valorem* trade margin on imported intermediates from sector i, and

P_{NMj} denote landed prices of imported intermediates.

Then, the pricing relationships are

$$P_{NDi} = \Sigma_j A_{ji}(1 + t_{NDj})PQ_j \tag{24}$$

$$P_{NMi} = \Sigma_j AM_{ji}(1 + t_{NMj} + t_{mj})P_{NMj} \tag{25}$$

To finalize the production side, we need to specify that capital stocks (or land in the agriculture sector), and infrastructure outputs are given as quasi-fixed factors. Actually, the input of infrastructure is linked to the output of the infrastructure sector and distributed across receiving sectors according to fixed quantity shares, so we have that

$$K = \bar{K} \qquad (26)$$

and

$$G = a_G X_{\text{infrastructure}} \qquad (27)$$

where a_G are the fixed sectoral allocation shares for infrastructure.

3.2.4 Links with the rest of the model

To see how the production block above ties in with the rest of the model, it may be worthwhile to count equations and unknowns. Clearly, we have twenty-two equations (equations 6 to 27). Here are the twenty-six unknowns with a tentative reference to where they are determined:

Q	composite output	(7)
P_Q	price of composite output	(rest of model)
X	domestic output	(6)
P_X	price of domestic output	(10)
M	final imports	(8)
P_M	price of final imports	(rest of model)
Z	non-infrastructural inputs	(9)
P_Z	price of non-infrastructural inputs	(13)
G	infrastructural inputs	(27)
P_G	price of infrastructural inputs	(11)
V	value added	(12)
P_V	value-added price	(16)
N	intermediates	(14)
P_N	intermediates price	(22)
S	land/capital/labor composite	(15)
P_S	returns to land/capital/labor composite	(19)
LW	employment of wage labor	(17)
W	wage rate	(rest of model)
K	capital stock	(26)
P_K	returns to capital	(20)
LS	self employment	(18)
P_{LS}	returns to self employment	(rest of model)
ND	domestic intermediates use	(23)
NM	use of imported intermediates	(21)
P_{ND}	price of domestic intermediates	(24)
P_{NM}	price of imported intermediates	(25)

Note that this pairing of equations to unknowns is only meant to be suggestive. In reality, the full model is simultaneous, and it does not make any sense to say that a single equation has determined a single variable. However, from a systems point of view, it may be convenient to think of the individual building blocks of the model as generating a set of variable values conditional on getting other values.

In the ordering above, we have suggested that the production block depends on the rest of the model being able to generate the market price of composite output, the price of imports, the wage rate, and the return to self employment. The economic intuition is that wage rates are generated in the labor markets to be discussed in section 3.5.2 below, that import prices are determined by world markets, modified where applicable by the availability of administered imports allowed by the government, while the interactions between supply and demand jointly determine output prices and quantities. For a given price, market clearing determines output, and vice versa. An equally appropriate statement would be that the production side determines the output price, and that market clearing determines the quantity.

One point deserves mention. For some sectors, final imports are administered, i.e., $M = \bar{M}$. For those sectors, clearly (8) will not determine the level of imports but rather determine the scarcity premium on them, i.e., the level of premia that the different sectors are willing to pay for imports over and above the landed-cum-tariff price. In principle, these premia may be allocated to different agents (households or the government or both). Disregarding such distributional aspects and assuming that all premia accrue to the government, the import administration formally corresponds to endogenizing the tariff rate in equation (36) below. For sectors with administered imports, the premium may be positive or negative. For sectors where imports are not administered, the premium will be zero, and (8) determines the level of imports. For simplicity, we shall not pursue this issue further in the description of the core model.

3.3 Income generation

In this subsection, we take a look at the generation of income for households and revenues for the government and the rest of the world.

3.3.1 Household income

As was seen in the SAM in table 4.1, we can distinguish four sources of household income. These are (1) labor income, (2) capital and land revenues, (3) income from government subsidies in the form of infrastructure, and (4) non-production-related income in the form of transfers, workers remittances, etc. In addition, all the models of this study cover more than a single household type. The distinction may be between urban and rural households or agricultural, unskilled labor, skilled labor, and capitalist households. Here, we are not concerned about the specific distributional mechanisms adopted in the individual models but rather with the common theme, which is that the different households receive shares of the different income types corresponding to their fixed initial endowments.

In general, for factor income, the gross disposable income by sector is generated as factor returns times factor employment. Particular factor taxes are then netted out prior to distribution to households. We therefore have that the sectoral net factor incomes may be written as

$$Y_{\text{self-employed},\,i} = P_{LSi}LS_i(1 - t_{LSi}) \tag{28}$$

$$Y_{\text{wage},\,i} = W_i LW_i(1 - t_{LWi}) \tag{29}$$

$$Y_{\text{capital},\,i} = PK_i K_i(1 - t_{Ki}) \tag{30}$$

Here, Y denotes current income, i denotes sector, and t denotes factor tax rates. Beyond pure factor income, infrastructural rents are generated. The share allocated to households is

$$Y_{\text{infrastructure},\,i} = PG_i G_i(1 - t_{\text{infrastructure}}) \tag{31}$$

where $t_{\text{infrastructure}}$ denotes the share of infrastructure rents retained by the government. Next, consider transfers. In general, transfers in the models are linked to some price index, typically the GDP deflator for domestic transfers and the US GDP deflator for foreign transfers. Let

T_G denote current government transfers,
T_W denote transfers from the rest of the world,
P_{GDP} denote the domestic GDP deflator,
P_{GDP}US denote the exogenously given US GDP deflator.

Then, we have that

$$P_{GDP} = \Sigma_i PV_i V_i / \Sigma_i PV_{01} V_0 i \tag{32}$$

Here, the 0 subscript indicates base year values. Therefore, the current value of real transfers (denoted by a subscript 0) is

$$T_G = T_{G0} P_{GDP} \tag{33}$$

$$T_W = T_{W0} P_{GDPus} \tag{34}$$

For now, we will not consider interhousehold transfers. Although their numerical significance can be considerable, as noted in the case of Kenya in chapter 3, they do not add anything analytically new to the model. With that simplification we can apply the fixed coefficients approach (derived from the fixed initial household endowments) to allocate the sectoral and transfer incomes to households. Each income type may be allocated differently across households, since in general the households have different initial endowments of the various factors. Let

h denote households,
t denote income type (self employed, wage, capital infrastructure),
$a_{ti,h}$ denote the share of income of type t from sector i accruing to household h,
a_{Th} denote the share of transfer income accruing to household h.

Then household income at current prices for household h is given as

$$Y_h = \Sigma_t \Sigma_i a_{ti,h} Y_{ti} + a_{Th}(T_G + T_W) \tag{35}$$

Clearly, taking prices and factor employment as given from the rest of the model, these eight equations are used to establish eight unknowns ($Y_{\text{self-employed}}$, Y_{wage}, Y_{capital}, $Y_{\text{infrastructure}}$, P_{GDP}, T_G, T_W, and Y_h).

3.3.2 Government revenues

The SAM in figure 4.1 shows that government revenue originates from four sources: commodity taxes in the form of taxes and tariffs on intermediates, final import tariffs,[5] factor taxes in the form of labor and capital taxes; income taxes, consumption, export, and investment taxes; and retained infrastructure rents. Here, we spell them out in that order. It should be mentioned first, however, that all taxes are assumed to be of the proportional *ad valorem* type.

Tax revenues from domestic intermediates are found by noting that the tax is levied on market prices, according to the usage of intermediates in each sector. The tax rate may vary across delivering sectors. We thus have that tax revenues from domestic intermediates may be written as

$$\Sigma_i ND_i \Sigma_j A_{ji} P_{Xj} t_{NDj}$$

where t is the tax rate. Similarly, tariff revenue from imported intermediates is given by

$$\Sigma_i NM_i \Sigma_j AM_{ji} P_{NMj} t_{NMj}$$

Tariff revenue from imported final goods is given by

$$\Sigma_i t_{Mi} P_{Mi} M_i$$

Therefore, the domestic price of final imports is

$$P_{Mi} = P_{Mi}(1 + t_{Mi}) \tag{36}$$

This determines one of the variables left undetermined in the production block above.

As was mentioned above, factors may also be taxed. We have that the total tax revenue from factors is

$$\Sigma_i P_{LSi} LS_i t_{LSi} + W_i LW_i t_{LWi} + PK_i K_i t_{Ki}$$

Final goods taxes include consumption taxes, income taxes, export taxes, and investment good taxes. Consumption tax revenues are

$$\Sigma_i t_{Fi} P_{Qi} \Sigma_h C_{ih}$$

where

$t_{Fi} =$ the final goods tax rate on commodity i (assumed to be common to consumption and investment)

$C_{ih} =$ consumption of commodity i by household h

Similarly, revenues from investment taxes amount to

$$\Sigma_i t_{Fi} P_{Qi} (I_i + DS_i)$$

Here, I and DS are fixed investment and stock changes, respectively. Export taxes amount to

$$\Sigma_i t_{Ei} PQ_i E_i$$

where E denotes exports. Note that when t_E is negative, we have an export subsidy. Similarly, income taxes amount to

$$\Sigma_h t_{Yh} Y_h$$

An increase in export taxes (or a drop in export subsidies) will reduce export demand, thus lowering aggregate demand directly and indirectly because of reduced household incomes via the contraction of production. The response may vary across sectors and affect different households differently. A secondary effect comes in via the adjustment of factor prices.

The final component of government revenues is from retained earnings from infrastructure, amounting to

$$\Sigma_i PG_i G_i t_{\text{infrastructure}}$$

In total, government revenues amount to

$$Y_G = \Sigma_i \{ ND_i \Sigma_j A_{ji} PQ_j t_{NDj} +$$
$$NM_i \Sigma_j AM_{ji} P_{NMj} t_{NMj} +$$
$$t_{Mi} PM_i M_i +$$
$$t_{LSi} P_{LSi} LS_i +$$
$$t_{LWi} W_i LW_i +$$
$$t_{Ki} PK_i K_i +$$

$$t_{Fi}P_{Qi}(\Sigma_h C_{ih} + I_i + DS_i) +$$
$$t_{Ei}PQ_iE_i\} +$$
$$\Sigma_h t_{Yh}Y +$$
$$\Sigma_i PG_iG_i t_{\text{infrastructure}} \tag{37}$$

Taking prices and quantities as given for this submodule, we have one equation in one unknown (Y_G).

3.3.3 Rest-of-the-world revenues

The SAM in table 4.1 tells us that the rest of the world receives revenues from the economy in question in the form of earnings on imports for intermediate uses and from final imports. For simplicity, we ignore government and other final demand imports. We measure all rest-of-the-world revenues in world prices. Therefore, revenues from intermediate imports amount to

$$\Sigma_i NM_i \Sigma_j AM_{ji}P_{NMj}$$

where P_{NMj} are world prices of intermediate imports. Similarly, revenues from final imports amount to

$$\Sigma_i P_{Mi}M_i$$

Thus, total rest-of-the-world revenues are

$$Y_W - \Sigma_i P_{Mi}M_i + NM_i - \Sigma_j AM_{ji}P_{NMj} \tag{38}$$

Again, we have one equation in one unknown (Y_W).

3.4 Institutional behavior

Having now established income for the different institutions of the economy, we can proceed to take a look at how they spend that income. We will first describe household behavior, before turning to the government, and then to the rest of the world. Finally, we describe investment.

3.4.1 Household behavior

The SAM tells us that households consume composite commodities, pay consumption and income taxes, and save. As was the case above, we ignore interhousehold transfers.

The individual models differ strongly in their exact specification of household behavior. Therefore, in this section, we will describe consumption and savings behavior in blanket form. In section 5 below, we shall provide more precise details.

In general, we may assume that households select per capita consumption in response to per capita disposable income. The response may be related either to the level of or changes in income. Also, it may be linear or non-linear. For our purposes it is sufficient to state that for each household

$$CM = E(YM(1 - t_Y)) \tag{39}$$

where CM is real per capita consumption expenditure, $E()$ is the expenditure function, and YM is real per capita income. t is the proportional income tax rate for the household class in question. Also, we have that $0 < E' < 1$, i.e., the marginal propensity to save and consume are both positive.

Note that YM is defined as household income at fixed (base-year) prices (Y^F) divided by the population of the household class (n)

$$YM = Y^F/n \tag{40}$$

Income at base-year prices is generated by applying equations (28)–(35) but substituting base-year prices for current prices

$$Y^F = YF(P^O{}_{LS}, LS, t_{LS}, W0, LW, t_{LW}, \ldots) \tag{41}$$

Since the consumption function is in real terms, it is being assumed that consumers have no money illusion.

Next, given the real per capita level of consumption, a demand system is applied to determine consumption of individual commodities. The demand system is derived from a direct or indirect utility function, as the solution to the consumer's problem of maximizing utility subject to the budget constraint

Maximize $U = U(C)$

such that $PC.C = Y^*$

Here

U is utility,
C is a column vector of consumption,
PC is a row vector of consumer prices, and
Y^* is total expenditure (income less savings less taxes).

In solving the problem, the consumer takes market prices and the budget as given. The solution is the usual condition that marginal rates of substitution be equal to consumer price ratios.

To implement this, we need to establish total expenditure. This is done by noting that CM above is per capita real expenditure. To establish total current expenditure, we need to reinflate to current prices and multiply by population. Reinflation may be done by deriving the consumer price index, implied by the utility function U, i.e.

$$P^* = f(PC) \tag{42}$$

Here, PC is the tax-inclusive price of output

$$PC = PQ(1 + t_F) \tag{43}$$

Then, Y^* is given by

$$Y^* = CMP^*n \tag{44}$$

The solution to the consumer's problem may now be expressed as a function of income and prices (in addition to various parameters from the utility function)

$$C_H = C(PC, Y^*) \tag{45}$$

Here, C_H is a vector of consumption demands by household class.

Note that depending on the specification of the consumption function and the utility function, the consumption system may have quite different income and own- and cross-price elasticities. For example, in the Turkey model, the consumption function is linear in income and the utility function is Cobb–Douglas. This leads to income elasticities of 1 and own-price elasticities of -1 with zero cross-price elasticities. In the Kenya model, the utility function leads to a Stone–Geary linear expenditure system, where these simple relations do not hold anymore. Indeed, in that model all consumer goods are net substitutes and normal, and each good is inelastic in its own price.[6]

As in the case of production above, one should be careful in asserting that these partial relationships are also general equilibrium relationships. Assume for example that the price of a consumption good increases. This leads to a drop in consumption demand of that good and probably increased demand for other goods. Production must adjust, which leads to a decrease of consumer income, as well as a price reduction for this good and price increases for other goods. Therefore, both incomes and relative prices change, violating the *ceteris paribus* assumption behind the derivation of partial income and price elasticities. The net effect on the composition of the consumption bundle is not easily determined but is likely to be smaller than indicated by the partial elasticities.

The final step in describing consumers' behavior is to determine savings. This may be done directly or indirectly through the balancing constraint for households, i.e., the constraint that all income must be spent. Thus, we have that household savings, S_H, are

$$S_H = Y(1 - t_Y) - PC.C_H \tag{46}$$

This gives us eight equations per household to determine CM, YM, Y^F, P^*, PC, Y^*, C_H, and S_H, given output prices and incomes.

3.4.2 Government behavior

The government consumes, makes transfers to households, and saves. Here we do not consider direct government imports, although in the Turkey model, the government imports oil.

Transfers have already been considered in the discussion on household income above. The total amount transferred is

$$\Sigma_h T_{Gh}$$

It is essentially exogenous, although the current value of transfers is linked to the GDP deflator, i.e., the amount of real transfers is a policy variable. Similarly, government consumption of each commodity is exogenous in real terms. The reason is that government consumption (and transfers) are policy instruments that can be varied exogenously. Government expenditure could be linked to the state of the economy and particular policy targets, thus making it endogenous, but that is not implemented in any of the models. The current value of government consumption is

$$\Sigma_i P_{Qi} C_{Gi}$$

Finally, government savings, S_G, are determined residually from the budget balance constraint

$$\Sigma_h T_{Gh} + \Sigma_i P_{Qi} C_{Gi} + S_G = Y_G \tag{47}$$

It may be noted that the specification of government behavior implies a marginal savings propensity of 1. In the setting of the overall model this means that a redistribution of income from household to government, for instance via taxation, will be contractionary. On the other hand, it also means that the model may have certain Keynesian features, since the fixed real government consumption, and the proportional taxes on the revenue side, stabilize the economy. This is not always the case, however, since it depends on the way the model is closed. We return to this subject in section 3.6.1.

3.4.3 Rest-of-the-world behavior

The rest of the world buys exports from the economy, pays export taxes (or receives export subsidies), makes international transfers, and saves.

International transfers were covered in section 3.3.1 on household income. The total amount transferred to households at world prices (but in national currency) is T_W.

The rest of the world is assumed to choose, in effect an optimal allocation between own production and commodities exported from the economy in question. The two goods are assumed to be imperfect substitutes. In addition, foreign agents are assumed to take prices as given. In that case, the rest-of-the-world's cost minimization of the bundle of foreign goods and exports has the same solution as that shown for the producers' problem in (3') above. It is seen that these assumptions about behavior in the rest of the world imply a downward-sloping demand curve for exports with a constant price elasticity. Consequently, the demand curve for exports implemented in the models is

$$E = E_0(P_{E0}/P_E)^e \qquad (48)$$

Here

E = export volume of the given commodity
E_0 = a measure of export scale (for instance base-year exports)
P_{E0} = base-year export prices (measured in national currency)
P_E = export prices
e = the export price elasticity

Note that the elasticity of exports is again a partial one. The general equilibrium export elasticity is lower than the partial elasticity. This is because an increase in export prices lowers export demand and hence also the supply price of exports via the effects on production income, demands, etc.

The export price, P_E, may include trade margins and export taxes

$$P_E = P_Q(1 + t_{ME} + t_E) \qquad (49)$$

To balance income and expenditure, foreign savings (in national currency) are given by

$$T_W + \Sigma_i P_{Ei}E_i + S_W = Y_W \qquad (50)$$

Summing up, we have three equations. (48) "determines" E, and (49) "determines" P_E. In some cases, when the model is run in "investment driven" mode, (50) determines foreign savings, and sometimes, when it is "savings driven," (50) determines total investment. These terms are further explained in section 3.6.1.

3.4.4 Investment

Investment in the models is described in a very simple manner. Essentially, investment demands across sectors are fixed quantity proportions to total investment demand. This is true of fixed investment and also of stock changes. A more rigorous treatment of investment would make it dependent on interest rates, income, expectations of the future, etc. However, although the models are multiperiod, they are not intertemporal. Therefore, the interest rate, which is inherently intertemporal, cannot be determined in the models. Neither can rational expectations. Therefore, those variables are considered exogenous in the model, and do not vary in any single period. Consequently, they do not affect investment. It may be noted, however, that chapter 7 on Thailand includes policy simulations in which total investment is indeed determined by intertemporal general equilibrium mechanisms. The investment equations of the core model are

$$I_i = a_{Ii} b_I I^* \tag{51}$$

$$DS_i = a_{DSi}(1 - b_I) I^* \tag{52}$$

Here

a_I is the sectoral allocation key for fixed investment, summing to 1,
a_{DS} is the sectoral allocation key for stock changes, summing to 1,
b_I is the share of total investment going to fixed investment,
I^* is total real investment, and
DS is real stock changes.

In addition to these two types of investment, investment takes place in infrastructure. The total value at base year prices is $\Sigma_i G_i$.

The savings–investment balance is now

$$S_H + S_G + S_W = \Sigma_i P_{Ci} I_i + P_{Qi} D_{Si} + P_Q \text{ infrastructure } \Sigma_i G_i \tag{53}$$

We thus have two equations in two unknowns (I, DS), per sector in addition to the savings–investment balance and the variable I^*. In some cases, the model is run as investment driven, (i.e., I^* is fixed), and in other cases, I^* is variable (when foreign savings are fixed, and the model is run as savings driven). As mentioned above, when I^* is fixed, the balance of payments constraint (50) determines foreign savings. Otherwise, when I^* is variable, but foreign savings are fixed, that equation determines I^*.

Note, because of Walras' law, that the savings–investment balance is implied by the rest of the model. It, therefore, should not be counted as an independent equation.

3.5 Market clearing

Having stated the production technology, producers' behavior, income generation, and the behavior of the different institutions of the economy, we can now turn to the clearing of commodity and factor markets. These are the only remaining blocks of the core model. We first describe commodity market clearing, before turning to factor markets.

3.5.1 Commodity markets

Commodity markets clearance is ensured by the condition that aggregate supplies equal aggregate demands for each composite commodity. Total supplies consist of composite output plus stocks carried over from the previous year

$$Q_i + DS_{0i}$$

Aggregate demands consist of final domestic demands, exports, additions to stocks, demands for domestic intermediates, and in addition, for the trade and transportation sector, trade and transport margins, and for the infrastructure sector, demands for infrastructure.

Final domestic demands are given as the sum of private consumption, government consumption, and fixed investment

$$FD_i = \Sigma_h C_{ih} + C_{Gi} + I_i \tag{54}$$

Total trade and transport margins are given by

$$TMP_Q \text{ trade/transport} = \Sigma_i tm_{FI} P_{Qi} FD_i + \Sigma_i tm_{Ei} P_{Qi} E_i + \Sigma_i tm_{Mi} P_{Mi} M_i$$
$$+ NM_i \Sigma_j AM_{ji} P_{Mj} tm_{NMj} \tag{55}$$

where

TM is total real trade margins, and
tm is trade margins by sector and usage type.

Similarly, total infrastructure demands are

$$G^* = \Sigma_i G_i \tag{56}$$

Therefore, the commodity market-clearing constraint is

$$Q_i + DS_{0i} = FD_i + E_i + DS_i + TM \tag{57}$$

for i being the trade and transportation sector,

$$Q_i + DS_{0i} = FD_i + E_i + DS_i + G^* \tag{57'}$$

for i being the infracstructure sector, and

$$Q_i + DS_{0i} = FD_i + E_i + DS_i \tag{57''}$$

for all other sectors. Here, DS_0 signifies stocks at the beginning of the period. These are described further in section 4.1 below.

We may think of (57)–(57″) as determining P_Q in all sectors, thus yielding another one of the variables left over from the production block.

3.5.2 Factor markets

Since the capital stock is exogenous in every year of the model, we have already covered the market for capital. It remains to describe the labor markets.

Labor markets feature some special characteristics. The wage rate of some labor types is linked to a price index, while the wage rate of other types is free to vary to clear markets. In addition there are certain spillover mechanisms between those two segments. Thus, for instance, if skilled labor cannot be fully employed at the going wage rate, those who cannot find a job may become self employed. This increases the supply of self-employed labor, and, in order for that market to clear, the return to self employment must drop. In other cases, no spillover is possible, so open unemployment may exist.

The precise descriptions of labor markets vary from model to model so here we shall only consider one description. We return to the specifics in section 5.4.2 below. In our case, the urban labor markets are cleared through spillovers within the urban area: hired labor wage rates are indexed, while self-employment rates vary to clear markets. The total supply of urban labor is fixed. Therefore, the market-clearing condition may be written

$$L_U = LW_U + LS_U \tag{58}$$

where

L_U is the supply of urban labor,
LW_U is urban wage labor, and
LS_U is urban self-employed labor.

The indexation of wage rates of hired labor in both the urban and rural areas follows the consumer price index of that area

$$W/W_0 = 1CPI/CPI_0 \tag{59}$$

Here, 1 is an indexation rate parameter, and CPI is the consumer price index, given by

$$CPI\Sigma_i C_i = \Sigma_i P_{ci} C_i \tag{60}$$

for each area. The subscript 0 denotes initial values.

To end the description of labor markets, we only need to state that the supply of rural self-employment labor is fixed. The idea is that, in the rural area, self employment takes place on own land, making the transition from wage labor to self employment in that area very difficult.

$$LS_R = 1_{sR} \tag{61}$$

The situation may be described as follows. Take the urban area first. Since the wage rate of hired labor is essentially fixed, the demand for that labor type is determined from the production function and producers' behavior (in equation (17) above). Now, those who cannot be employed swell the ranks of the urban self employed, and the market-clearing equation (58) determines the returns to urban self employment (P_{LSU}). (The mechanism also works the other way around: if there is overemployment of hired labor, some potentially self employed will take jobs as hired labor.)

In the rural area, wage rates are also essentially given, so (17) determines the employment of rural hired labor. However, the amount of rural self-employed labor is fixed, and there is a market-clearing condition for rural labor. Therefore, (17) determines the returns to rural self employment.

It may be noted that the rural sector may have open unemployment of hired labor. These unemployed rural laborers do not get any unemployment compensation. This induces quite strong income effects for households supplying that labor. Therefore, policies that increase consumer prices relative to other prices may have strong distributional effects.

3.6 The overall workings of the model

In this section, we offer an overview of the workings of the model as a whole. We begin by discussing model closure. Second, we turn to the question of determining prices. Third, we compare the model with partial equilibrium modeling approaches.

3.6.1 Closure

The above specification of labor markets has determined everything that was left open from the production system. The only remaining issue is to decide on model closure. Counting equations and unknowns, we find a total of as many equations as unknowns. However, one of the equations is redundant (functionally dependent on the rest of the system) by Walras' law. Therefore, the model really has one more variable than independent equations, and one more equation is needed to close the system.

Traditionally, computable general equilibrium models use two different closures.[7] Either investment is fixed, and the model is said to be "investment driven," or foreign savings are fixed, and the model is said to be "savings driven." The choice of closure affects the workings of the model. Typically, when the model is investment driven, it features some Keynesian characteristics, whereas when it is savings driven, it works more along the lines of neoclassical theory.

Thus, with investment fixed, an increase in government demand reduces government savings. In order to satisfy the savings–investment balance, other savings must increase. This can happen in a number of ways. For example, income may rise so that private savings increase, imports may rise so that foreign savings increase, or prices may rise so that exports are reduced and foreign savings increase.

With foreign savings fixed, an increase in government demand again reduces government savings. The primary response will then be a decrease of investment.

The model response is, however, a little more complicated than this. Since the total supply of urban labor is given, and, since the capital stock is also given, output in urban sectors is also virtually fixed, although by substitution between hired and self employed, and between value added and intermediates, some productivity response may be obtained. This implies that, on the one hand, prices must bear a relatively large adjustment in response to various shocks, and, on the other hand, that redistributions among different kinds of demands are important, regardless of closure.

For example, if investment is fixed, and government consumption increases, one may expect Keynesian inflationary effects: prices increase, reducing exports, and increasing imports. This increases foreign savings, but probably not by enough to offset the reduction of public savings. In order to satisfy the savings–investment balance, private savings must, therefore, in principle increase. In a pure Keynesian world this would happen through multiplier effects which increase output and private income. However, with a limited output response, this cannot be the only adjustment in the economy. Instead, what may happen are stronger inflationary responses but occurring differentially across sectors. In this manner, the value of investment and government consumption may increase relatively little while foreign savings may increase relatively more. In addition, household income may rise more than the value of consumption. Thus, in the new equilibrium, one might expect limited Keynesian multiplier effects, occurring differentially across sectors, with strong effects on relative prices and trade, and with relatively little effect on households.

On the other hand, when foreign savings are fixed and government consumption increases, the reduction in government savings will immediately crowd out investment. However, if investment demands and government demands do not have the same sectoral composition, the limited output response will imply some price adjustment as well. Some prices will increase while others decrease. Depending on the composition of labor used in the different sectors, household income, and hence private savings, will be affected. Thus, it is possible that aggregate private savings will increase to offset some of the reduction in government savings. However, in general it may be expected that income effects would be smaller in a savings driven economy than in an investment driven economy.

3.6.2 Price determination

The above discussion has mentioned consumer price indices and inflationary effects. At the same time, no mention has been made of the exchange rate, although traditional analysis would imply exchange-rate effects as a response to various shocks.

It is important to recognize that inflation and exchange-rate effects may not be directly analyzed in the model set out here. Inflation is a monetary phenomenon. So is the exchange rate. Our CGE model, however, has no monetary transactions.

In its present form it is therefore only capable of determining relative prices, not the price level. All prices in the model are measured relative to one another. In order to anchor the price level, we need to select a numeraire, i.e., a price against which all other prices are measured. In effect, we choose to use world prices as the numeraire (note that all world prices are fixed in the model). Now, assume that we were to allow for an endogenous exchange rate in the model. Doubling the exchange rate would imply the following: all landed foreign goods prices would double. If, as a result, all domestic prices would double, it is easily verified that nothing would happen to real quantities in the model. All production decisions are based on relative prices. So are all household decisions. and, since no relative price has changed, the economy is still in equilibrium, although at twice the price level as before. So obviously, a possible effect of exchange-rate changes is that nothing happens to real quantities, but all prices simply change *pro tanto*. In fact, if the model is correctly specified, this is the only possible effect from exchange-rate changes. For that reason, the exchange rate is nothing but a way to scale the numeraire of the model, and, consequently, we do not need it in the model (implicitly, that sets the exchange rate to an arbitrary value of 1). That said, the introduction of wage–price rigidities, for example, can allow nominal exchange-rate movements to change relative prices and therefore to have important real effects in the model.

Returning to the present model, while it does not include any nominal exchange rate for the above reasons, it does admit of real exchange rates that may vary according to market conditions. The latter may variously be defined as a trade weighted index of domestic prices relative to world prices (as in the Turkey country study of chapter 9) or an index of the prices of traded versus non-traded goods. The real exchange rate, being a relative price, influences the allocation of resources across different sectors of the economy.

3.6.3 Comparison with partial equilibrium models

To further illustrate the workings of the general equilibrium model, it proves instructive to compare it to partial equilibrium models of the economy. To do so, we will consider an input–output model. In this model, it is assumed that inputs are used in fixed proportions, i.e., the technology is Leontief. Prices are determined by that technology. Some final demands are price responsive, while others are not. We use the following notation.

A = matrix of input–output coefficients for intermediates,
A_M = row vector of non-competitive import coefficients,
A_V = row vector of primary factor coefficients,
C = column vector of private consumption,
G = column vector of government and investment demand,
E = column vector of exports,
X = column vector of output,
V = row vector of value added,
M = row vector of intermediate imports,
P = row vector of output prices,
P_V = row vector of value-added prices, and
P_M = row vector of import prices,
I = identity matrix

For simplicity, we will not consider taxes, final imports, transfers, etc.

In this model, the market-clearing condition that total supply equals total demand is given by

$$X = AX + C + G + E \tag{62}$$

implying that

$$X = (I - A)^{-1}(C + G + E) \tag{62'}$$

Also, prices are given by

$$P = P_V \hat{A}_V + P_M \hat{A}_M (I - A)^{-1} \tag{63}$$

where the caret indicates diagonalization. Now, consumption and exports may be dependent on prices. For example, assume that we use some expenditure system to generate consumption

$$C = C(Y, P) \tag{64}$$

with

$$Y = P_V V' \tag{65}$$

where V' is $A_V X$.

Also, we may make exports responsive to prices.

$$E = E(P) \tag{66}$$

Although we have chosen to use fixed coefficients in this model, conceptually very little would change in the following if factor substitution were allowed. In this model, consider an external oil price shock. From (63), we get an increase of all output prices, including direct and indirect effects. This reduces demands for consumption and exports (from (64) and (66)). Next, to clear markets, a multiplier process takes over, reducing output in each sector (by (62')). This again affects household income, cutting consumption, again reducing production, until an equilibrium has been reached. In that equilibrium, savings will equal investment.

Next, consider an increase in government consumption. Since this is final demand, the model will exhibit only quantity responses: from (62'), output will increase. This affects household income and consumption, giving rise to a new round of output adjustments. However, since there is no price response, exports are not affected.

How is this story different from that emerging from a general equilibrium model? In the partial equilibrium model commodity markets clear, and income–expenditure balancing constraints are (implicitly) enforced. However, factor markets are missing. Furthermore, prices are determined by a full forward shifting of costs. It is possible in the model to allow for full backward shifting of certain costs into returns to primary inputs, thus directly affecting household income without affecting prices.[8] In contrast, in the general equilibrium model, prices are determined endogenously together with transacted quantities, and using a comprehensive set of feedbacks.

In the general equilibrium model, an oil price shock would first affect the economy in a manner very similar to the picture of the partial equilibrium model. Domestic prices would rise and demands would drop. The resulting adjustment of production, however, leads to a reduction in demand for primary inputs. Factor market clearance then requires that factor prices be reduced. This is where the feedback starts. As factor prices are reduced the output price is lowered, and if substitution possibilities are present, more factor inputs are demanded. The initial income loss for households, and the price reductions, increase private consumption and exports, thus offsetting some of the initial reduction. This process of simultaneous adjustment to goods and factor prices and quantities continues until all markets are simultaneously cleared.

In the case of a government spending increase, the first-round effects are again similar to those in the partial equilibrium model. However, the demands for various factors will increase, thus increasing the returns to those factors. This starts an increase in output prices which, via the input–output system, is magnified across sectors. The price increase offsets some of the gains from production on household income, and also reduces export demands. As a consequence production is reduced and a new round of adjustment takes place.

It should be evident that the general equilibrium model offers a considerably more nuanced picture of the adjustment of the economy to shocks. Also, in line with our comments at several places above, the quantity and income responses of the CGE are dampened relative to those of partial analysis (for the same set of parameters). This is because price adjustments crowd out some of the quantity effects.

4 Dynamics

Previous sections have laid out the core structure of the static model used in the study. We have mentioned that the model is run for many periods as a sequence of static equilibria. We shall now describe more closely how the dynamics of the model are specified.

The key point with regard to the dynamics of the model is that investment in one period adds to the stock of available inventories in the next period. Another issue is that a number of the parameters of the model change exogenously over time. In the first section we shall be concerned only with the linkage of investment to capital. The next section describes how, in principle, the model is calibrated to track actual economic history. Third, we describe the module for simulating foreign debt and service payments thereon. Fourth we briefly discuss some possible shortcomings of the multiperiod simulations.

4.1 Stock updating

The models all assume that fixed capital depreciates exponentially over time. Therefore, the available existing capital in year $t+1$ is $(1-d)K_t$. However, after a one-year gestation period, investment made in year t enhances the capital stock in year $t+1$. Note that the investment I above is by sector of origin. In order to translate these demands into sector of destination a fixed coefficient allocation scheme is applied. We therefore have that

$$K_{it} - (1-d_K)K_{it-1} + a_{Ki}\Sigma_j I_{jt-1} \qquad (67)$$

For inventories we apply a first-in first-out principle. Therefore, all old stocks are used within each period, so the new inventory level by sector is

$$DS_{0it} = a_{DSi}\Sigma_j DS_{jt-1} \qquad (68)$$

It is assumed that old and new capital have the same productivity, so no endogenous changes to factor productivity coefficients occur as a result of investment.

4.2 *Tracking history*

To run the model over several time periods, and provide a base-case replication of economic history of the country in question, the model needs to be calibrated to match reality. For a number of accounts, the required coefficients, or exogenous variables, can be found in official statistical sources. However, for other parameters of the model, no available sources support a particular choice of values. This, for instance, is the case for total factor productivities, which are likely to change over time, consumers' marginal savings propensities, etc. On the other hand, history provides excellent information on some variables determined endogenously in the model, like GDP growth rates, total private consumption, total exports, etc.

It is not easy to apply standard econometric techniques to estimate the parameters of the full general equilibrium to replicate the given data series on GDP and other variables. There are several reasons for this. First, data are not generally available for all the required series to do such a regression. We would need disaggregated price and production series, details on household expenditure year by year, and so on. Second, the regression itself is not easily undertaken, because the system to be estimated is strongly simultaneous and non-linear. Third, we do expect certain parameters to vary over time, while standard regression techniques assume that the coefficients are constant over time.

Given these circumstances, another approach is taken to calibrate the model to replicate history. The idea is to select a number of parameters and coefficients, for which we do not have very good data, for example, sectoral factor productivity parameters or savings rates for different categories of households and apply non-linear optimization techniques to find the values of those parameters which result in as good a tracking performance as possible, given the rest of the model. The optimal tracking performance is determined as the least-weighted sum of squared deviations from a number of selected target variables.

The procedure is roughly this: First, take a guess at the sought after parameter values, and use the general equilibrium model to generate an estimate of the tracking variables (say, GDP and private consumption growth rates). Next, see if the weighted sum of squared deviations from the target values of these tracking variables can be reduced by other parameter values. If so, choose these values and rerun, if not, the resulting parameter values are used in the model for this year. Next, go to the next year, and redo the calibration. While such intertemporal calibration is standard practice among applied general equilibrium modelers, we have formalized the procedure by resorting to an explicit minimization.

The actual choice of target variables and tracking parameters differs from model to model. Specifics are given in the chapters on the individual models. However, there are typically more tracking parameters than target variables, so an actual optimization can indeed be performed. Also, the range of possible values for the tracking parameters may be bounded.

4.3 The debt module

Two of the models (the India and Thailand models of chapters 6 and 7 respectively) are connected to a module that simulates how foreign debt and interest and principal payments thereon evolve over time as a result of historical and model-generated financing needs. For those purposes, it distinguishes between medium-term government debt, medium-term private debt, and short-term debt.

The module is based on a few simplifying assumptions. First, any new borrowing in a given year is split between the different types of debt in the same proportions as those actually prevailing in the particular year. Second, all debt is assumed to follow a service profile whereby, for the first few years, only interest payments are made (the grace period), followed by a period of amortization, during which the total of interest and principal payments make up an annuity (i.e., the total payment is constant). Third, it is assumed that new debt of a given type has the same grace period and maturity as well as interest rate and currency composition as actual historical debt.

To formalize this, we first describe the payments for a single new loan, and next aggregate to find payments on total outstanding debt.

Let

r denote the interest rate,
g denote the grace period in years,
T denote maturity (years from now including the grace period)
t denote number of years from now ($t=0$ is today),
D_t denote outstanding debt on this loan at time t,
S_t denote total service payment on this loan at time t,
I_t denote interest payment at time t, and
P_t denote principal payment at time t.

By straight accounting, we have that

$$I_t = rD_{t-1} \tag{D1}$$

and

$$D_t = (1+r)D_{t-1} - S_t \tag{D2}$$

where

$$S_t = I_t + P_t \tag{D3}$$

For the grace period, only interest payments are made, i.e.

$$P_t = 0$$
$$S_t = I_t = rD_0$$
$$D_t = D_0, \quad t = 1, 2, \ldots, g$$

During the amortization period, S is constant by the assumption of annuity. In order to achieve full retirement of the loan, we have that $D_T = 0$. Using (D2) to find the evolution of debt over the amortization period, we have that

$$D_{g+1} = (1+r)D_0 - S$$
$$D_{g+2} = (1+r)D_{g+1} - S$$
$$\quad\quad = (1+r)^2 D_0 - (1 + (1+r))S$$
$$D_{g+3} = (1+r)D_{g+2} - S$$
$$\quad\quad = (1+r)^3 D_0 - (1 + (1+r) + (1+r^2))S$$

$$\cdots\cdots\cdots$$

$$D_t = (1+r)^{(t-g)}D_0 \sum_{i=0}^{t-g-1} (1+r)^i S$$

$$\quad = (1+r)^{(t-g)}D_0 - S((1+r)^{(t-g)} - 1)/r$$

Now, $D_T = 0$ implies that

$$S = \alpha_{g,T,r}D_0$$

where $\alpha_{g,T,r}$ is the annuity factor

$$\alpha_{g,T,r} = r/(1 - (1+r)^{(T-g)})$$

Hence, we have that

$$S_t = \begin{cases} rD_0 & \text{for } t = 1, \ldots, g \\ \alpha_{g,T,r}D_0 & \text{for } t = g+1, \ldots, T \\ 0 & \text{for } t > T \end{cases} \tag{D4}$$

In addition, given our above expression for the evolution of outstanding debt, we find that the interest payments over the amortization period evolve according to

$$I_T = rD_{T-1}$$
$$\quad = r((1+r)^{(t-1-g)} - \alpha_{g,T,r}D_0, \quad t = g+1, \ldots, T$$
$$\quad = \frac{1 - (1+r)^{(T+1-t)}}{1 - (1+r)^{-(T-g)}} rD_0$$

Thus

$$I_t = \beta_{g,T,r,t} D_0 \tag{D5}$$

where β is the interest accumulation factor,

$$\beta_{g,T,r,t} = \begin{array}{ll} r & t = 1, \ldots, g \\[2mm] \dfrac{1 - (1+r)^{-(T+1-t)}}{1 - (1+r)^{-(T-g)}} \, r & t = g+1, \ldots, T \\[2mm] 0 & t > T \end{array}$$

Finally, using (D3), the principal payment, P, is found.

This completes the calculations needed for a single loan. To compute total debt service payments, we need to aggregate overall outstanding issues, including historical and new debt.

To do that, we need to introduce a vintage classification index, k. We then have that

$$TS_t = \Sigma_k \alpha_{gk}, T_k, r_k D_{0k} + S^*_t \tag{D6}$$

Here, S^* is an error term determined to make S_t match its observable value. Also, for total interest payments, we get

$$TI_t = \Sigma_k \beta_{gk}, T_k, r_k, t D_{0k} + I^*_t \tag{D7}$$

Here, I^*_t is an error term used to match historically observed interest payments. To use the debt module in conjunction with the above general equilibrium model, we need to specify how new borrowing comes about. This follows the accounting balances

$$TD_t = TD_{t-1} + NFB_t \tag{D8}$$

where TD is total outstanding debt, and NFB is net foreign borrowing, and

$$NFB_t = CA_t + I_t + DR_t - S_t \tag{D9}$$

where CA is the current-account deficit, DR is the change in reserves, and I and S are defined above.

NFB, DR, and I can be found from the historical data. In addition, the historical calibrated run of the general equilibrium model yields a path for CA_t. Hence, (D9) is used to residually determine S_t to match the historical run. The above system of debt-accounting equations is then used to determine S^* and I^* residually from (D6) and (D7).

It may be noted that there is only a one-way link between the CGE model and the debt module. The debt module uses the foreign savings generated in the CGE to keep track of debt, but the implied debt servicing is not fed back to the CGE. Therefore, when performing a counterfactual, we first determine the sequence of equilibria in the CGE model. The foreign savings corresponding to those equilibria can be used, via (D9), to determine net foreign borrowing in each year. Using actual historical shares, total net foreign borrowing is split into subtypes. In the rest of the computations, DR, S^*, and I^* are kept at the calibrated levels, and the debt module used in a straightforward manner to determine outstanding debt as well as principal and interest payments. In conjunction with the CGE results, the ratio of debt service to macroeconomic variables such as GDP and exports can then be determined.

4.4 *Multiperiod simulations: caveats*

It will be seen in chapters 6 to 9 that the tracking performance of the models is quite satisfactory on most counts. For many of the tracking indicators, growth rates are tracked well, indicating that the models are able to capture some important historical trends. This is not however the case for all the indicators. One reason may lie in the fact that the tracking parameters are bounded. Another reason could be that some of the other coefficients of the model, which are not calibrated, are not adjusted to precisely match the historical developments.

Even though the models track history well and therefore provide a good baseline for counterfactuals, it is appropriate to raise two caveats about the multiperiod simulations done in the study.

First, when using a sequence of static equilibrium models for dynamic simulations, it should be made clear that the relevant time period is "equilibrium" time, i.e., the time that it takes the economy to return to an equilibrium after a shock. In the simulations, these periods are taken to be one year each. However, nothing in the CGE models dictates that it takes exactly one year for the economy to adjust. Instead casual empiricism suggests that the relevant period is longer than that. Furthermore, it might be conjectured that the larger the shocks the longer are equilibrium times. This point should be borne in mind when interpreting the results of the counterfactual experiments in the chapters on the individual countries. In particular, it is preferable to look at the broad contours of the results over several years rather than strictly on a year-to-year basis.

Second, although the models are able to capture historical trends, many parameter estimates and guesstimates are single-year point estimates. Some parameter values are chosen with reference to econometric studies, while others are obtained from calibrating the model to replicate the base-year SAM. In order to do so, the procedure is first to specify a particular functional form for, say, consumption, and next, given a set of prices, incomes, and actual consumption, to derive the relevant coefficients for the chosen functional form to replicate the SAM.

Note, however, that any functional form can be calibrated to the SAM, but with quite different marginal characteristics. For example, both a system with constant value shares (Cobb–Douglas utility function) and a linear expenditure system (Stone–Geary utility function) are easily calibrated to the SAM. But, as indicated in our discussion on consumers' behavior above, the implications for income, own- and cross-price elasticities can be very different. Therefore, when doing counterfactuals, two models which both replicate history equally well do not necessarily have equally good comparative static or dynamic characteristics. This should not be seen as a criticism specific to the tracking procedure or the assumed dynamics used in this study. It applies equally to econometrically estimated models. In the ultimate analysis, the counterfactual performance of any economic model depends on particular choices made by the model-builder which, in turn, reflect the latter's intuition and view of the world.

5 Differences among the country-specific models

The focus so far has been on integrating the individual country models in order to provide a common frame of reference. However, since the models used in this study have been tailored to answer questions of adjustment for specific countries, each of them differs in certain respects from the general framework above. This is obviously true for the data and the various parameters and coefficients that differ from country to country. But in addition to that, certain structural and behavioral aspects vary across models as well. In this section, we provide an overview of the main differences.

We follow the same outline as that in the discussion of the static code model, namely, (1) production, (2) income generation and distribution, (3) institutional behavior, and (4) market clearing. We also attempt to evaluate the qualitative effects of each departure from the core model.

5.1 Production

All models cover the following six production sectors/commodity types:

1 Agriculture
2 Consumer goods
3 Capital goods
4 Intermediate goods
5 Public infrastructure
6 Services

The sectoral disaggregation follows agriculture–industry–service lines. Industry is disaggregated by source of demand into sectors (2)–(4) to capture the differential impact of policies on different parts of the industrial sector. The capital-goods sector includes construction and produces outputs which are used as investment goods in all sectors. Infrastructure (irrigation, roads, etc.) is singled out to isolate possible bottlenecks to expansion of other sectors necessary for adjustment.

In addition to these six sectors, the Turkey model also considers a seventh sector, namely, a petroleum sector. This is treated separately because petroleum played a particularly prominent role in the foreign exchange crisis of the late 1970s in Turkey.

In all the models, the domestic production technology and producers' behavior is as described in the core model. The only exception is for the petroleum sector in Turkey, and in that case only at the lowest levels of the CES tree. Instead of allowing for imperfect substitution between imported and domestic intermediates, the petroleum sector is allowed to use imported and domestic intermediates in fixed quantity proportions. This may affect the exact numbers coming out of the model. For example, an oil price shock may hit the economy harder, *ceteris paribus*, because it is less easy to substitute away from petroleum imports. However, it does not change the overall qualitative behavior relative to the other models.

A more substantial difference between the models lies in the treatment of final imports. The India, Kenya, and Thailand models all assume that the capital-goods sector has free access to final imports and that these are imperfect substitutes for domestically produced capital goods. For the rest of the sectors, the India and Kenya models assume that final imports are administered, giving rise to the existence of licensing premia. Since the import quantities are fixed, gross output in those sectors will react more rigidly than if imports had been allowed to respond to prices. Consequently, prices of final goods react more strongly to shocks. In addition, in the India model, licensing premia are allocated to the government, which, with fixed government consumption and investment, has a marginal consumption propensity of zero. In the Kenya model, the licensing premia are treated as capital income and thus allocated to households that own capital. These households typically have higher savings propensities than the average household. In both models, therefore, the savings propensity of the economy is increased, other things being equal.

As an illustration, consider an increase in government consumption. With final imports fixed, there is a relatively strong price impact and increased pressure on import licenses. The import license premia divert resources from households to the government. Furthermore, the rise in price affects the competitiveness of the economy adversely. Thus, increased government spending is not as expansionary as in a similar economy without quantity restrictions on imports. On the other hand, the economy is more insulated from the effects of increases in world prices of imports because the resulting rise in domestic prices of those imports reduces import demands and depresses the premium on import licenses. This offsets some of the impact of international price increases on domestic prices.

In the Turkey model, imports may also be restricted. However, in that model, the assumption is that import premia arise because total capital inflow may be controlled. In addition all premium income is allocated to one household group (capitalists), which has a higher savings propensity than other households. Therefore, mechanisms along the above lines operate in the Turkey model as well. Note also that the assumption that license premia accrue exclusively to one group, e.g., capitalists, intensifies the distributional effects of various policies. The quantitative significance of these effects depends on the relative size of administered imports in the economy. Thus, in India, imports were of relatively minor importance in the period studied, so that the above effects are likely to have been quite small in that country.

In the Thailand model, final imports are assumed to be imperfect substitutes for domestic consumption, and free to vary in response to changes in relative prices.

5.2 Income generation and distribution

5.2.1 Households

Table 4.2 shows the differences in classification of households across the models.

It will be seen that the classification of households in the Kenya and Turkey models parallels that for factors. The classification in Thailand is more aggregated but not very different in spirit from these two models. In contrast, the total of thirty household types in the India model allows for a comprehensive analysis of distributional issues. The thirty Indian household types are separated into two groups, rural and urban. For rural households, the distinguishing feature is essentially land ownership. For urban households, the classification follows income percentiles.

In all four country studies, the distribution of income follows the fixed share approach outlined in the core model.

5.2.2 Government revenues

Although the number of tax instruments differs from one model to the other, government revenues roughly follow the description provided for the core model above. These differences are of minor importance for the present study. More importantly, as has already been mentioned, in the

Table 4.2 *Household classification in the country studies*

India	Turkey	Kenya	Thailand
15 classes of rural households	Agricultural households	Rural small landholders and landless	Rural households
15 classes of urban households	Unskilled labor households	Rural larger landowners	Urban households
	Skilled labor households	Urban low-income households	
	Capitalists	Urban medium- and and high-income households	

India model, import-licensing premia accrue to the government. Similarly, in the Turkey model, the government owns the petroleum sector and may decide on discretionary oil imports, the net revenues from which accrue to the government.

5.2.3 Rest-of-the-world revenues
All the models essentially follow the description of the core model.

5.3 Institutional behavior

5.3.1 Household behavior
As indicated before, the description of household consumption behavior varies a good deal across the models. Here, we shall first consider the Turkey model, next turn to the Kenya and Thailand models, and finally describe the detailed mechanisms of the India model.

Turkey
The simplest description of household consumption demands is that of the Turkey model. Here, consumers are assumed to pay a fixed proportional income tax to the government, and save a fixed proportion of disposable income. The rest is allocated to consumption expenditure, according to a Cobb–Douglas utility function for each household type

$$U_h = \prod_i C_{ih}^{c_{ih}}$$

$$\Sigma_i c_{ih} = 1$$

Here

U_h is utility for household h,
C_{ih} is the quantity of good i consumed by household h, and
c_{ih} is a fixed parameter.

Utility maximization subject to the budget constraint

$$\Sigma_i P_i C_{ih} = Y_h (1 - t_h)(1 - s_h)$$

yields a demand system with constant value of consumption

$$P_i C_{ih} = c_{ih} Y_h (1 - t_h)(1 - s_h)$$

where

P_i = consumer price of good i
Y_h = gross income of household h
t_h = proportional income tax rate for household h,
s_h = marginal = average savings rate for household h,

Note in this formulation that the own-price elasticity is -1 and all cross-price elasticities are 0. Moreover, the income elasticity is 1.

Kenya and Thailand

In the Kenya and Thailand models, savings are again proportional to income net of proportional taxes. Domestic expenditure, E, is given by disposable income less savings less the value of any direct consumption imports

$$E_h = Y_h (1 - t_h)(1 - s_h) - P_M M_h$$

Next, it is assumed that utility is Cobb–Douglas, not in total consumption as in the Turkey model, but in consumption above the subsistence level

$$U_h = \prod_i (c_{ih} - N_h \gamma_{ih})^{c_{ih}}$$

$$\Sigma_i c_{ih} = 1$$

where

γ_{ih} = per capita subsistence, or committed, consumption of good i by a member of household h,
N_h = population of household group h.

Utility maximization, subject to the budget constraint

$$\Sigma_i P_i C_{ih} = E_h$$

yields the Stone–Geary linear expenditure system,

$$P_i C_{ih} = P_i \gamma_{ih} N_h + c_{ih}(E_h - \Sigma_j P_j \gamma_{jh} N_h)$$

The first term on the right-hand side is the value of committed consumption of commodity i by household class h. The expression in parenthesis is the supernumerary income, i.e., expenditure over and above total committed expenditure. It is seen that supernumerary income is allocated in fixed value proportions across commodities, and that committed consumption is added to this to arrive at total consumption of the item in question.

In this demand system, values of the own-price elasticities are less than 1 as long as committed consumption can be met (which is the case in all experiments of the models). Also, cross-price elasticities are greater than 0. Finally, the income elasticity is positive but may be less than, equal to, or greater than 1. Also note that this consumption description is more general than the one for Turkey, to which it reduces as a special case when committed consumption is set equal to zero. It therefore also allows for a wider set of consumer responses to changes in prices and incomes.

India

The treatment of consumption in the Indian model is quite elaborate. Some of the complexities stem from the fact that income data are available for the fifteen households in each of the urban and rural areas, whereas other data sources report consumption for only five rural and five urban groups of households. In an attempt to match these two sources of data, the analysis rests on an assumption that the distribution of population according to per capita income and per capita consumption is bivariate lognormal. From this assumption, it is possible to describe how changes in the household income distribution translate into changes in the distribution and level of consumption.[9]

We shall proceed by first defining the relevant means and standard deviations of per capita income and consumption. Using that information, we can derive the cumulative distributions of population, consumption, and total income according to per capita consumption (i.e., by consumption group). Given the cumulative distributions and the mean per capita consumption, we can next derive per capita consumption and income levels by consumption group. Finally, we employ the linear expenditure system above, to determine consumption of different commodities by each consumption group. Since the story is the same for both rural and urban households, we shall not make a distinction between the two in what follows.

Step 1 Given the constant share income allocation scheme, we know the per capita income of each of the fifteen household classes of the area in question. Hence it is easy to find the mean per capita income and its variance. Let Y_h be per capita income by household class h, and ϕ_h be the share of households in that category in the total population. Then the mean per capita income is

$$\bar{Y} = \Sigma_h \phi_h Y_h \qquad \text{(C1)}$$

with a variance of

$$V = \Sigma_h \phi_h (Y_h - \bar{Y})^2 \qquad \text{(C2)}$$

Since the distribution of income and expenditure is assumed to be bivariate lognormal, the mean of the logarithm of per capita income, and its variance are given by

$$\mu_Y = \log \bar{Y} - 1/2\sigma_Y^2 \qquad \text{(C3)}$$

$$\sigma_Y^2 = \log(1 + V/Y^2) \qquad \text{(C4)}$$

The bivariate lognormality assumption implies that log income and log expenditure are linearly related, so the mean and variance of log per capita expenditure are given by

$$\mu_C = \alpha + \beta\mu_Y \qquad \text{(C5)}$$

$$\sigma_C = K\sigma_Y \qquad \text{(C6)}$$

Thus, the mean per capita level of consumption expenditures is

$$\bar{C} = \exp(\mu_C + 1/2\sigma_C{}^2) \qquad \text{(C7)}$$

Step 2 Given the means and standard deviations of income and expenditure, we can derive the distributions of population, consumption, and total income by consumption groups. The share of population that has per capita expenditure no more than c is given by

$$\eta_c = N(\log c - \mu_C/\sigma_C) \qquad \text{(C8)}$$

where $N(x)$ is the standardized cumulative normal distribution (mean zero, standard deviation 1). Similarly, the share of consumption by households that have per capita expenditure no more than c is

$$\theta_c = N((\log c - \mu_C)/\sigma_C - \sigma_C) \qquad \text{(C9)}$$

and the share of total income accruing to those households is

$$\delta_c = N((\log c - \mu_C)/\sigma_C - \rho_{YC}\sigma_Y) \qquad \text{(C10)}$$

where ρ_{YC} is the correlation coefficient between income and consumption.

Step 3 Using the above, we can now find the per capita levels (in contrast to the cumulative shares above) of income and consumption by the five consumption groups. This is easily done by

$$\bar{C}_c = \bar{C} d\theta_c / d\eta_c \qquad \text{(C11)}$$

and

$$\bar{Y}_c = \bar{Y} d\delta_c / d\eta_c \qquad \text{(C12)}$$

where the d indicates differencing ($d_c = x_c - x_{c-1}$).

Step 4 What has been accomplished so far is that income data on fifteen household income groups and consumption data on five household consumption groups have been brought together to determine per capita income and expenditure for those five household consumption groups. It remains to determine how each of these five groups allocates expenditure across commodities. When this is done, we have a formal mechanism for translating the income distribution for fifteen household classes as derived from the model into consumption demands. To do this, the India model assumes the Stone–Geary linear expenditure system as described above for each member of the consumption classes

$$P_i \bar{C}_{ic} = P_i \gamma_{ic} + \beta_{ic} (\bar{C}_c - \Sigma_j P_j \gamma_{jc}) \qquad \text{(C13)}$$

where $\bar{C}_{ic}$ is per capita consumption of commodity i by members of consumption class c.

The final step is, therefore, to derive total consumption demands

$$\bar{C}_i = \Sigma_c d\eta_c N C_{ic} \qquad \text{(C14)}$$

where C_i is total consumption demand by commodity. Note that $d_{\eta c} N$ is the population of consumption class c.

Beyond the technicalities of this distribution and expenditure system, it is quite instructive to see what is accomplished by (C1)–(C14) by means of an example. Assume that an external shock or a change in economic policy affects sectoral production and prices in ways given by the model. Factor incomes will then be affected and, in turn, via the fixed allocative scheme, map into changed household incomes for the fifteen rural and fifteen urban household income classes. This affects the mean and variance of household income (by (C1) and (C2) above). Consequently, the mean and standard deviation of log per capita income will change (by (C3) and (C4)). This translates into changed means and standard deviations of log per capita expenditure (by (C5) and (C6)), and also the mean per capita expenditure level (in (C7)).

Since the parameters of the bivariate lognormal distribution change in this manner, so will the cumulative distributions of per capita income, expenditure, and population (by (C8)–(C10)). Since both mean per capita expenditure and its distribution have changed, consumption demands will be affected (through (C11)–(C14)). This feeds back through the model in the ways described earlier: some demands may have risen while others may have fallen. Therefore, a new round of adjustment takes place, including price and quantity changes that again affect factor incomes; hence, income and expenditure levels and their distribution. This continues until the economy settles into a general equilibrium. In that equilibrium, we can determine sectoral production patterns, relative prices, and so on, just as in the core model. But in addition, we may derive various measures of inequality such as the Gini coefficient as resulting from a consistent treatment of all the repercussions on prices, production, and other economic magnitudes, due to the shock.[10] This makes the India model well suited for analyzing questions of socioeconomic incidence, in addition to questions of macroeconomic efficiency and sectoral allocation of resources. It may also be noted that, since the India model includes a linear expenditure system, it includes the consumer behavior of all the other country models as special cases.

5.3.2 Government behavior

All models use the assumptions of government behavior described in the core model. Thus transfers are indexed, and tax rates and government consumption are fixed exogenously except in one experiment. In the latter we analyze the effects of using revenue-raising and expenditure-reducing instruments simultaneously to adjust domestic savings to help finance a given level of investment. In this fiscal experiment, all tax rates and government consumption are allowed to be scaled by a common proportionality factor which is determined endogenously in the model. The experiment is described in detail in section 6.2 below.

5.3.3 Rest-of-the-world behavior

All models use the assumptions about rest-of-the-world behavior laid out in the discussion of the core model above. Thus, the country is small in import markets (world prices of imports are fixed) but faces a downward-sloping constant elasticity demand curve for its exports.

5.3.4 Investment

Standard runs of the models all use the same assumptions from the core model about fixed sectoral distribution of investment. Similarly, the models may be run in either of the two closure modes. When investment driven, investment is fixed. When savings driven, foreign savings are fixed,

Table 4.3 *Labor types in the country models*

India	Turkey	Kenya	Thailand
Self-employed labor	Agricultural labor	Self-employed labor	Rural labor
Wage labor	Unskilled labor	Wage labor	Urban informal sector labor
	Skilled labor		Blue-collar labor
			White-collar labor

and the level of investment may vary, but still be subject to the same constant sectoral allocation.

There are two exceptions to this. One is that, in a particular experiment done on all the models, the allocation of investment is allowed to vary according to sectoral differences in rates of return to capital. We shall describe this in detail in section 6.3 below. The other exception is an experiment with the Thailand model, where an optimal path of investment and borrowing is calculated. This is described in chapter 7 on Thailand.

5.4 *Market clearing*

5.4.1 Commodity markets

The commodity market-clearing conditions are identical in all models, save the case of Turkey, where the inclusion of government imports of oil increases the gross supplies of the petroleum sector.

5.4.2 Factor markets

All models use the assumptions of the core model with regard to capital. The capital stock in each sector is fixed and infrastructural inputs are allocated with fixed ratios. However, the country models differ in their description of labor markets. The differences cover, first, the types of labor considered and, second, the ways in which different market segments interact. We now describe those differences.

The labor types distinguished in the models are shown in table 4.3.

For the Turkey model, there is a close correspondence between labor types and household types. Thus, agricultural households supply agricultural labor, whereas skilled and unskilled labor households supply skilled and unskilled labor, respectively. Capitalists receive rents from capital and import licenses and do not supply labor.

The India and Kenya models use only a functional classification, i.e., self-employed labor and wage labor. However, due to their sectoral employment pattern, these can be further distinguished as rural and urban labor types.[11] The reason is that the agriculture sector (mainly) employs rural labor while all other sectors (mainly) employ urban labor. Similarly, in the Thailand model, rural labor is only employed by the agriculture sector, whereas the other three labor types are all urban.

Table 4.4 provides an overview of the main assumptions of the workings of labor markets in the individual models. Labor market assumptions are classified according to the following criteria. The first depends on whether or not migration between the rural and urban area occurs. The only model that allows for migration is the Thailand model. The assumptions about this are closely related to the spillover mechanisms in that model which are described below.

The second criterion is the degree to which factor returns are indexed. All models allow for some degree of indexation of particular rates. Since that implies that the real wage rate is not perfectly flexible, unemployment may exist for such labor types. In the Kenya model, it should be mentioned that the rural self-employed wage rate is not indexed directly, but instead linked to the urban wage rate. Also, wage labor rates are not fixed in all experiments with that model.

Next, table 4.4 shows which labor types are assumed to have flexible wage rates. These labor types will therefore not be unemployed.

Although they differ in assumptions about the fixity of individual labor supplies, all models assume that the total labor supply is fixed. There are, therefore, no incentive effects to supply more labor when the real wage rate increases. The fact that total labor supplies are fixed implies, as described in the discussion of the core model, that gross domestic output is virtually fixed, and can therefore only adjust sluggishly to demand changes.

As was mentioned above, the indexation of particular wage rates may imply unemployment. However, not all unemployment need be visible. Instead, some unemployed may move to supply labor of a different type. The mechanics are described in the discussion of spillover effects below. However, in some segments of the market, open unemployment may persist. Since no unemployment benefits are assumed for any of the models, unemployment implies strong income effects. It may be noted that'open unemployment may exist for rural wage labor in the India model, for any type of rural labor in the Kenya model, and for both rural and white-collar labor in the Thailand model. In the Turkey model, there is no open unemployment.

Conversely, when the wage rate is flexible, it is assumed to be determined so as to preserve full employment. The labor types for which full

Table 4.4 *Workings of the labor market in the country models*

	India	Turkey	Kenya	Thailand
Migration between rural and urban areas	No	No	No	Yes
Indexation	Wage labor rates	Skilled labor rates	Wage labor rates, Rural self-employed rates	Rural wage rates White-collar rates
Flexible rates	Self-employed rates	Agriculture rates Unskilled rates	Urban self-employed rates	Informal sector rates, Blue-collar rates
Labor supplies	Fixed aggregate supply by area	Fixed aggregate supply	Fixed aggregate supply by area	Fixed supply by labor type
Open unemployment	Rural wage labor	None	Rural wage and self-employed labor	Rural labor, White-collar labor
Spillovers	Urban wage labor to urban self-employed labor	Skilled labor to unskilled labor	Urban wage labor to urban self-employed labor	Agricultural labor to informal labor, white-collar labor to blue-collar labor
Wage differentials across sectors	None	Fixed	Fixed	None

employment obtains are therefore the same as those shown under the flexible wage rate criterion in table 4.4.

Spillover effects between market segments determine to what degree unemployment is absorbed by employment into other labor types. For instance, in the case of the Turkey model, skilled labor real wage rates are fixed. However, unemployed skilled labor is assumed to be absorbed into the supply of unskilled labor, a category for which rates are flexible. Thus, an increase in the real wage rate of skilled labor, leading to unemployment, ultimately has the effect of increasing the supply of unskilled labor and causing a drop in the wage rate in that market segment.

The spillover may be full or partial. The most general spillover mechanism considered here is that of the Thailand model. It assumes that a fixed fraction of unemployed white-collar workers becomes blue-collar workers, hence allowing some open unemployment for white-collar workers. For agricultural workers, the spillover effect depends on the relative wage rates of rural workers and urban informal workers. More specifically,

$$l_r = 1 - \exp(w_r - \phi w_u)$$

where

l_r is the ratio of underemployed agricultural labor that spills over into the supply of informal labor,
w_r is the agricultural wage rate,
w_u is the urban informal-sector wage rate, and
ϕ is a constant of proportionality.

Assume that the urban wage rate (suitably scaled) is higher than the agricultural wage rate. In that case, the parenthesis is negative, and the exponent low, so the spillover coefficient becomes close to 1. When the agricultural wage rate is higher than the urban wage rate, the exponent becomes large and the spillover coefficient gets close to zero.

Now, given the spillover coefficients, the labor market structure of the Thailand model becomes

$$L_r = \Sigma_i L_{ri} + U_r$$

(agricultural labor supply equals agricultural employment plus agricultural unemployment – accounting identity)

$$L_u + l_r U_r = \Sigma_i L_{ui}$$

(informal-sector labor supply augmented by spilled-over agricultural unemployment equals informal-sector employment – equilibrium condition determining the informal-sector wage rate)

$$L_w = \Sigma_i L_{wi} + L_w^G + U_w$$

(white-collar labor supply equals employment of white-collar labor in private production and the government plus unemployment – accounting identity)

$$L_b + l_w U_w = \Sigma_i L_{bi} + L_b^G$$

(blue-collar labor supply augmented by spilled-over unemployed white-collar labor equals employment of blue-collar labor in private production and the government – equilibrium condition determining the blue-collar wage rate).

It is seen that there are two "hard" labor market segments in this model: the rural and urban informal segment and the blue- and white-collar segment. In addition, each of those two hard segments contains two "soft" segments with partial spillover mechanisms.

The spillover mechanisms in the other models are all special cases of this arrangement. Thus, in the Kenya model, the rural segment is isolated from the urban segment, which in turn is characterized by a full spillover from wage labor to self-employed labor (i.e., the spillover coefficient is 1).

It might be noted that the labor market specifications are not merely a way to reshuffle income among factors. Indeed, they play a role in determining how cost shocks to production are shifted forward into output prices or backward into factor returns. Roughly speaking, the more flexible wage rates are, the more is the burden of adjustment placed on factor income. On the other hand, the less flexible wage rates are, the more is that burden placed on output prices. The pattern of adjustment affects different demands differently. Thus, when factor income is affected most, household income changes and private consumption is affected quite directly through income effects. However with output price adjustment, export demands and private demands are directly affected through price effects, but since some demand categories such as consumption and investment are not sensitive to prices, household welfare effects are likely to be less than in the case of factor price adjustment.

The last item that differentiates the specification of labor markets in the models is the treatment of sectoral wage rate differentials for the same type of labor. Table 4.4 shows that the Turkey and Kenya models both include a sectoral wage differential scheme. In both models it is implemented by assuming a set of constant proportionality factors giving the ratio of sectoral wage rates to the average wage rate

$$W_i = a_{W_i} W$$

The India and Thailand models do not include such mechanisms. Although sectoral wage rate differentials may appear to be important, they are really just a convenient way of generating numbers that resemble those in labor statistics. The constant wage differentials do not in any way affect the workings of the general equilibrium model. To see why, note that in calibrating the model to actual data, the total sectoral wage sum is given. This is split into a wage and an employment figure by postulating a wage rate and calculating what the corresponding employment figure is. Next, given employment figures, and numbers for other real inputs as well as real outputs, the production function parameters are determined in a way that makes the factor composition consistent with the first-order conditions for profit maximization. In short, this means that for a given wage sum, a particular wage rate postulate is mirrored in a particular marginal productivity. If the wage rate is high (low), the marginal productivity measure will be high (low). In all runs of the model, the cost-minimizing behavior of producers implies that real product wage rates are equal to marginal products. A parallel scaling on both sides of this condition, as implied by the constant proportion sectoral wage differentials, does not affect the producer's choice.

6 Prototypical experiments

In this section, we provide a brief overview of some typical experiments undertaken in the rest of this study. Our aim is both to illustrate how the models may be used for analyzing different scenarios as well as to provide a point of reference for some experiments that are common to the country analyses. It is not our intention to specify the experiments fully – that is done in the individual country chapters.

We will sketch three such prototypical experiments. The first experiment examines whether external shocks could have accounted for the economic performance of the country in question. The second experiment analyzes the role of fiscal policy in country adjustment to external shocks. The third experiment focuses on whether market-oriented investment policies could have improved economic performance.

6.1 Analysis of the impact of external shocks

To find out how much of the historical performance could be explained by external shocks alone, it is natural to run a counterfactual, where external shocks do not occur, and compare the model results with the historical run obtained from the tracking procedure described in section 4.2 above.

To set up the experiment, it may be assumed that a no-shock case is characterized by a smooth growth of certain exogenous variables, e.g., prices and perhaps world export prices. For example, it may be assumed that oil prices grow by the same rates over the period of analysis as they did "historically." This establishes a new set of values for the relevant exogenous variables over the period analyzed. Since the absence of shocks would also most likely have affected borrowing, some adjustment is made to the path of discretionary shock-related borrowing as well.

All other exogenous variables and parameters are then kept constant, and the model run to trace out a new sequence of equilibria. The new set of sectoral outputs and demands, as well as prices, factor returns, household incomes, and the like thus allow a detailed analysis of the impact of external shocks on the economy. The results can be used to compare macro-economic performance, sectoral allocation of production, and income distribution *vis-à-vis* the historical run.

6.2 Analysis of the impact of fiscal policies

The impact of fiscal policies in explaining historical performance can be analyzed in several ways. One is to use some rule to select a different path of government spending and tax rates than what actually occurred. In that case, the experiment can be set up in a way very similar to the experiment to analyze the impact of external shocks. The new set of exogenous government consumption and tax rates is used in conjunction with the unchanged values of all other exogenous variables to find a new sequence of equilibria that can be compared to that of the historical run.

Another interesting way to approach the analysis is to ask what would have happened if the government had used revenue mobilization and expenditure reduction to target a more stable trajectory of foreign borrowing and investment than was historically the case. This experiment, which is undertaken for Kenya in chapter 8, can be performed with the model by first specifying what the target trajectories of foreign savings and investment should be and then fixing those two variables to their target trajectories. Note that this leaves the model overdetermined since it is normally run either in investment-driven or savings-driven mode, but not both at the same time. When both variables are thus fixed, another one must be allowed to vary. Since the aim is to use revenue mobilization and expenditure reduction as the instruments for achieving the investment and borrowing targets, it is natural to allow all or a subset of tax rates and public consumption levels in the economy to be adjusted in proportion to their historical values.

With all exogenous variables and parameters fixed at historical levels, and investment and foreign savings pegged at their target values the model solves for a new equilibrium. In so doing, it also finds the (common) proportion by which tax rates would have had to be increased and public consumption scaled back. As usual, comparing the evolution of various indicators in this run with the historical run allows one to evaluate the consequences of this mode of adjustment.

It may be noted that the principal adjustment mechanism in this experiment is one of income redistribution between the government and the private sector, since the government savings propensity is 1 and thus much higher than that of households. The domestic savings rate increases with tax increases and expenditure reductions.

6.3 Analysis of investment allocation

One feature of all the models used in the subsequent study is that the allocation of investment across sectors is exogenously given as a policy decision. A valid hypothesis might therefore be that, by responding to market signals in the sectoral allocation of investment, a higher degree of economic efficiency and growth might have been achieved. Since the allocation does not respond to market signals regarding the relative scarcity of capital in different sectors, this leads to quite different rates of return on capital across sectors, as well as over time in the historical run.

That proposition might be tested in different ways. One would be to allow the sectoral allocation of investment to be determined by the model in a way that would equalize rates of return on capital across sectors. That would indeed be the case in a frictionless world with perfect mobility of capital. However, recognizing that the capital markets of the countries analyzed here are not frictionless, a "softer" rule may be imposed. The rule applied in the country analysis is as follows

$$y_i = 1 - \exp(1 - \lambda x_i) \tag{I1}$$

where

y_i is the share of the volume of investment allocated to sector i,
x_i is the relative rate of return on capital in sector i, defined below, and
λ is a factor that ensures that the allocation shares add to one.

The relative rate of return on capital in sector i is given by a normalization of the implicit price of capital in that sector to the economy-wide returns

$$x_i = P_{Ki}/\Sigma_j P_{Kj} \tag{I2}$$

In the experiments in chapters 6 to 9, the investment allocation rule above is not applied to every sector in the economy but to groups of sectors. In that case, the normalization rule applies to those groups, and the sectoral allocation within each group follows the capital stock proportions in the base year.

For given x_i's and a given λ, the allocation rule may not find a set of y_i's which add to one. When this is the case, λ is adjusted to ensure that shares add to one.

To understand the rule, assume that returns to capital in a given sector are high relative to the economy-wide returns. In that case, x_i is high and for a given λ, the parenthesis of (I1) is low. This translates into a high allocation to the sector, y_i. The opposite is the case for a sector where the return to capital is lower than the average. Consequently, the rule allocates much investment to sectors where capital is presently relatively scarce so that the rate of return is high, and little investment to sectors where rates of return are low. Note, however, that the reallocation is done sluggishly. It does not imply factor price equalization across sectors. Note also that the rule is myopic. It does not take into account intertemporal effects. On the one hand, this means that the allocation pattern implied by the rule may in principle change a lot from year to year. On the other hand, it implies that the rule is possibly more easily implementable in practice.

To run an experiment with this more market-oriented investment allocation rule, all exogenous parameters, as well as investment are fixed at historical levels. After solving each year of the counterfactual, the above rule is used to generate additions to capital across sectors in response to the rates on return to capital that result in the equilibrium. Next, capital stocks are updated in the way described in the section on dynamics, and the next year is solved. This continues for every year of the simulation. It may be noted that in this experiment, even though total investment is fixed at historical levels in every year, the total capital stock need not be the same as in the historical run. The reason is that each sector may have different depreciation rates. For example, if the allocation rule above implies higher allocations to sectors with lower depreciation rates, the total capital stock may increase in this experiment relative to the historical run.

7 Concluding remarks

This chapter has introduced the framework used in the country studies to analyze the impact of and policy responses to changes in oil prices and other external shocks. We have described the common analytical core of the models and also discussed specific features that distinguish them from one another, with a view to guiding intuition for how particular results in the country analyses come about. We have stressed that intuition from the more commonly used partial equilibrium analysis may be misleading. Computable general equilibrium models like the ones developed in this study forge linkages among production sectors, final demands, and factor markets by establishing a set of market-clearing relative prices. These are particularly important when analyzing the effects of oil price increases. A partial equilibrium will imply quite sharp price increases throughout the economy and may indicate production cuts, primarily due to a reduction of competitiveness of the economy. However they neglect the impact of price shocks on factor markets. In contrast, a general equilibrium analysis will continue where the simple model leaves off and let factor markets adjust to reduced demands. New relative factor prices are the result, implying changes to income and production incentives. These simultaneous adjustments in all markets allow the model to provide a more comprehensive assessment of the sectoral and distributional impacts of relative price shocks. Similarly, the consequences of particular policy responses can also be evaluated more adequately. Thus, the general equilibrium approach allows a fuller analysis not only of how external shocks affect economic performance but also of the extent to which adverse effects are neutralized by particular economic policies. The country studies that follow will be seen to use the models to those ends.

Notes

1 This chapter is technically the most demanding in the book. Readers uninterested in those details may wish to look at descriptions of general structure and then proceed directly to chapter 5.
2 The model is called "Ganges: A Macroeconomic Framework for India."
3 For a detailed description of social accounting matrices, see Pyatt and Round (1985).
4 This is so because addition of all row sums simply sums all numbers in the matrix. The same applies to the addition of all column sums.
5 For simplicity, we ignore sales taxes here, since they do not add anything conceptually new.
6 A standard reference on demand analysis is Deaton and Muellbauer (1980).
7 For a fuller discussion, see Taylor and Lysy (1979).
8 This would be the case, for example, for exportables facing fixed prices on world markets.
9 A standard treatment on the lognormal distribution is Aitchison and Brown (1969) to which the reader is referred for technical details.
10 Since we are operating in a two-parameter lognormal world where the entire Lorenz curve is uniquely determined by the distribution parameter σ, the Gini coefficient and the headcount ratio measure of poverty would mostly move in the same direction, given a prior specification of the poverty line.
11 The qualification arises from the fact that 46 percent of labor income in the consumer-goods sectors in the India model accrues to the rural labor force.

5   Country studies

Introduction

The next four chapters study the adjustment experience of four selected developing countries at different income levels and characterized by varying structures of trade and production: (1) Turkey, a semi-industrial country ($600),[1] (2) Thailand, a middle-income primary producing country ($270), (3) India, a partially industrialized low-income country ($120), and (4) Kenya, a low-income sub-Saharan African country ($170). They assess the relative magnitude of external shocks *vis-à-vis* other exogenous or policy-induced developments in the economy, compare the particular policies chosen with alternatives in terms of their macroeconomic, sectoral, and distributional consequences, highlight the difficulties of maintaining a coherent policy stance in the light of positive and negative external developments, describe the role of post-1973/4 policies in shaping adjustment to the 1979/80 round of external shocks, and explore the role of more market-oriented schemes for the sectoral allocation of investment in the light of changes in the international environment. The intention is to subject the conclusions of chapter 2 to closer scrutiny within a richer framework that allows an explicit comparison of policy alternatives. As before, we proceed by applying a common methodology to the study of all four countries. The methodology is that of chapter 4.

Comparative structure

Tables 5.1 to 5.4 present macroeconomic aggregates, sectoral composition, and distributional characteristics for all four countries in their respective base years.[2] Consumption accounts for roughly 80 percent of GDP in all countries – with the mix being most weighted in favor of public consumption in Kenya (almost entirely services), followed by Turkey, with the two Asian countries, India and Thailand, being characterized by public

Table 5.1 Selected features of the economy: India, 1973

I National accounts aggregates

	Private consumption	Government consumption	Total investment	Exports	Imports
Ratios to GDP at market prices	0.72	0.08	0.22	0.04	0.06

II Sectoral composition

	1	2	3	4	5	6
Shares in selected macroeconomic aggregates						
Share in value added	0.52	0.05	0.06	0.06	0.03	0.28
Share in private consumption	0.57	0.22	0.02	0.04	0.02	0.14
Share in exports	0.13	0.56	0.05	0.26	0.0	0.0
Share in intermediate imports	0.13	0.17	0.14	0.52	0.0	0.04
Share in final imports	0.26	0.04	0.36	0.0	0.34	0.0
Share of value added in gross output	0.76	0.32	0.32	0.30	0.53	0.71
Share of intermediate imports in gross output	0.01	0.04	0.04	0.12	0.0	0.01
Share of private consumption in gross output	0.72	0.86	0.08	0.16	0.27	0.32
Share of exports in gross output	0.01	0.09	0.01	0.06	0.0	0.0

III Distributional characteristics

Shares of different classes in

	Income	Consumption	Population
Urban			
C1	0.01	0.01	0.06
C2	0.03	0.04	0.12
C3	0.09	0.12	0.22
C4	0.25	0.28	0.32
C5	0.63	0.55	0.29
Gini coefficient	0.47	0.37	
Rural			
C1	0.03	0.05	0.13
C2	0.12	0.14	0.24
C3	0.27	0.29	0.32
C4	0.38	0.36	0.25
C5	0.20	0.16	0.06
Gini coefficient	0.38	0.30	

IV Budget

Revenue composition

Domestic indirect taxes	79.1%
Tariffs	7.0%
Direct taxes	13.9%

Expenditure composition

Public consumption	78.6%
Transfers	21.4%

Note: "—" implies "not defined." C1–C5 denote five urban and five rural groups of households, where the groups are ranked in ascending order with respect to per capita expenditure

Table 5.2 Selected features of the economy: Thailand, 1973

I National accounts aggregates

	Private consumption	Government consumption	Total investment	Exports	Imports
Ratios to GDP at market prices	0.68	0.09	0.24	0.20	0.21

II Sectoral composition

	1	2	3	4	5	6
Shares in selected macroeconomic aggregates						
Share in value added	0.50	0.07	0.16	0.07	0.06	0.14
Share in private consumption	0.38	0.18	0.18	0.02	0.05	0.19
Share in exports	0.12	0.39	0.03	0.20	0.0	0.26
Share in intermediate imports[a]	0.05	0.09	0.21	0.50	0.09	0.06
Share in final imports	0	0.10	0.61	0.21	0.0	0.08
Share of value added in gross output	0.75	0.18	0.37	0.13	0.35	0.36
Share of intermediate imports in gross output	0.01	0.04	0.08	0.16	0.09	0.03
Share of private consumption in gross output	0.51	0.43	0.36	0.04	0.24	0.43
Share of exports in gross output	0.05	0.27	0.02	0.09	0.0	0.17

III Distributional characteristics

	Share of different classes in	
	Income	Consumption
Own account urban	0.21	0.20
Informal urban	0.03	0.02
Blue collar	0.20	0.21
White collar	0.09	0.10
Own account rural	0.44	0.43
Informal rural	0.03	0.04

IV Budget

Revenue composition

Domestic indirect taxes	52.2%
Tariffs	24.2%
Direct taxes	18.6%

Expenditure composition

Public consumption	101.4%
Transfers	−1.4%

Note: [a]Petroleum is included in sector 4, intermediate goods.

Table 5.3 Selected features of the economy: Kenya, 1976

I National accounts aggregates

	Private consumption	Government consumption	Total investment	Exports	Imports
Ratios to GDP at market prices	0.62	0.17	0.20	0.32	0.31

II Sectoral composition

	1	2	3	4	5	6
Shares in selected macroeconomic aggregates						
Share in value added	0.42	0.05	0.05	0.05	0.07	0.35
Share in private consumption	0.36	0.25	0.02	0.06	0.07	0.24
Share in exports	0.33	0.09	0.02	0.10	0.25	0.21
Share in intermediate imports	0.05	0.15	0.16	0.16	0.41	0.07
Share in final imports	0.32	0.19	0.50	0.0	0.0	0.0
Share of value added in gross output	0.86	0.18	0.19	0.30	0.25	0.66
Share of intermediate imports in gross output	0.03	0.13	0.16	0.23	0.38	0.03
Share of private consumption in gross output	0.46	0.54	0.04	0.22	0.15	0.29
Share of exports in gross output	0.25	0.12	0.20	0.20	0.33	0.14

III Distributional characteristics

| | | Share of different classes in | |
	Income	Consumption	Population
Urban poor	0.27	0.28	0.08
Urban rich	0.15	0.08	0.02
Rural small	0.38	0.45	0.77
Rural large	0.20	0.19	0.13

IV Budget

Revenue composition

Domestic indirect taxes	42.3%
Tariffs	25.8%
Direct taxes	31.9%

Expenditure composition

Public consumption	58.1%
Transfers	41.9%

Table 5.4 Selected features of the economy: Turkey, 1973

I National accounts aggregates

	Private consumption	Government consumption	Total investment	Exports	Imports
Ratios to GDP at market prices	0.71	0.12	0.19	0.09	0.11

II Sectoral composition

	1	2	3	4	5	6
Shares in selected macroeconomic aggregates						
Share in value added	0.27	0.06	0.10	0.09	0.04	0.44
Share in private consumption	0.27	0.24	0.05	0.10	0.03	0.32
Share in exports	0.20	0.44	0.0	0.11	0.05	0.21
Share in intermediate imports	0.09	0.11	0.28	0.36	0.02	0.14
Share in final imports	0.02	0.03	0.34	0.37	0.16	0.08
Share of value added in gross output	0.68	0.20	0.44	0.37	0.79	0.81
Share of intermediate imports in gross output	0.02	0.02	0.09	0.11	0.03	0.02
Share of private consumption in gross output	0.52	0.59	0.17	0.33	0.41	0.47
Share of exports in gross output	0.05	0.14	0.0	0.05	0.09	0.04

III Distributional characteristics

	Shares of different classes in	
	Income	Consumption
Agricultural households	0.30	0.37
Urban unskilled	0.09	0.10
Urban skilled	0.29	0.29
Capitalist	0.33	0.24

IV Budget

	Revenue composition
Domestic indirect taxes	36.2%
Tariffs	17.7%
Direct taxes	46.1%

Note: The Turkey model (chapter 9) distinguishes a seventh sector, viz., petroleum, which in the above table is included with sector 4, intermediate goods.

consumption shares which are less than 10 percent of GDP. Investment averaged 20 percent of GDP, with the share being the highest in India and Thailand. The above figures on the shares of consumption and investment imply that the trade gap (the difference between imports and exports) was a modest proportion of GDP – 2 percent in India and Turkey, 1 percent in Thailand, and – 1 percent in Kenya.

The sectoral breakdown generally distinguishes (1) agriculture, (2) consumer goods, (3) capital goods, including construction, (4) intermediate goods, (5) infrastructure, and (6) services.[3] Agriculture accounts for the bulk of value added in India and Thailand and is the dominant sector in Kenya. It also features most importantly in private consumption, with consumer goods and services also being significant. Consumer goods make the largest contribution to exports in India, Thailand, and Turkey; that role is played by the agricultural sector in Kenya. The bulk of intermediate imports goes into the capital-goods and intermediate-goods sectors, although their role in infrastructure in Kenya is also significant. The same sectors are important in final imports as well.

Turning to distributional characteristics, an inspection of table 5.1, as well as the Gini coefficients, shows greater equality in urban compared to rural India. Ninety percent of Kenya's population is in rural areas: of this smallholders comprise 85 percent of the rural population and 65 percent of rural income. Some 45 percent of income and consumption in Thailand is accounted for by own-account rural workers. Roughly 37 percent of rural consumption in Turkey goes to agricultural households.

Figures on the composition of tax revenues in the base year for each country show that direct taxes are the most important in Turkey (46.1 percent) and Kenya (31.9 percent), followed by Thailand (18.6 percent) and India (13.9 percent). Domestic indirect taxes are overwhelmingly important in India and Thailand. Trade taxes bring in only 7 percent of tax revenue in India: this is due primarily to the low share of trade, a feature to which attention was drawn in table 5.1 above. In turn, the importance of international trade in Kenya and Thailand is reflected in the fact that tariffs contribute around 25 percent of tax revenue in both countries.

Why these countries?

Among the four countries considered here, Turkey belongs to the ranks of the semi-industrial nations.[4] A high share of manufacturing in both GDP and merchandise exports made for potential flexibility in adjusting to shocks, as well as creditworthiness in private capital markets in the 1970s and early 1980s. India, a populous low-income country, has a significantly higher share of manufacturing in merchandise exports, a feature that gave it a wider range of adjustment options than many other countries at that income level. It is also, however, much more heavily dependent on the agricultural sector in terms of both GDP and employment. Both countries built up a diversified industrial base through a strategy of import-substituting industrialization, fostered by protective trade barriers. The share of imports and exports was around 10 percent of GDP in Turkey and roughly 5 percent in India. The inward-looking strategy led to a pattern of boom-and-bust cyclical growth in Turkey, where industrial expansion and its associated import demand would lead to a foreign exchange crisis, a major devaluation, and a slowdown in growth. In India, too, any cuts in foreign assistance would lead to a decline in public investment and growth, as no sustained effort was made to promote export expansion to help finance imports. But, in addition, developments in agriculture exerted a dominant role in macroeconomic policy-making in India. It will be seen that the character of adjustment to external shocks was conditioned in Turkey by perceptions shaped by recurrent foreign exchange crises and in India by the view that food and foreign exchange were the principal constraints to growth.

The two primary producing countries, Kenya and Thailand, offer an interesting contrast with respect to adjustment. The agricultural sector is an important determinant of economic performance in both countries. Imports and exports were around 30 percent of GDP in Kenya and roughly 20 percent in Thailand. However, Thailand's development strategy involved outward-looking policies and diversification of exports: the share of the three most important commodities in export earnings was less than 40 percent, compared to 70 percent for countries such as Ghana, the Ivory Coast, and Sri Lanka. This set of policies provided raw materials for processing industries, generated a home market for industrial output, and earned foreign exchange for imported inputs for manufacturing industries. In Kenya, too, three commodities accounted for around 40 percent of the country's exports. But in contrast to Thailand, Kenya moved from being an open economy in the 1960s to one where the incentive system had begun to be tilted against cash crop exports and in favor of production of manufactured goods for the domestic market. The coffee boom of 1975–7 was largely responsible for a 93 percent overall increase in export prices and implied that the resulting favorable shock was at least as great as the terms-of-trade movements associated with the 1973–4 and 1979–80 increases in the price of imported fuels. The boom, in addition to the policy weaknesses noted later, undermined any sense of urgency in adjusting to oil price shocks and complicated the task of maintaining a coherent response to external shocks.

The questions asked

All four country studies describe the development policies followed prior to the 1970s so as to embed the discussion of adjustment in historical perspective. The analysis of shocks and adjustment is carried out using a general equilibrium model implemented on a consistent data base for each country over the eight- to ten-year period under review.[5] The magnitude of terms-of-trade shocks is then quantified and assessed *vis-à-vis* other shocks, such as harvest failure, or favorable developments, such as growth in arable land, in order to determine how much adjustment was necessary. The appropriateness of the policies pursued by each country is then compared with a different pattern of adjustment, involving *inter alia*, exchange-rate adjustment, greater growth orientation, the mix between domestic savings and foreign borrowing, and the greater use of market signals to guide investment in different sectors of the economy. The policy conclusions emerging for each country are discussed in the relevant country chapters. The general lessons emerging from the studies for adjustment to external shocks, as well as their relationship to those of chapter 2, are collected in chapter 10.

Relationship to the literature

In a survey of the literature, Westoby (1984) finds two broad kinds of attempts to analyze the macroeconomic impact of increases in oil prices.[6] One type involves comparative analysis using shock-adjustment approaches of the Balassa type, for example, World Bank (1981b), Lin (1981), and Dell and Lawrence (1986). The second type, exemplified by Gupta and Togan (1983), Dick and Gupta (1984), and Hoffman and Jarass (1983) studies adjustment in groups of countries using a common general equilibrium framework.[7] The present study combines both approaches, harnessing the insights made available by the former to motivate the questions asked of the latter and using the results from both to elicit applicable lessons for policy. But it also extends each of the two approaches in significant ways. First, we have seen that the approach of chapter 2, while following the comparative analytic tradition, enriches it by introducing savings and investment, thus bringing it closer to the basic framework of international economics. Second, the general equilibrium analysis of adjustment in the four countries covers a broader range than that of current comparative modeling. We track historical developments for an eight- to ten-year period starting from 1973 in order to define a historical run which serves as a benchmark for the evaluation of counterfactual policies. Next, we use the models to assess the relative importance of external shocks of various kinds. The heart of the analysis is the comparison of alternative policies specified and run over an eight- to ten-year period. Particular attention is paid in some of the models to questions of income distribution, workings of the labor market, the evolution of debt, and the optimal time-phasing of investment and external borrowing.[8] Furthermore, to encourage readers to use these techniques to analyze similar episodes elsewhere, we provide a reference (Brooke, Kendrick, and Meeraus, 1988) which may be consulted for the relevant software and full model documentation.

Notes

1 Figures in parentheses are per capita GNP figures for 1973.
2 The base year is 1973 for Turkey and Thailand, 1973/4 for India, and 1976 for Kenya.
3 There are some slight variations in the sectoral breakdown across the four countries. Details were provided in chapter 4.
4 In their cross-country statistical analysis of industrialization and growth, Chenery, Robinson, and Syrquin (1986) include all four countries, but comment that Turkey alone meets their criteria for semi-industrial economies.
5 For a formal discussion of the methodology, calibration, and multiyear data-tracking procedures, see chapter 4. The implementation for each country is presented in the relevant country chapter.
6 That paper covers analyses of adjustment for industrial countries as well. We do not focus on those countries here.
7 Mention may also be made, for example, of Hideshima and Inoue (1982) and Pearce and Westoby (1985) which use simpler Keynesian-type simulation models.
8 The need to explore some of these questions in a comparative modeling framework was noted by Sanderson and Williamson (1985) in their survey of World Bank models of adjustment to external shocks.

6 Adjustment with growth or stagnation?: India, 1973/4 to 1983/4

1 Adjustment experience

Introduction

In common with other oil-importing countries, India was adversely affected by the two oil price increases of 1973/4 and 1979/80. The first was associated with a terms-of-trade deterioration of 1.5 percent of GDP in 1974/5 and 1.9 percent in the immediately succeeding years, and a doubling in the share of oil imports in export earnings between 1972/3 and 1973/4. The corresponding figures for the second were a terms-of-trade deterioration of 2.8 percent of GDP in 1979/80 and a rise in the share of oil imports in export earnings from 29 percent during 1974/5 to 1978/9 to 78 percent in 1980/1. However, turning to policy-related outcomes, while the current-account balance went from a deficit of 1.2 percent of GNP in 1974/5 to a surplus of 0.1 percent of GNP in 1975/6, it moved from a deficit of 0.2 percent of GNP in 1978/9 to a deficit of 2 percent of GNP in 1980/1 and 1981/2, in which range it remained in subsequent years.

These figures suggest that the magnitude of the shocks was significant. They also indicate a different pattern of balance-of-payments adjustment to the two sets of shocks. At the same time, average annual growth, which had dipped from 3.9 percent during 1950/1 to 1964/5 to 3.3 percent during 1964/5 to 1973/4, rose to 4 percent in the period 1973/4 to 1983/4. It is necessary to interpret these figures carefully because they include rapid growth in services, especially public administration and defense, compared to the two earlier periods. However, industry too played its part. While its performance failed to match the 6.7 percent recorded during 1964/5 to 1973/4, the average annual growth of GDP in the secondary sector accelerated from 3.5 percent during 1964/5 to 1973/4 to 4.2 percent in 1973/4 to 1983/4. In other words, industrial growth during the decade of adjustment, though better than that of the preceding decade, fell well short of that witnessed in the first decade and a half of planning. The intermediate

146

nature of this outcome explains the ambiguity posed in the title of the chapter.

To what extent can the intermediate growth performance of the middle 1970s be attributed to terms-of-trade shocks and balance-of-payments adjustment? Is that pattern of adjustment better understood as a response to harvest failure that occurred alongside the first oil shock or to the already overheated economy on which it was superimposed?

What would have been the implications of a more investment- and growth-oriented strategy in the aftermath of 1973/4, underwritten by greater foreign borrowing and the reserves of foreign exchange that were allowed to accumulate from 1976/7 onwards? Would the resulting depletion of reserves have prevented the economy from adopting an outward-oriented adjustment strategy of the kind pursued after 1979/80?

Economic background before 1973/4

India exemplifies the findings of comparative analysis that economies with a large population and diversified natural resources generally rely less heavily on international trade than the average developing country (Chenery, Robinson, and Syrquin, 1986). In addition, reliance on foreign trade had been further limited by a strategy of import substitution – a strategy adopted in part because of the "export pessimism" prevailing in the 1950s. Recurrent foreign exchange crises, arising partly out of this approach to industrialization, were met by an intensification of import and foreign exchange restrictions of various kinds. Those restrictions provided protection to domestic producers of import-competing products and, notwithstanding certain *ad hoc* concessions, discriminated against exports.[1] Foreign assistance substituted for export expansion as a source of financing for imports. At the same time that import restrictions protected domestic producers from international competition, industrial licensing controlled the entry of additional domestic producers and thereby stifled domestic competition as well. This combination of policies gave rise to a diversified yet highly protected industrial structure and to an economy effectively insulated from the international environment.

During those years, the economy was vulnerable to two types of exogenous shocks: (1) a weather-induced failure of the agricultural harvest, such as the two successive droughts in the agricultural years (July–June) 1965/6 and 1966/7, and (2) cuts in foreign assistance, such as a cessation of US foreign aid following India's wars with Pakistan in 1965 and again in 1971. The former was capable of triggering both an inflationary price spiral as well as a recession in a virtually closed and predominantly agrarian economy and was to lead to an extension of irrigation and the provision of

Table 6.1 Trend rate of growth for selected periods and variables

Variable	Period I 1950/1 to 1964/5 ROG[b]	Period II 1964/5 to 1973/4 ROG[b]	Highest rate of growth observed 1964/5 to 1981/2 ROG[b]	Period
1 Aggregate GDP	3.85	3.32	3.59	1964/5 to 1983/4
2 Per capita GDP	1.86	1.08	1.34	1964/5 to 1978/9
			1.34	1964/5 to 1983/4
3 GDP in agriculture	2.40	2.79	2.84	1964/5 to 1978/9
4 GDP in manufacturing (total)	6.75	3.47	4.08	1964/5 to 1979/80
5 GDP in manufacturing (registered)	7.98	3.78	4.08	1964/5 to 1981/2
6 GDP in primary sector	2.50	2.78	4.27	1964/5 to 1981/2
7 GDP in secondary sector	6.67	3.53	2.82	1964/5 to 1978/9
8 GDP in tertiary sector	4.87	4.01	3.92	1964/5 to 1979/80
9 GDP in trade and communications	5.78	3.94	4.72	1964/5 to 1981/2
10 GDP in finance and real estate	3.94	4.58	4.76	1964/5 to 1981/2
11 GDP in community and personal services	4.06	3.79	4.57	1964/5 to 1979/80
12 GDP in public administration and defense	6.26	6.50	4.75	1964/5 to 1981/2
13 Gross fixed capital formation (GFCF)[ac]	6.68		7.13	1964/5 to 1981/2
14 Gross domestic capital formation (GDCF)[ac]	7.16		4.12	1964/5 to 1979/80
15 Public-sector GFCF[c]	11.40		4.87	1964/5 to 1981/2
16 Gross investment in manufacturing (destination)	10.52	3.40	4.20	1964/5 to 1978/9
			5.25	1964/5 to 1981/2
17 Gross investment in registered manufacturing (destination)	10.55	−0.30	6.83	1964/5 to 1977/8

Notes:

[a] Gross fixed capital formation and gross domestic capital formation are measured at 1960/1 prices. All other items are at 1970/1 prices.

[b] ROG is the trend rate of growth in percent per year. It is given by the coefficient of the time variable when the logarithmic transform of a given variable (GDP, etc.) is regressed against time.

[c] Trend growth rates are not shown for lines 13–15 for period II because the levels were virtually stagnant.

incentives to farmers to adopt chemical–biological technology in the 1960s in order to increase domestic output and reduce its dependence on the weather. The latter typically led to significant cuts in public investment, the consequences of which were to be manifested in the shortages of infrastructure starting in the decade of the 1970s. A sequence of such events shaped perceptions that food and foreign exchange were the two principal constraints on Indian economic development, an idea that will be seen to have influenced macroeconomic policy in the mid 1970s.

The vulnerability of the economy's development prospects to those shocks is illustrated by table 6.1 which compares the trend growth rates of certain variables for the years 1950/1 to 1964/5 (period I) with those for the years 1964/5 to 1973/4 (period II). The net result of both shocks is reflected in a slowdown in the trend growth rate of aggregate GDP from 3.85 percent in period I to 3.32 percent in period II, and of per capita GDP from 1.86 percent to 1.08 percent, with much greater variability around the lower rates. Indeed, period II, the decade preceding the first oil crisis, is marked by a deceleration in the trend rate of growth of almost all the macroeconomic aggregates. Gross fixed capital formation in the public sector (line 15) virtually stagnated in the second period, as did gross investment in registered manufacturing (not included in the table). The only sectors that registered a higher growth rate in period II than in period I were GDP in agriculture (line 3), the result of a successful policy of boosting crop output; the primary sector, of which agriculture is a dominant component (line 6); finance and real estate (line 10); and public administration and defense (line 12). The reasons underlying this deceleration have been the subject of extensive discussion.[2]

The oil shocks
Balance-of-payments consequences

Tables 6.2, 6.3, and 6.4 provide a description of the balance-of-payments consequences of the two oil price increases. The resulting *terms-of-trade* loss amounted to 1.5 percent of GDP in 1974/5 and 1.9 percent in the two subsequent years; these were far exceeded during the second oil shock when the figure reached 2.83 percent. *Import outlays on petroleum, oil, and lubricants (POL)* more than quadrupled between 1972/3 and 1974/5, although the amount of crude imports rose by less than 8 percent a year, while imports of petroleum products actually declined by more than 13 percent a year. Similarly, the import bill for POL doubled between 1978/9 and 1979/80 and increased by over 60 percent between 1979/80 and 1980/1. When expressed as a proportion of export earnings, POL imports more than doubled between 1972/3 and 1973/4. They subsequently averaged 29 percent during 1974/5 to 1978/9, largely due to

Table 6.2 *Terms-of-trade effect*

Year (1)	Terms-of-trade effect (Rs. crores at 1970/1 prices) (2)	GDP (Rs. crores at 1970/1 prices) (3)	Gross disposable income [(2)+(3)] (4)	(2)÷(4) % (5)
1970/1	0	40,623	40,623	0.00
1971/2	168	41,196	41,364	0.41
1972/3	328	40,901	41,229	0.80
1973/4	0	42,370	42,370	0.00
1974/5	−608	42,437	41,829	−1.45
1975/6	−879	46,574	45,695	−1.92
1976/7	−877	47,124	46,247	−1.90
1977/8	−309	51,017	50,708	−0.61
1978/9	−486	54,407	53,921	−0.90
1979/80	−1,421	51,598	50,177	−2.83
1980/1	−1,102	55,098	53,996	−2.04
1981/2	−743	58,292	57,549	−1.29
1970/1 to 1973/4	496		165,586	0.30
1974/5 to 1978/9	−3,159		238,400	−1.33
1979/80 to 1981/2	−3,266		161,722	−2.02
1974/5 to 1981/2	−6,425		400,122	−1.61

Note: Terms-of-trade effect indicates a surplus (+) or deficit (−) of import capacity in relation to volume of exports, or

$$\frac{X}{Pm} - \frac{X}{Px}$$

where X = value of exports,
Pm = unit value index for imports,
Px = unit value index for exports.

1 crore = 10 million.

the relative stability of oil prices during the years 1975/6 to 1978/9. This figure rose to 51 percent in 1979/80 and 78 percent in 1980/1. *The trade deficit on merchandise account* as a proportion of GDP at market prices rose from 0.24 percent in 1972/3 to 1.88 percent in 1974/5 and from 1.25 percent in 1978/9 to a record 5.14 percent in 1980/1. Although it declined gradually to 3.4 percent by 1983/4, its level was still twice as high as the peak of 1.9 percent reached in 1974/5 in the aftermath of the first oil shock. The movement of the trade deficit during the first oil shock, combined with a deficit on the invisibles account, led to a *current-account deficit* which, as a

Table 6.3 *Crude oil: import bill, net import availability ratios, and production–consumption ratios*

Year (1)	Import bill on petroleum, oil, and lubricants as % of		Domestic crude oil production as % of domestic consumption in crude equivalent (4)	Ratio of net import to availability in million tons of crude (5)
	Total merchandise imports (2)	Total merchandise exports (3)		
1970/1	8.34	8.88	35.45	63.14
1971/2	10.64	12.07	33.83	63.95
1972/3	10.92	10.35	31.09	62.27
1973/4	18.96	22.20	29.93	65.86
1974/5	25.61	34.76	32.28	64.61
1975/6	23.86	31.12	35.19	61.71
1976/7	27.86	27.49	34.41	61.22
1977/8	25.78	28.70	39.29	57.42
1978/9	24.69	29.36	38.36	55.76
1979/80	35.77	50.95	36.98	57.80
1980/1	41.97	78.48	31.75	60.72
1981/2	38.14	66.48	46.53	45.69
1982/3	39.04	62.92	56.93	28.15
1983/4	30.64	48.96	68.18	18.71

Sources: (a) Columns (2) and (3) based on value of merchandise imports and exports given in various issues of the *Economic Survey*, Ministry of Finance, Government of India.
(b) Column (4) is from table 13 in Ahluwalia (1986).
(c) Column (5) based on various issues of the *Economic Survey*, Ministry of Finance, Government of India.

proportion of GDP, rose to 1.2 percent in 1974/5, a figure which, though not significant in comparison with other oil-importing developing countries, was large by India's historical standards. Continuing workers' remittances allowed the current-account deficit to be contained at around 2 percent of GDP in 1979/80 and 1980/1. However, it showed no signs of being converted into a surplus, as it had done by 1975/6 after the first oil shock, for reasons examined below.

The first oil shock: initial conditions

The peak agricultural harvest of 1970/1 was followed by a slight reduction in 1971/2 and a severe drought in 1972/3. Real income originating in agriculture declined by over 6 percent in 1972/3 when

Table 6.4 *Current-account balance, 1970/1–1983/4 (in Rs crores)*

Year	On A/C of goods and non-factor services (1)	On current A/C (NAS) (2)	On merchandise A/C (NAS) (3)	On merchandise A/C (Economic Survey) (4)	GDP at current market prices (5)	As percentage of GDP			
						(1)	(2)	(3)	(4)
1970/1	−45	−424	−99	−99	36,736	−0.12	−1.15	−0.26	−0.26
1971/2	−212	−519	N.A.	−216	39,263	−0.54	−1.32	N.A.	−0.55
1972/3	+176	−327	−104	−103	43,241	+0.41	−0.76	−0.24	−0.24
1973/4	−346	−425	−432	−432	53,772	−0.64	−0.79	−0.80	−0.80
1974/5	−944	−748	−1,190	−1,190	63,263	−1.49	−1.18	−1.88	−1.88
1975/6	−852	+77	−1,222	−1,222	66,370	−1.28	+0.12	−1.84	−1.84
1976/7	+525	+1,275	+72	+69	71,464	+0.73	+1.78	+0.10	+0.10
1977/8	+84	+1,417	−621	−616	80,666	+0.10	+1.76	−0.78	−0.76
1978/9	−311	−180	−1,088	−1,085	87,046	−0.36	−0.21	−1.25	−1.25
1979/80	−1,478	−627	−2,499	−2,724	94,978	−1.56	−0.66	−2.58	−2.87
1980/1	−4,550	−2,151	−5,813	−5,839	113,584	−4.01	−1.89	−5.12	−5.14
1981/2	−4,626	−2,665	−5,868	−5,802	130,583	−3.54	−2.04	−4.49	−4.41
1982/3	N.A.	N.A.	N.A.	−5,448	144,393	N.A.	N.A.	N.A.	−3.77
1983/4	N.A.	N.A.	N.A.	−5,897	173,420	N.A.	N.A.	N.A.	−3.40

Note: N.A. not available.
1 crore = 10 million.
Sources: Columns (1), (2), (3) and (5) are based on National Accounts.
Column (4) is based on data in the Economic Survey.

compared even with the indifferent harvest of previous years. The influx of refugees in 1971 from what was then East Pakistan, resulting in the creation of Bangladesh, led to a steep rise in defense spending and concomitant increases in central bank credit to the government. Consequently, the annual rate of inflation, as measured by the wholesale price index, accelerated progressively from 2 percent in April 1971 to about 17 percent by September 1973, the beginning of the oil price increase.[3]

The quadrupling of oil prices between September 1973 and March 1974 coincided with a number of other unfavorable developments. While the agricultural harvest of 1973/4 managed to restore real income in agriculture to the level of 1970/1, it again dipped marginally in 1974/5. There were political difficulties in the western state of Gujarat and significant food shortages in neighboring Maharashtra. These exogenous shocks accentuated the inflationary pressures that had been accumulating since 1972; the annual inflation rate soared from 17 percent in September 1973 to an all-time high of nearly 34 percent a year later. The Economic Surveys of this period produced by the Ministry of Finance give the impression that policy-makers viewed the poor harvests as the primary cause of inflation and, as will be seen below, orchestrated macroeconomic policies to help offset those effects. The Report of the Committee to Review the Working of the Monetary System (Reserve Bank of India, 1985) states, for example, that "the buildup of inflationary pressures in 1971–3 under the delayed and perhaps inadequate response of the central bank to the emerging inflationary situation probably contributed to a greater extent than the 1973 oil shock to the steep rise in prices in 1973/4." It is not clear whether the oil price increase was seen as contributing principally to inflation through its cost–push impact or to recession brought about by the need to transfer higher payments to the oil-importing countries. In any event, there was an expectation that it was mainly a transient phenomenon requiring short-term borrowing.

The first oil shock: policy response
The record current-account deficit of 1974/5 was, however, converted into a current-account surplus in 1975/6 and remained so for the next two years before turning into a small deficit on the eve of the second oil shock of 1979/80 (table 6.4). A series of policies contributed to this remarkedly rapid turnaround in the current account.

The macroeconomic policy package comprised five post-budget measures in 1974/5 that were designed to reduce private disposable income. The government (a) froze all wage increases and half of additional cost-of-living increases in the public sector; (b) limited dividend distributions by companies; (c) introduced a new scheme of compulsory (frozen)

Table 6.5 *Rates of gross domestic capital formation*
(at 1970/1 prices (Rs. crores))

	Gross domestic capital formation	GDP at market prices	Rate of gross capital formation
1970/1	7,344	40,263	18.24
1971/2	7,959	41,196	19.32
1972/3	7,479	40,901	18.29
1973/4	8,739	42,370	20.63
1974/5	8,947	42,437	21.08
1975/6	9,388	46,574	20.16
1976/7	9,847	47,124	20.90
1977/8	10,096	51,017	19.79
1978/9	11,633	54,407	21.38
1979/80	11,489	51,598	22.27
1980/1	12,192	55,098	22.13
1981/2	12,218	58,292	20.96
1982/3	12,230	59,953	20.40
1983/4	12,998	64,543	20.14

Note: 1 crore = 10 million.
Source: Government of India, *National Accounts Statistics* (Central Statistical Organization), various issues.

deposits on a graduated basis for all income taxpayers; (d) raised excise duties and railway freight rates; and (e) taxed the interest income of commercial banks. This strong dose of demand management occurred in the face of a bumper agricultural harvest in 1975/6 and, subsequently, in 1977/8 and 1978/9. It was further supplemented by selected imports of certain key consumer goods in temporarily short supply such as foodgrains, edible oils, and fibers.

Second, this period was marked by deceleration in the rate of growth of public-sector fixed capital formation (table 6.1, line 15). This was reflected in the rate of growth of domestic capital formation (lines 13 and 14) and investment in total and registered manufacturing (lines 16 and 17). The fall in the ratio of gross domestic capital formation to GDP in real terms during the years 1975/6 to 1977/8 is evident from table 6.5 which shows the rate of domestic investment fluctuating around 20 percent as indeed did private gross investment, especially in the registered manufacturing sector. This was mirrored in the virtual stagnation of imports, especially of intermediates and capital goods, with the peak level for imports of the latter, reached in 1973/4, not being restored even by 1979/80.[4]

This constellation of demand-management policies and favorable harvests led to a sharp fall in the rate of inflation; indeed, prices were actually falling by September 1975. Double-digit rates of inflation were not to return until June 1979.

Third, the nominal effective exchange rate which was initially pegged to the pound sterling and to a basket of currencies thereafter, was allowed to depreciate between 1974 and 1978. However, the price stability brought about by anti-inflationary policies, compared to that of India's trading partners, converted this to a nearly 25 percent depreciation in the effective real exchange rate. This was partly responsible for a rate of growth of export earnings of more than 25 percent between 1972/3 and 1976/7, a situation that was aided by underutilized capacity in manufacturing. While the first three years were marked by rising unit values rather than volume, the situation was reversed in the last two years. The rate of growth of export earnings was to slowdown considerably in 1977/8 and 1978/9, a period that witnessed relative stagnation in the real effective exchange rate compared to the earlier years.

Fourth, almost half of the current-account deficit in 1974/5 was financed from unconditional or low conditionality facilities of the International Monetary Fund.

Finally, the slowdown in export earnings in 1977/8 and 1978/9 was more than compensated for by an unanticipated yet continuous rise in current private transfers from abroad, especially remittances from migrants to oil-importing countries. This helped keep the current-account balance in surplus.

In sum, adjustment to the first round of inflation, harvest failure, and terms-of-trade deterioration was facilitated by (1) the management of domestic demand prompted by internal inflationary pressures, (2) a concomitant slowdown in the rate of real gross domestic investment and imports of intermediates and capital goods, (3) an acceleration in export earnings brought about through real exchange-rate depreciation, (4) significant recourse to low-conditionality external financing, and (5) an increase in current private transfers, especially remittances from migrants to the oil-exporting countries. Notwithstanding the slowdown in investment, year-to-year growth rates of GDP showed some increase during this period. Although industrial growth fell well short of the average 8 to 10 percent rate achieved in the ten years preceding 1965, it almost doubled from an annual average rate of 2.85 percent in 1970/4 to 5.26 percent in 1974/9. This was achieved primarily through better capacity utilization rather than new capacity creation.

The second oil shock: initial conditions
Initial conditions facing the Indian economy were more favorable at the time of the second oil shock than that of the earlier one. First, India had continuously accumulated foreign exchange reserves – the result of unanticipated private remittances between 1974/5 and 1978/9. Second, following the two bumper harvests of 1977/8 and 1978/9, the government's foodgrain stocks had reached a record of 21.5 million tons by the end of July 1979. Third, the annual rate of inflation had fallen to less than 10 percent. As against the above, the second major increase in the price of oil in 1979/80 coincided with a severe drought, causing real income originating in agriculture to drop by more than 13 percent from the level of the previous year. The combination of the two shocks led to the annual rate of inflation rising from around 5 percent in April 1979 to a peak of 25 percent by January 1980.

The first two of the favorable initial conditions noted above imply that the food and foreign exchange constraints, traditionally considered in India to be among the two most important bottlenecks to economic development were relaxed on the eve of the second oil shock, thereby permitting a bolder response to the latter. However, the accumulation of such reserves occurred precisely because of the economy's inability to step up industrial investment. A plausible explanation for such a policy stance derives in part from the adjustment to the first round of shocks and in part subsequently from uncertainty regarding how long both the food and the foreign exchange reserves could be expected to last. Sensitivity to inflationary pressures especially after the experience of 1972/3 and 1974/5, led policy-makers to believe that the alternative of increased industrial investment would lead to uncontrollable inflationary pressures in the event of rapid exhaustion of food stocks. And depletion of foreign exchange reserves would make it difficult to relieve this situation with food imports. In summary, a perception that the traditional food and foreign exchange constraints might return to abort the investment–cum–growth process conditioned macroeconomic policy responses in 1977/8 and 1978/9. The tradeoff in terms of growth foregone was, however, intertemporal, for the reserves in question made possible a less conservative response to the 1979/80 round of external shocks.

The second oil shock: policy response
The policy response to the second oil shock was different than before, for at least two reasons. *First*, as noted before, the accumulated food and foreign exchange reserves provided favorable initial conditions when the economy was hit by the shock and therefore enlarged the set of available policy options. *Second*, there appears to have been a growing realization

that the import-substituting strategy of industrialization followed since the 1950s had not helped insulate the economy from external shocks. This change in perception may have been shaped by progressively rising terms-of-trade losses (see table 6.2), by the increasing share of imports and exports in GDP after 1973, and, possibly, by continuing stagnation in investment and growth when viewed in historical perspective.

The government's response comprised (1) efforts to raise public-sector investment in real terms, (2) the importation of food, edible oil, and fiber to ease potential shortages and curb inflationary pressures, (3) relaxation of the rigors of quantitative controls on imports to promote efficiency by exposing domestic producers to international competition, (4) increased domestic oil exploration to reduce dependence on imported crude, and (5) measures to switch energy use away from POL and toward domestically available coal and electricity. Thus the adjustment strategy evidently comprised a combination of "supply-side" measures (1) to (3), together with output switching into and expenditure switching away from POL-based energy [(4) and (5)].

Outcomes in the wake of the second oil shock were as follows. First, notwithstanding government intentions to the contrary, the rate of real gross investment declined from 22 percent between 1979 and 1981 to 20 percent by 1983/4 (table 6.5). The real fixed investment of the private sector did not show any buoyancy either.

Second, the rate of industrial growth showed some deceleration in 1979–83 compared with the years 1974–9. The deceleration was experienced by most groups of industries (table 6.6). This may be explained by three factors. First, certain high-cost, import-competing industries were affected by import liberalization in the face of global recession-induced falling international prices. Second, with exports relatively unimportant in relation to the domestic market, fluctuations in agricultural harvests brought about corresponding fluctuations in the market for industrial goods. Third, the two droughts of 1979/80 and 1982/3 adversely affected hydropower generation and accentuated the infrastructural bottlenecks originating in the coal–railway–power complex during the 1979–83 period. The above combination of supply and domestic demand constraints had a deleterious impact on industrial output.

Third, the rate of domestic inflation was brought down from its peak of 25 percent in January 1980 to under 10 percent by 1983/4. Although measures of monetary control were instituted in 1979/80, the first half of 1980/1, and in 1981/2, the decline in inflation was more the result of the bumper harvests of 1980/1, 1981/2, and 1983/4, combined with the selective importation of foodgrains, i.e., policies of supply management. However, unlike after the first oil shock, this was not enough to prevent a 15 percent

Table 6.6 *Growth rates of index of industrial production*

	1970–4	1974–9	1979–82	1979–83
1 General index of industrial production	4.49	5.58	4.78	4.71
2 Manufacturing subgroup	2.85	5.26	4.03	3.82
Selected components of manufacturing groups				
(a) Chemical and chemical products	4.88	8.77	5.03	4.61
(b) Petroleum products	3.10	6.30	4.45	5.20
(c) Basic metals industries	1.03	6.30	4.43	3.32
(d) Metal products except machinery	5.10	5.93	−1.01	0.65
(e) Non-electrical machinery	11.20	6.03	5.29	5.15
(f) Electrical machinery	3.13	7.62	3.34	2.08
(g) Transport equipment	2.18	2.86	4.30	4.10
(h) Miscellaneous	3.15	5.58	8.18	n.a.
3 Use-based classification				
(a) Basic industries	3.38	7.87	7.00	6.62
(b) Capital goods	6.68	4.37	3.94	4.04
(c) Intermediate goods	2.94	4.43	2.13	3.54
(d) Consumer goods	2.34	4.28	4.75	3.64
(i) Durable	4.60	4.60	2.33	1.79
(ii) Non-durable	1.90	4.24	5.09	3.91
4 Input-based classification				
(a) Agro-based	1.10	3.99	4.23	4.24
(b) Metal-based	5.97	4.57	3.03	3.14
(c) Chemical-based	5.31	8.28	5.27	4.67
5 Sectoral indicators				
(a) Transport equipment and allied industries	4.31	2.58	4.55	5.16
(b) Electricity and allied industries	6.24	7.42	5.77	5.05
(c) Energy output	4.51	7.54	8.22	7.96

Note: These are point-to-point growth rates per annum because continuous time series were not available to compute trend growth rates.

real exchange-rate appreciation between 1979 and 1981, particularly as the nominal exchange rate did not move significantly during this period. This contributed to a slowdown in the rate of growth of export earnings, a feature that was aggravated by recession in the industrial countries.

Fourth, imports rose much faster than export earnings because of trade liberalization, higher POL prices, imports of essential items to control inflation, and imports of capital goods and intermediates due to modernization and an accelerated import substitution program in the energy sector.

Consequently, the trade deficit widened considerably between 1979 and 1984 (table 6.4).

Finally, a 12 percent annual growth in domestic production of crude oil as against a virtual stagnation in net imports of crude between 1973/4 and 1983/4 brought down import outlays on POL in relation to merchandise export earnings from the record level of 78 percent in 1980/1 to just under 49 percent in 1983/4. But even this level of 49 percent was considerably higher than the previous peak level of nearly 35 percent recorded in 1974/5. In other words, the import bill for POL rose faster than export earnings after 1979/80.

The current-account deficit was financed by the following. First, India negotiated a variety of short- and medium-term facilities with the International Monetary Fund (IMF). A total of about Rs 47 billion or about 55 percent of the cumulative deficit in the four-year period 1980/1 to 1983/4 was obtained from the IMF. Second, there was a continued increase in private remittances. Third, unlike after the first oil shock, there was recourse to commercial borrowing to a noticeable extent, with new commitments averaging $1 billion a year.

Macroeconomic performance, 1973/4 to 1983/4

Macroeconomic performance in 1973/4–1983/4 resulting from these policies is marked by three notable features. First, although economic growth at 3.97 percent surpassed the growth rate attained before 1964/5, much of that increase was attributable to the tertiary sector. Notwithstanding some recovery after 1973/4, industrial sector GDP grew much more slowly compared to the period 1950/1 to 1964/5. Even if attention is confined to the period 1973/4 to 1983/4, while real gross fixed capital formation grew around 6.7 percent a year in the public sector, it barely reached 2.5 percent a year in the private sector (see table 6.7).

Second, and more favorably, notwithstanding the significant rise in energy prices, the trend rate of growth of wholesale prices (all commodities) was maintained at 7.66 percent per annum.

Third, while India's net barter terms of trade *vis-à-vis* the rest of the world deteriorated about 1.5 percent a year from 1973/4 to 1981/2, a steady 8 percent annual expansion in exports since 1973/4 caused the income terms of trade to improve at a trend rate of 4.5 percent a year. While a variety of other export incentives were in place, this performance may be attributed mainly to a depreciation in real exchange rates in general (table 6.8) and in exchange rates with reference to the US dollar and pound sterling in particular. However, adjustment for various fortuitous elements[5] not only brings down the trend growth rate of export earnings but also increases their variability around the lower trend growth rate.

Table 6.7 *Trend growth rates in real GDP and gross fixed capital formation (% per annum)*

Aggregate GDP	1970/1 to 1981/2	3.59
Aggregate GDP	1973/4 to 1981/2	3.98
Aggregate GDP	1970/1 to 1983/4	3.68
Aggregate GDP	1973/4 to 1983/4	3.97
GFCF, public sector	1970/1 to 1981/2	6.20
GFCF, public sector	1973/4 to 1981/2	6.66
GFCF, public sector	1970/1 to 1983/4	6.30
GFCF, public sector	1973/4 to 1983/4	6.67
GFCF, private sector	1970/1 to 1981/2	2.97
GFCF, private sector	1973/4 to 1981/2	3.25
GFCF, private sector	1970/1 to 1983/4	2.52
GFCF, private sector	1973/4 to 1983/4	2.46
GFCF, public and private	1970/1 to 1981/2	4.37
GFCF, public and private	1973/4 to 1981/2	4.78
GFCF, public and private	1970/1 to 1983/4	4.24
GFCF, public and private	1973/4 to 1983/4	4.42
GDP in primary sector	1973/4 to 1983/4	2.24
GDP in secondary sector	1973/4 to 1983/4	4.15
GDP in tertiary sector	1973/4 to 1983/4	5.95

Source: Based on the data available in the various issues of Government of India, *National Accounts Statistics* (Central Statistical Organization).

Table 6.8 *Trend rates of appreciation (+)/depreciation (−) of exchange rates*

Description of exchange rate	Period	Type	Trend growth rate (% p.a.)	Source
Export weighted (4 currencies)	1970–83	Nominal	−2.49	Ahluwalia, table 7
Export weighted (4 currencies)	1975–83	Nominal	−1.82	Ahluwalia, table 7
Export weighted (4 currencies)	1970–83	Real	−2.22	Ahluwalia, table 7
Export weighted (4 currencies)	1975–83	Real	−0.86	Ahluwalia, table 7
Export weighted (15 currencies)	1975–83	Nominal	0.47	Verghese, pt. I, table 6

Table 6.8 (*cont.*)

Description of exchange rate	Period	Type	Trend growth rate (% p.a.)	Source
Export weighted (15 currencies)	1975–83	Real	−0.99	Verghese, pt. I, table 6
Import weighted (15 currencies)	1975–83	Nominal	−0.43	Verghese, pt. I, table 6
Import weighted (15 currencies)	1975–83	Real	−1.59	Verghese, pt. I, table 6
Total trade weighted (15 currencies)	1975–83	Nominal	−0.42	Verghese, pt. I, table 6
Total trade weighted (15 currencies)	1975–83	Real	−1.32	Verghese, pt. I, table 6

Sources: Lines 1 to 4 based on table 7 in Ahluwalia (1986).
Lines 5 to 10 based on table 6, p. 1099 in Verghese (1984).

2 Generating the historical run

Tracking history

Before answering the questions of the introductory section, it is necessary to reproduce the principal historical developments in the Indian economy between 1973/4 and 1983/4 within the framework of the model described in chapter 4. This simulation of historical developments, referred to below as the historical run, provides the model with a benchmark against which the results of counterfactual experiments can be compared. In as much as counterfactual policy simulations need to be compared with such a benchmark rather than with actual experience, the derivation of an historical run is a necessary intermediate step.[6]

Tables 6.9 and 6.10 report selected features of the base year 1973/4, or the conditions describing the Indian economy at the beginning of the period being analyzed. These and other features are satisfied by the model in the process of "benchmarking" to the base-period data set. Table 6.11 shows the expenditure side of the national accounts at constant prices – GDP at market prices and its components, which are private consumption, total investment, exports, and imports. These are the five macroeconomic target

Table 6.9 India: selected features of the economy, 1973–4

	Sector 1	Sector 2	Sector 3	Sector 4	Sector 5	Sector 6	Average
Share of value added in gross output	0.76	0.23	0.32	0.30	0.53	0.71	0.57
Share of hired wage income in value added	0.19	0.50	0.44	0.51	0.66	0.50	0.34
Share of intermediate imports in gross output	0.01	0.04	0.04	0.12	0	0.01	0.03
Share of private consumption in gross output	0.72	0.86	0.08	0.16	0.27	0.31	0.50
Share of exports in gross output	0.01	0.09	0.01	0.06	—	—	0.03
Share of private consumption accounted for by sector	0.57	0.22	0.02	0.04	0.02	0.14	—
Share of private exports accounted for by sector	0.13	0.56	0.05	0.26	—	—	—

Table 6.10 *India: selected features of the economy, 1973–4 share of consumption by sector and group (constant prices)*

	Sector 1	Sector 2	Sector 3	Sector 4	Sector 5	Sector 6
Urban						
C1	0.70	0.14	0.01	0.05	0.02	0.08
C2	0.66	0.17	0.01	0.05	0.02	0.09
C3	0.60	0.20	0.01	0.05	0.02	0.12
C4	0.53	0.24	0.02	0.05	0.02	0.16
C5	0.41	0.25	0.02	0.04	0.02	0.27
Rural						
C1	0.74	0.12	0.01	0.05	0.03	0.06
C2	0.72	0.15	0.01	0.04	0.02	0.07
C3	0.65	0.20	0.01	0.04	0.02	0.09
C4	0.58	0.23	0.02	0.03	0.02	0.12
C5	0.47	0.26	0.03	0.03	0.02	0.20

Note: C1–C5 are five groups of rural and urban households whose expenditure levels and sectoral consumption patterns are identified by the model. The groups are ranked in ascending order with respect to per capita expenditure.

variables whose growth rates must be replicated as closely as possible by the historical run of the model. Figures 6.1 through 6.5 present a comparison between the realized growth rates and those generated by the model for these variables at constant prices and show that the correspondence is quite satisfactory.

Table 6.12 displays the characteristics of the model-generated historical run which is henceforth taken to be a reasonable replication of the broad contours of development during the period. The proximity of the ratios on the expenditure side of the national accounts to their counterparts in the data is a function of the degree of success achieved by the model in tracking the target variables. Although the model was not constrained to mimic the composition of value added among agriculture, manufacturing (the sum of sectors 2, 3, and 4), infrastructure, and services, it nevertheless successfully captures the declining share of agriculture and the growing importance of services over time. But it understates the growth of manufacturing to some extent and overstates the growth of infrastructure correspondingly. Table 6.12 further displays the model-generated Gini coefficients of income and consumption inequality among the five urban and five rural groups of households in the historical run. This indicates no change in inequality over this period. While there are no time-series data against which this result can be directly checked, other research (Bhalla and Vasistha, 1988) suggests

Table 6.11 *India: tracking indicators (growth rates in percent)*

	1974-5	1975-6	1976-7	1977-8	1978-9	1979-80	1980-1	1981-2	1982-3	1983-4
GDP (market prices)										
Data	-0.6	9.9	1.3	8.2	6.6	-5.2	7.2	5.5	4.3	7.6
Model	1.7	14.5	1.8	7.8	7.3	-2.1	7.6	3.4	4.3	9.1
Private consumption										
Data	-4.2	3.7	-2.4	15.2	2.7	-10.1	10.8	6.4	3.4	8.8
Model	-1.0	10.7	-1.3	13.8	4.0	-4.5	10.9	3.4	4.2	11.1
Total investment										
Data	6.3	19.4	4.2	0.0	19.0	0.4	8.7	5.3	1.3	6.1
Model	6.0	17.8	3.1	1.0	18.1	-0.2	10.2	4.2	0.2	5.4
Exports										
Data	8.1	16.5	19.7	-3.8	8.2	16.8	-0.3	-0.2	3.2	4.9
Model	6.8	16.6	22.3	-2.9	7.6	15.0	-1.4	1.5	3.3	4.4
Imports										
Data	-13.1	1.2	-0.2	30.3	8.5	-4.1	46.7	8.0	0.2	4.1
Model	-11.2	-0.3	-3.6	30.3	8.7	-3.5	48.5	7.5	0.1	4.4

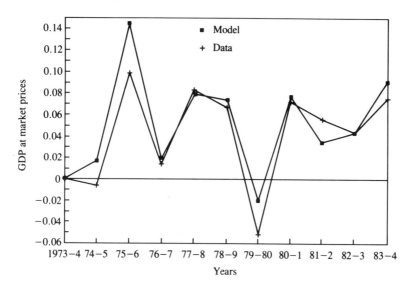

Figure 6.1 India: tracking 1973/4–1983/4 GDP at market prices (growth rate)

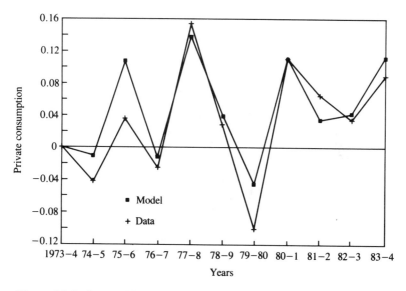

Figure 6.2 India: tracking 1973/4–1983/4 private consumption (growth rate)

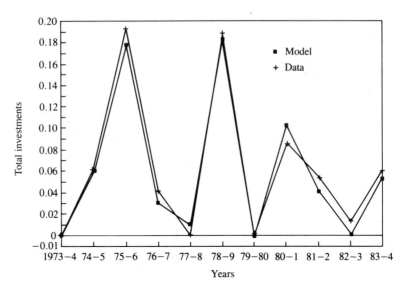

Figure 6.3 India: tracking 1973/4–1983/4 total investment (growth rate)

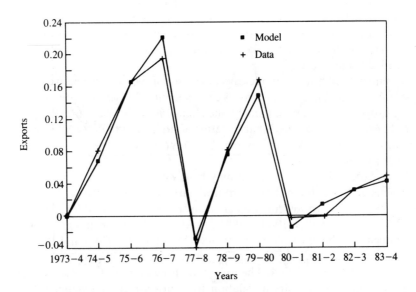

Figure 6.4 India: tracking 1973/4–1983/4 exports (growth rate)

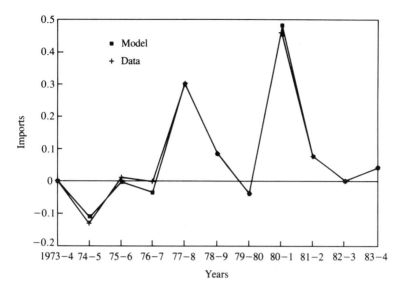

Figure 6.5 India: tracking 1973/4–1983/4 imports (growth rate)

this to be broadly consistent with the evidence. Finally, tables 6.13 and 6.14 profile the stock of debt and debt service payments respectively in the historical run, broken down by medium- and long-term debt, both official and private, as well as short-term debt with a maturity of one year or less. IMF debt is shown separately from 1980/1, when India negotiated an Extended Fund Facility.

To understand how the model effects a close correspondence between the historical run and the data, it proves convenient to restrict our attention to three exogenous variables, namely, the change in real agricultural output, the change in the economy's barter terms of trade, and the ratio of foreign savings to gross domestic product. The time series for these variables appear in table 6.12.

The years under consideration may be divided into two groups: those characterized by a dip in the agricultural harvest (1974/5, 1976/7, 1979/80, and 1982/3) and those enjoying a recovery in agricultural production (1975/6, 1977/8, 1978/9, 1980/1, 1981/2, and 1983/4). In the first group, the downturn was the most severe in 1979/80, followed by 1974/5 and 1976/7, whereas in the second, the most pronounced increases occurred in 1975/6, 1977/8, 1980/1, and 1983/4. The following discussion looks separately at these two groups of years in relation to terms-of-trade movements and foreign savings inflows.

Table 6.12 India: selected features of the historical run (model-generated)

	1973–4	1974–5	1975–6	1976–7	1977–8	1978–9	1979–80	1980–1	1981–2	1982–3	1983–4
1 Ratios to GDP (market prices)											
Private consumption	0.72	0.70	0.68	0.66	0.69	0.67	0.65	0.67	0.67	0.67	0.69
Government consumption	0.08	0.08	0.09	0.10	0.09	0.09	0.09	0.09	0.09	0.10	0.10
Total investment	0.22	0.23	0.24	0.24	0.22	0.25	0.25	0.26	0.26	0.25	0.24
Exports	0.04	0.05	0.05	0.06	0.05	0.05	0.06	0.05	0.05	0.05	0.05
Imports	0.06	0.06	0.05	0.05	0.05	0.06	0.05	0.08	0.08	0.07	0.07
2 Ratios to total value added											
VA (agriculture)	0.52	0.49	0.47	0.47	0.48	0.46	0.46	0.43	0.43	0.44	0.43
VA (manufacturing)[a]	0.17	0.19	0.15	0.17	0.16	0.16	0.18	0.20	0.19	0.16	0.17
VA (infrastructure)	0.03	0.04	0.05	0.04	0.04	0.05	0.05	0.05	0.04	0.05	0.04
VA (services)	0.28	0.28	0.33	0.32	0.32	0.33	0.31	0.32	0.34	0.36	0.36
3 Gini coefficients											
Income											
Urban	0.47	0.47	0.45	0.47	0.47	0.46	0.47	0.46	0.46	0.47	0.46
Rural	0.38	0.39	0.38	0.38	0.38	0.37	0.38	0.38	0.37	0.37	0.36
Consumption											
Urban	0.37	0.37	0.36	0.37	0.37	0.36	0.37	0.36	0.36	0.37	0.36
Rural	0.30	0.31	0.30	0.30	0.30	0.30	0.30	0.30	0.29	0.29	0.28
4 Change in gross output of agriculture (%)	0	−6.3	11.6	−5.0	11.0	3.1	−10.2	10.4	3.6	−2.0	13.6
5 Change in net barter terms of trade (%)	0	−27	−3	−4	20	−9	−28	8	20	8	−2
6 Foreign savings to GDP at market prices (%)[b]	0.8	1.5	0.6	−0.7	−0.6	−0.3	−0.2	1.2	1.1	0.7	0.7

Notes:
[a] Manufacturing is the sum of sectors 2, 3, and 4.
[b] The numerator is foreign savings at 1973–4 prices multiplied by the model-generated investment inflator; the denominator is model-generated GDP at current market prices.

Table 6.13 *India: debt profile: historical run*
(tens of millions of 1973–4 rupees)

		Medium- and long-term		
	IMF	Official	Private	Short-term
1973–4		7,897.35	208.24	
1974–5		8,017.29	198.87	
1975–6		7,847.67	193.78	
1976–7		8,075.38	183.46	
1977–8		8,375.01	204.03	
1978–9		8,253.23	182.94	141.52
1979–80		7,786.90	169.23	124.41
1980–1	478.71	7,881.33	247.83	170.21
1981–2	729.52	7,281.54	320.87	238.94
1982–3	1,566.89	7,772.01	480.03	546.40

Table 6.14 *India: total debt service: historical run*
(tens of millions of 1973–4 rupees)

		Medium- and long-term		
	IMF	Official	Private	Short-term
1973–4		437.91	70.01	
1974–5		464.02	64.33	
1975–6		444.09	50.87	
1976–7		419.61	50.31	
1977–8		433.51	46.77	
1978–9		469.54	52.12	
1979–80		473.72	46.36	142.32
1980–1		446.48	41.91	128.12
1981–2	12.26	397.05	36.48	177.47
1982–3	51.17	411.53	74.97	278.68

In addition to harvest failures, 1974/5 and 1979/80 were both characterized by a sharp deterioration in the economy's terms of trade. The extent of
harvest failure was more severe in 1979/80. There was a marked decline in
GDP and private consumption, a fall in imports, stagnation in investment,
and a growth in exports of 15 percent over the previous year. In contrast,
the years 1974/5 and 1976/7 witnessed a modest increase in model-
generated GDP and a healthy increase in investment. However, these two
years differed greatly in the movement of the terms of trade, which led to a

much more drastic curtailment of imports in 1974/5. The surge in investment in 1974/5, its respectable growth in 1976/7 in the face of a small current-account surplus and modestly rising income, and its stagnation rather than decline in 1979/80 were generally brought about in the historical run of the model through a combination of increased factor productivity in capital goods and consumer goods production, together with some increases in the productivity of intermediate goods production and, in 1975/6 and 1979/80, in the savings propensity of the private sector.

As for the years of agricultural recovery, 1975/6, 1977/8, 1980/1, and 1983/4 stand out as those when GDP and private consumption increased very substantially. But there are striking differences on the foreign trade side. Foreign savings, though positive, were much smaller in 1975/6 than in 1980/1 and 1983/4 (see table 6.15). This was partly the result of the difference in the strategies of adjustment to the first and second oil shocks and is reflected in the relative export and import figures for those years. Also, the large improvement in the barter terms of trade in 1977/8 allowed India to sustain an import boom despite a decline in exports triggered to some extent by the pressure of domestic demand. The savings–investment balance for these years was brought about in the historical run of the model by mechanisms analogous to those in periods of agricultural decline. Whereas 1975/6 was marked by a massive growth of investment with comparatively limited foreign savings, precisely the opposite was true for 1980/1 and 1983/4. The balance was attained through some increase both in factor productivity in capital goods production and in the private savings propensity in 1975/6 and through a decline in both parameters in 1980/1. The productivity parameters also fell in 1977/8 and 1983/4.

3 Policy simulations

The results of the policy simulations of this section are usually presented in two tables. The first reports deviations of the macroeconomic aggregates (GDP, private consumption, investment, exports, and imports) and of the sectoral output levels from the 1973/4 to 1983/4 historical run. The second reports the cost-of-living index of each of the five rural and five urban groups identified by the analysis. For every year, these numbers show the percentage change in the cost of attaining historical run utility levels for the same year at the prices corresponding to the experiment. That table also reports movements in the Gini coefficients of consumption and income inequality in rural and urban areas.

Simulation 1 No external shocks and accommodating borrowing
To what extent can the intermediate growth performance of the middle 1970s be attributed to adverse terms-of-trade shocks and associated

balance-of-payments adjustment? To answer this question, the counterfactual is defined to be a situation in which (a) terms of trade remain at their 1973/4 level;[7] (b) foreign savings are set below their historical levels by an amount equal to the sum of the IMF's Oil Facility, external assistance from the oil-exporting countries, and borrowing from the IMF's Extended Fund Facility, net of amortization and interest charges; while net current transfers (which include workers' remittances) are set at their 1973 level; (c) government-controlled oil imports are determined with reference to the growth in GDP and the relative price of oil, using income and price elasticities of 1.3 and −0.3 respectively.[8]

Table 6.15 reports the time series of foreign savings, net current transfers, terms-of-trade and oil imports in both the historical run and the no external shock-cum-accommodating borrowing counterfactual. Notice that foreign savings are much lower in the counterfactual than in the historical run, especially in 1975/6 and in the years following the second oil shock.[9]

The results, which are shown in table 6.16, display two broad patterns. First, the period up to 1976/7 and also the year 1979/80 are characterized by higher GDP, private consumption, and investment as well as by higher gross output in virtually all sectors of the economy, than in the historical run. Second, and contrastingly, the years 1977/8 and 1978/9 and the period 1980/1 to 1983/4 witness generally lower macroeconomic aggregates as well as reduced sectoral output.

These patterns may be explained by the relative dominance of terms-of-trade movements *vis-à-vis* changes in foreign savings relative to the historical run. There was a marked deterioration in the terms of trade relative to 1973/4 in the historical run, particularly up to 1976/7 and also in 1979/80. In removing that element, the experiment enriches the economy in proportion to the importance of external trade. This has the effect of increasing aggregate demand and, hence, outputs and prices. Secondly, the restoration of the terms of trade, inasmuch as it is brought about by a reduction in the prices of imported intermediate inputs, shifts the economy's supply curve outwards, with a particularly favorable impact on sectors 3 and 4. Thus both sets of effects increase output in all sectors of the economy. The increase in income leads to a substantial increase in private savings as well as in government savings, with part of the latter being brought about through a rise in public profits on domestic sales of government-controlled imports. These developments lead to a sufficient rise in investment.

In contrast, the terms of trade did not worsen much in the historical run *vis-à-vis* the no-external-shock scenario in 1977/8 and 1978/9 and the period 1980/1 to 1983/4. Hence much of the difference between the two developments may be attributed to changes in foreign savings, although it must be noted in addition that, by 1977/8, the capital stock, for reasons

Table 6.15 India: no external shock-cum-accommodating borrowing simulation: selected features (Rs crores)

	1973–4	1974–5	1975–6	1976–7	1977–8	1978–9	1979–80	1980–1	1981–2	1982–3	1983–4
Foreign savings[a]											
Historical run	479	961	579	−1,031	−903	−575	−299	1,996	2,412	2,370	2,650
No external shock	479	605	−36	−1,277	−1,111	−676	−361	1,134	1,747	505	1,604
Net current transfers[a]											
Historical run	192	274	528	739	1,022	1,042	1,624	2,257	2,221	2,527	2,527
No external shock	192	192	192	192	192	192	192	192	192	192	192
Terms of trade											
Historical run	1.00	0.80	0.73	0.84	1.02	1.00	0.84	0.92	0.98	1.01	1.03
No external shock	1.00	1.00	1.00	1.00	1.00	1.00	1.00	1.00	1.00	1.00	1.00
Sector 5 imports											
Historical run	417	421	410	422	436	441	485	489	460	404	291
No external shock	417	349	304	320	345	315	312	355	382	387	457

Notes: [a]There are nominal magnitudes which are treated with the appropriate deflators in the model. 1 crore = 10 million.

Table 6.16 *India: no external shock-cum-accommodating borrowing simulation (percentage deviation from historical run)*

	1974-5	1975-6	1976-7	1977-8	1978-9	1979-80	1980-1	1981-2	1982-3	1983-4
GDP	1.3	1.3	-1.8	-0.6	-0.7	1.2	-0.7	-1.2	-1.8	-3.5
Private consumption	0.5	0.4	0.3	-0.1	0.1	0.0	-0.7	-0.8	-1.0	-2.5
Investment	5.8	5.7	7.6	-8.1	-7.0	4.3	-8.0	-8.1	-16.5	-19.1
Exports	13.0	20.2	3.6	6.0	3.4	4.9	7.9	-2.1	11.8	16.1
Imports	18.1	26.1	9.8	-17.3	-14.0	3.3	-18.4	-19.9	-30.4	-27.5
Gross output of										
Agriculture	1.1	1.2	0.8	-0.1	0.1	0.9	0.2	-0.1	-0.2	-1.1
Consumer goods	3.4	3.8	0.4	-0.1	-1.3	-0.1	-1.0	-2.7	-1.3	-2.9
Capital goods	6.5	6.0	8.1	-7.2	-6.3	5.2	-7.2	-7.4	-16.3	-19.5
Intermediates	4.7	4.6	4.9	1.3	0.9	6.1	-0.2	-1.6	-4.4	-8.5
Infrastructure	13.3	17.0	15.7	11.6	16.5	28.5	18.4	9.1	0.1	-19.1
Services	2.6	2.9	1.9	0.7	1.3	2.7	1.1	0.2	0.5	-2.0

Table 6.17 India: no external shock-cum-accommodating borrowing simulation: distributional characteristics (percentage deviation from historical run)

Cost-of-living indices Groups	1974–5	1975–6	1976–7	1977–8	1978–9	1979–80	1980–1	1981–2	1982–3	1983–4
Urban
C1	−18.3	−17.9	−16.8	−27.6	−21.8	−19.5	−19.8	−13.8	−13.7	−9.6
C2	−18.3	−17.9	−16.9	−27.6	−21.8	−19.5	−19.8	−13.8	−13.7	−9.6
C3	−18.3	−18.0	−16.9	−27.6	−21.9	−19.6	−19.8	−13.8	−13.7	−9.4
C4	−18.4	−18.1	−17.0	−27.6	−21.9	−19.6	−19.8	−13.7	−13.8	−9.3
C5	−18.5	−18.3	−17.1	−27.6	−22.1	−19.9	−20.0	−13.8	−13.8	−9.1
Rural
C1	−18.2	−17.8	−16.7	−27.5	−21.7	−19.3	−19.7	−13.8	−13.7	−9.7
C2	−18.1	−17.8	−16.8	−27.6	−21.8	−19.4	−19.8	−13.8	−13.7	−9.7
C3	−18.2	−17.8	−16.8	−27.5	−21.8	−19.4	−19.7	−13.7	−13.7	−9.5
C4	−18.3	−17.9	−16.9	−27.5	−21.8	−19.5	−19.8	−13.7	−13.7	−9.4
C5	−18.4	−18.1	−17.0	−27.6	−22.0	−19.7	−19.9	−13.8	−13.8	−9.3
Gini coefficients
Urban
Income	−0.1	−0.4	−0.2	0	−0.2	−0.6	−0.3	−0.1	0.6	0.3
Consumption	−0.1	−0.5	−0.2	0	−0.2	−0.6	−0.2	−0.1	0.6	0.3
Rural
Income	−0.3	−0.5	−0.4	−0.2	−0.3	−0.6	−0.4	−0.2	−0.2	0.3
Consumption	−0.4	−0.5	−0.4	−0.2	−0.3	−0.6	−0.4	−0.2	−0.2	0.2

Note: The cost of living index here and in Tables 6.20, 6.22, 6.25 and 6.27 is the cost of attaining "pre-simulation" utility levels at "post-simulation" prices.

Table 6.18 *India: makeup of sector 5 from 115 sector input–output table, 1973–4*

Sector no.	Name	Gross output (lakhs of rupees)	% of sector 5 gross output
023	Coal and lignite	30,350	17.4
024	Crude petroleum, natural gas	9,952	5.7
100	Electricity	99,413	56.9
101	Gas	1,098	0.6
102	Water supply	7,401	4.2
106	Communications	26,626	15.2
	Total	174,840	100.0

Note: 1 lakh = 100,000

described above, is higher in the experiment. As expected, GDP, investment, and, most noticeably, the output of the capital goods sector are lower than in the historical run in those years.

The two sets of patterns more or less offset one another inasmuch as the capital stock in 1984/5 is about 1 percent lower in the no-external-shock experiment than in the historical run. Table 6.17 shows that the cost of living is also lower. There is no change in the Gini coefficients of income and consumption inequality. The economy's stock of debt would have been nearly 21 percent lower than in the historical run, because of the substantially lower foreign borrowing. Finally, the historical run, compared with the no-shock-cum-accommodating-borrowing scenario, exhibits no discrimination in the movement of cost-of-living indices either between the rural and urban sectors or within each of the sectors. This pattern, which is repeated in other experiments, is commented on later.

As for the sectoral composition of output, it is clear that the movement of capital goods production mirrors that of investment. Furthermore, the historical run bids resources away from the infrastructure sector until 1983/4. This looks like negative import substitution in sector 5 in the historical run up to 1982/3. It is known, however, that domestic petroleum production increased substantially during this period. Since crude petroleum and natural gas accounted for only 6 percent of the gross output of sector 5 (see the components of this sector in table 6.18) the behavior of the sector in the historical run is certainly not inconsistent with positive import substitution in petroleum.

The no-external-shock-cum-accommodating-borrowing scenario is thus characterized by lower investment after 1976/7 and a lower aggregate

Table 6.19 India: alternative adjustment strategy (percentage deviation from historical run)

	1974–5	1975–6	1976–7	1977–8	1978–9	1979–80	1980–1	1981–2	1982–3	1983–4
GDP	0.6	1.3	1.2	2.1	6.4	0.4	0.2	0.1	2.2	0.8
Private consumption	0	0.4	0.3	0.4	0.3	0.3	0.3	0.2	1.4	0.4
Investment	8.0	5.8	4.4	12.4	6.4	0.4	0.2	0.1	2.2	0.8
Exports	−18.3	7.7	3.9	−6.5	4.6	8.7	4.5	−1.5	15.3	9.0
Imports	8.2	14.3	5.3	11.5	−0.6	6.9	3.8	−0.4	1.0	1.6
Gross output of										
Agriculture	0.6	−0.7	0	0	0.2	0	0	0.5	1.4	0
Consumer goods	−1.4	1.1	0	0	0	−1.4	0	0	0	0
Capital goods	7.5	5.7	4.6	12.4	0.8	0.7	0.5	0.2	3.1	1.2
Intermediates	2.1	2.5	1.2	3.5	0.2	0.3	1.1	0.5	2.6	0.8
Infrastructure	0.5	−0.6	−0.6	−0.4	−0.3	−0.1	0.5	0.5	0.7	−0.2
Services	−0.1	0.4	0.3	0.3	0.5	0.4	0.5	0.4	1.7	0.5
Foreign savings (levels, tens of million rupees)	1,295	1,285	−652	42	−713	434	2,380	2,334	1,990	2,757
Foreign savings in historical run (levels, tens of million rupees)	961	579	−1,031	−903	−575	−299	1,996	2,412	2,370	2,650

capital stock in 1984/5. This establishes that external shocks and the accompanying borrowing could not have accounted for the stagnation of investment in historical perspective. Indeed, the opposite appears to be true. It is then appropriate to ask whether agricultural shocks and the contractionary responses elicited by them in the middle 1970s contributed to such stagnation. This theme is explored in simulation 3 below.

Simulation 2 Alternative adjustment strategy

It has already been argued that policy-makers perceived the dip in the agricultural harvest in 1973/4 as more important than the oil price shock, especially given its potentially inflationary consequences, and applied a strong dose of demand management in response. The slowdown in public investment and the choking off of private investment generated a "deflationary" adjustment profile. This approach may be contrasted with the more investment and growth-oriented policy response to the 1979/80 round of shocks.

This simulation accordingly looks at the consequences of following a more expansionary investment strategy in response to the first round of shocks, supplemented by imports of essential consumer goods such as food and edible oils to combat inflationary pressures. The counterfactual is defined to be a situation in which (a) the ratio of real investment to GDP at constant market prices is set at its 1978/9 historical run value for the years 1974/5 to 1977/8, and after that at its historical run value for each year;[10] (b) government-controlled imports in sectors 1 and 2 are set so that per capita domestic availability (production plus net imports plus stocks) of goods in these sectors is at least as large as per capita availability in the historical run for every year; and (c) government-controlled oil imports are set so that their ratio to GDP equals the corresponding ratio in the historical run for every year. Since investment is determined by the requirement that it satisfy the ratios outlined in (a) above, the model solves for the amount of foreign savings consistent with equilibrium.

Table 6.19 displays the results. Since the investment to GDP ratio is kept at its historical run value in 1978/9 and in subsequent years, the deviation of investment from the historical run must equal that of GDP, starting in that year. In general, higher investment and the need to maintain the domestic availability of sector 1 and sector 2 goods at levels at least as large as those attained in the historical run call for higher foreign savings. However, since domestic availability can be met either by increasing imports or by reducing exports, both options are, in the absence of any further restrictions, exploited in the simulation.

Two broad patterns are discernible, depending on whether price-driven imports (those in sectors 3 and 4) dominate or are dominated by

Table 6.20 *India: alternative adjustment strategy: distributional characteristics (percentage deviation from historical run)*

	1974–5	1975–6	1976–7	1977–8	1978–9	1979–80	1980–1	1981–2	1982–3	1983–4
Cost-of-living indices Groups										
Urban										
C1	13.0	−6.0	−2.0	4.2	−2.0	−5.0	−3.0	1.4	−7.0	−5.0
C2	13.0	−6.0	−2.0	4.2	−2.0	−5.0	−3.0	1.3	−7.0	−5.0
C3	13.0	−5.0	−2.0	4.2	−2.0	−5.0	−3.0	1.3	−8.0	−5.0
C4	13.0	−5.0	−2.0	4.2	−2.0	−5.0	−3.0	1.1	−8.0	−5.0
C5	13.0	−5.0	−2.0	4.3	−2.0	−5.0	−3.0	1.1	−8.0	−5.0
Rural										
C1	13.0	−6.0	−2.0	4.2	−2.0	−5.0	−3.0	1.4	−7.0	−5.0
C2	13.0	−6.0	−2.0	4.2	−2.0	−5.0	−3.0	1.3	−7.0	−5.0
C3	13.0	−5.0	−2.0	4.2	−2.0	−5.0	−3.0	1.3	−8.0	−5.0
C4	13.0	−5.0	−2.0	4.2	−2.0	−5.0	−3.0	1.3	−8.0	−5.0
C5	13.0	−5.0	−2.0	4.2	−2.0	−5.0	−3.0	1.1	−8.0	−5.0
Gini coefficients										
Urban										
Income	0	−0.4	−0.1	−0.1	0.2	0.1	0	0.2	0.4	0
Consumption	0	−0.4	−0.1	−0.1	0.2	0.1	0	0.2	0.5	0
Rural										
Income	−0.1	−0.1	−0.1	−0.1	−0.1	−0.1	−0.1	−0.1	−0.4	−0.1
Consumption	−0.1	−0.1	−0.1	−0.1	−0.1	0	−0.1	−0.1	−0.4	−0.1

policy-determined imports (i.e., those in sectors 1, 2, and 5).[11] The years 1974/5 and 1977/8 correspond to the first pattern; investment is high compared with the historical run, compelling the economy to absorb the resulting foreign savings and price-driven imports through a decrease in competitiveness and a concomitant reduction in exports. The higher relative domestic prices implicit in such a loss of competitiveness are reflected in those two years as well as to a much lesser extent in 1981/2 (see table 6.19). In contrast, years such as 1975/6, 1979/80, 1982/3, and 1983/4 correspond to the second pattern, which is characterized by a large rise in exports. The gain in competitiveness that brings it about is not inconsistent with extra imports which, for those years, are mainly policy-determined rather than price driven. It may be noted that, notwithstanding a significant increase in the imports of capital goods that can substitute for the domestically produced variety with an elasticity of substitution of almost unity, the expansion of the domestic capital-goods sector called for by the accelerated investment program does not permit any increase in the domestic production of consumer goods relative to the historical run.

The behavior of the distributional characteristics is shown in table 6.20; the cost-of-living indices across the board are lower except in the years of significantly higher investment. As for sectoral aspects, the experiment channels variable factors such as labor and intermediates into capital goods production at the expense of infrastructure and, to some extent, of consumer goods. The economy is left with a capital stock in 1984/5 which is 1.8 percent higher than in the historical run. But the stock of terminal debt is 20 percent higher than in the historical run as well.

The debt figures calculated above take no account of the fact that India accumulated substantial quantities of foreign exchange reserves during the years 1976/7 to 1979/80, a feature to which attention was drawn earlier. Hence a part of the extra foreign savings required by the alternative adjustment strategy could have been provided, if necessary, by foreign reserves without entailing accumulation of debt. Table 6.23 shows the extra foreign savings that would have been available had the economy maintained reserves at a level equaling six months (row 4) and four months of imports (row 5). A comparison of the extra foreign savings called for by the alternative adjustment strategy (row 3) with those figures shows that the latter strategy would have fallen well short of generating any additional debt up to 1979/80, so that a cushion would still have been available to support an outward-oriented strategy in response to the 1979/80 round of shocks. However, inasmuch as their magnitude would have been less in the face of the second oil shocks, their use in supporting the alternative adjustment strategy during 1976/7 to 1979/80 would have added to the economy's debt burden in later years.

Table 6.21 *India: reserves decumulation (percentage deviation from historical run)*

	1976/7	1977/8	1978/9	1979/80	1980/1
GDP	1.7	3.6	4.1	3.7	
Private consumption	0.1	0.5	0.9	1.0	
Investment	11.2	28.2	28.2	23.0	
Exports	−10.3	−23.2	−26.2	−19.5	
Imports	10.9	33.1	38.3	29.0	
Gross outputs of					
Agriculture	0.1	0.2	0.9	1.2	
Consumer goods	−1.2	−1.9	−1.2	−1.0	
Capital goods	11.4	28.2	28.4	23.6	
Intermediates	3.1	7.9	8.9	9.5	
Infrastructure	0.1	2.2	3.5	4.0	
Services	−0.1	0.3	1.0	0.9	
Domestic production of capital					
goods	10.7	26.4	26.3	22.1	
Imported capital goods	18.2	47.7	49.8	38.6	
Total capital stock	0	8.3	2.9	5.0	6.4
Urban–to–rural per capita ratios					
Income	1.0	3.2	2.6	3.1	
Consumption	0	1.7	1.6	1.1	
Foreign savings (levels,					
tens of million rupees)	−87	1,561	2,577	2,115	
Foreign savings in the					
historical run (level,					
tens of million rupees)	−1,031	−903	−575	−299	

Simulation 3 Reserves decumulation between 1976/7 and 1979/80

What would have been the consequences of following a less cautious policy with respect to reserve accumulation during 1976/7 to 1979/80? To that end, the simulation asks what would have happened had reserves in the years 1976/7 to 1979/80 being maintained at a level equaling four months of imports. This is accomplished by adding the difference between actual reserves and the "four months" level of reserves to foreign savings and running the model in its "savings driven" mode. The policy simulation starts in 1976/7 with the historical run level of capital stock and reserves, so that the less cautious policy is followed from this year onwards. Although it is closely related to the theme of simulation 2, the fact that the issue of excess reserve accumulation has featured in policy discussions in its own right makes it desirable to explore this separately.

Table 6.22 *India: reserves decumulation: distributional characteristics* (*percentage deviation from historical run*)

Cost-of-living indices Groups	1976/7	1977/8	1978/9	1979/80
Urban				
C1	7.0	17.0	20.0	14.0
C2	7.0	17.0	20.0	14.0
C3	7.0	17.0	20.0	14.0
C4	7.0	17.0	20.0	14.0
C5	7.0	17.0	20.0	14.0
Rural				
C1	7.0	17.0	21.0	14.0
C2	7.0	17.0	21.0	14.0
C3	7.0	17.0	20.0	14.0
C4	7.0	17.0	20.0	14.0
C5	7.0	17.0	20.0	14.0
Gini coefficients				
Urban				
Income	−0.1	−0.2	−0.1	−0.1
Consumption	−0.1	−0.2	−0.1	−0.1
Rural				
Income	−0.1	−0.2	−0.3	−0.4
Consumption	−0.1	−0.2	−0.3	−0.4

Table 6.21 reports the level of foreign savings in the historical run as well as in the reserves simulation. It will be noticed that foreign savings are very substantially higher. As expected, those savings can be accommodated via a rise in domestic *vis-à-vis* international prices, or a relative decline in domestic competitiveness, resulting in an export profile which is much lower than in the historical run. The opposite is true for imports. Investment and GDP are both higher compared to the historical run – as well as gross outputs of sectors 3 to 5. Imports of capital goods, which can substitute for the domestically produced variety with an elasticity of nearly unity, increase much more than domestic production. The increased investment in this simulation leads to a capital stock at the beginning of 1980/1 that is higher than the corresponding figures in the historical run by 6.4 percent. The pattern of sectoral output indicates a massive expansion in the output of capital goods and a modest decline in the consumer-goods sector caused by the bidding away of variable factors of production. Comparison with the "investment-driven" results of table 6.19 shows a number of similarities.

Table 6.22 shows that the reserves simulation has a large impact on the cost of living *vis-à-vis* the historical run, especially in the years 1977/8 and 1978/9, although not on the Gini coefficients. There is a roughly 1.5 percent increase in the ratio of urban–to–rural per capita incomes but no differences in the relative movements of urban and rural cost-of-living indices.[12]

Simulation 4 No agricultural shocks

This experiment continues the exploration of the behavior of the economy in the absence of exogenous shocks. Since the case of no external shocks has already been examined, the focus here is on the case of no agricultural shocks. To that end, the factor productivity parameter in the agricultural production function, which is taken as a proxy for weather-related fluctuations, is set equal to its base year (1973/4) level of unity.[13] This helps bring out clearly the impact of fluctuations in agricultural output on the historical path of the economy. The results of this simulation and those of simulation 2 could easily be combined to answer the question: what would have been the consequences for investment and growth of pursuing an "expansionary" adjustment policy if the economy had experienced only external shocks between 1973/4 and 1983/4? Such a "no-agricultural-shock-cum-expansionary-adjustment" simulation would be an obvious counterpart to the "no-external-shock-cum-accommodating borrowing" simulation.

Recall from the discussion of the historical run that the period under consideration may be divided into those characterized by a dip in the agricultural harvest (1974/5, 1976/7, 1979/80, and 1982/3) and those that witnessed a recovery in agricultural production (1975/6, 1977/8, 1978/9, 1980/1, 1981/2, and 1983/4). The following discussion explains the results for the first group of years; qualitatively opposite effects obtain in the second group of years.

The supply curve of agricultural output moves outward in the first group of years in the experiment. Since the price elasticity of private consumption demand for food ranges across different groups from -0.13 to -0.26, the increased availability leads to a significant drop in price, decreasing the amount spent on food. Given that the share of food in total consumption is never less than 40 percent and exceeds 70 percent for the poorest urban and rural groups (see table 6.10), the favorable income effect of the fall in the price of food shifts the demand curve outward, further increasing output, but restraining the fall in the food price.

Table 6.24 shows that the recovery in agriculture in the first group of years leads to a rise in demand for all other sectors. Sectors 2 and 6 account for 22 percent and 14 percent of the value of total consumption respectively in the economy as a whole and hence experience expansion in output. But the sectors that benefit most are capital goods and intermediates. This is

Table 6.23 *Foreign savings under different scenarios (Rs. crores)*

	1976/7	1977/8	1978/9	1979/80
1 Historical run	−1,031	−903	−575	−299
2 Alternative adjustment strategy	−652	42	−713	434
3 Extra foreign savings required by alternative strategy ((2)–(1))	379	945	−138	663
4 Extra foreign savings available through decumulation of reserves to six months of imports	132	1,340	1,857	712
5 Extra foreign savings available through decumulation of reserves to four months of imports	944	2,464	3,152	2,414

Note: 1 crore = 10 million.

because the consumption deflator (in which food looms large) falls more than the GDP deflator, leading to an increase in savings and, since the model is savings driven, in investment. Since virtually all investment demand is satisfied by the capital-goods sectors, its output increases, exerting a favorable effect on the intermediate-goods sector.

Turning to the macroeconomic aggregates, there is a positive effect on GDP and, as discussed above, on consumption and investment. The favorable supply conditions in agriculture improve the relative competitiveness of exports. Since foreign savings are fixed in the experiment at historical levels, this is reflected in a drop in imports.

The impact effect on the cost of living is progressive as between rich and poor and the Gini coefficients decrease in both rural and urban areas. However, there is no difference in the rural versus urban impact when each of the sectors is taken as a whole (see table 6.25).

Table 6.24 shows that investment is mostly lower than in the historical run except in 1974/5, 1976/7, 1979/80, and 1982/3 – the first group of years. The economy's total capital stock is 6.5 percent lower at the beginning of 1984/5. This indicates that the cumulative effect of agricultural peaks dominated that of the troughs in the historical run, resulting in a relaxation of the wage goods constraint and thus permitting higher savings, investment, and terminal capital stock. From this it cannot be concluded, except on the basis of hindsight, that deflationary adjustment in the face of the adverse 1974/5 agriculture shock was necessarily inappropriate. However, its ferocity appears to have been a response as much to the inflationary pressures of 1971/3 caused by defense expenditures and the severe 1972/3 drought and the "delayed and inadequate"[14] response of the central bank rather than the particular developments of 1973/4 and 1974/5.

Table 6.24 *India: no agricultural shock simulation (percentage deviation from historical run)*

	1974/5	1975/6	1976/7	1977/8	1978/9	1979/80	1980/1	1981/2	1982/3	1983/4
GDP	2.9	-7.9	0.9	-3.3	-5.4	5.9	-6.1	-4.4	11.3	-3.3
Private consumption	0.9	-2.1	0.1	-0.7	-1.2	0.3	-2.0	-1.6	6.2	7.4
Investment	8.9	-25.9	3.4	-11.9	-17.5	19.4	-15.3	-11.2	20.2	-31.3
Exports	7.7	-15.0	2.0	-6.0	-9.4	17.9	-17.3	-10.0	16.5	-18.5
Imports	2.6	-5.7	0.8	-2.4	-2.8	3.1	-1.2	-1.9	2.9	-0.5
Gross output of										
Agriculture	2.2	-5.3	0.6	1.7	-3.0	3.1	-4.1	-3.0	3.7	-6.8
Consumer goods	2.4	-5.4	0.5	-1.9	-3.7	4.1	-4.9	-3.6	4.7	-7.5
Capital goods	8.5	-25.5	3.5	-12.2	-18.1	20.1	-15.8	-11.7	22.1	-38.3
Intermediates	5.2	-13.6	1.5	-5.2	-8.3	10.1	-9.1	-6.9	10.7	-17.5
Infrastructure	1.3	-3.4	0	-1.3	-2.7	2.3	-2.8	-2.3	3.1	-4.7
Services	0.4	-1.5	0	-0.5	-0.9	-0.5	-0.2	-0.9	1.5	-1.7
Memo item										
Agricultural efficiency parameter (level)										
Historical run	0.97	1.05	0.99	1.01	1.02	0.96	1.04	1.02	0.97	1.06
No agricultural shock simulation	1.0	1.0	1.0	1.0	1.0	1.0	1.0	1.0	1.0	1.0

Table 6.25 India: no agricultural shock simulation: distributional characteristics (percentage deviation from historical run)

Cost-of-living indices Groups	1974/5	1975/6	1976/7	1977/8	1978/9	1979/80	1980/1	1981/2	1982/3	1983/4
Urban										
C1	-6.0	15.0	-2.0	5.0	8.0	-8.0	16.0	8.0	4.3	-2.0
C2	-6.0	15.0	-2.0	5.0	8.0	-13.0	16.0	8.0	3.8	-1.0
C3	-6.0	14.0	-2.0	5.0	8.0	-12.0	15.0	8.0	2.8	1.0
C4	-5.0	13.0	-2.0	5.0	7.0	-12.0	14.0	8.0	1.7	0
C5	-5.0	12.0	-2.0	4.0	7.0	-11.0	13.0	7.0	-0.3	1.4
Rural										
C1	-6.0	16.0	-2.0	5.0	9.0	-13.0	16.0	9.0	4.9	-3.0
C2	-6.0	16.0	-2.0	5.0	9.0	-13.0	16.0	9.0	4.5	-2.0
C3	-6.0	15.0	-2.0	5.0	9.0	-13.0	16.0	9.0	3.6	-2.0
C4	-5.0	14.0	-2.0	5.0	8.0	-12.0	15.0	9.0	2.5	-1.0
C5	-5.0	13.0	-2.0	5.0	7.0	-12.0	14.0	9.0	0.8	0.3
Gini coefficients										
Urban										
Income	-0.4	1.6	-0.3	0.5	0.7	-1.4	1.1	0.6	-0.6	1.6
Consumption	-0.5	1.7	-0.3	0.5	0.8	-1.4	1.2	0.6	-0.6	1.1
Rural										
Income	-0.4	1.4	-0.1	0.4	0.7	-0.6	0.9	0.8	-0.9	1.9
Consumption	-0.4	1.4	-0.1	0.4	0.7	-0.6	0.9	0.8	-0.9	1.9

Table 6.26 India: investment reallocation simulation (percentage deviation from historical run)

	1974/5	1975/6	1976/7	1977/8	1978/9	1979/80	1980/1	1981/2	1982/3	1983/4
GDP	0.5	0.6	0.7	0.7	0.7	0.8	0.6	0.1	1.1	0.9
Private consumption	0.4	1.3	0.8	0.9	1.2	1.0	1.1	1.2	2.2	2.1
Investment	0.4	1.1	1.3	1.5	2.1	1.8	1.4	1.5	2.3	2.3
Exports	1.7	-7.4	-1.4	-2.6	-6.4	-3.3	-5.2	-9.2	-7.2	-9.8
Imports	-1.4	4.4	0.9	2.1	5.4	2.2	3.1	7.0	7.0	8.7
Gross output of										
Agriculture	0.2	0.4	0.3	0.3	0.2	0.4	0.5	0.3	0.6	0.6
Consumer goods	1.2	1.0	1.2	1.5	1.1	1.5	1.5	0.9	2.4	2.0
Capital goods	0.3	0.7	0.8	0.9	1.1	1.1	0.8	0.7	1.2	1.2
Intermediates	0.5	-0.2	0.6	0.4	0.1	0.9	0.8	-0.2	0.7	0.4
Infrastructure	0.2	0.5	0.1	0.0	-0.1	0.1	0.0	-0.3	0.6	0.3
Services	0.0	-0.1	-0.5	-0.9	-1.1	-1.1	-1.2	-1.7	-0.6	-0.8
Capital stocks in										
Agriculture	0.6	1.0	1.2	0.8	1.5	1.4	1.3	0.9	6.1	3.4
Consumer goods	15.5	21.7	26.4	34.3	36.7	35.8	31.7	31.5	47.6	43.6
Capital goods	15.3	21.2	25.8	32.8	34.6	33.0	30.2	31.0	45.7	41.5
Intermediates	15.1	21.0	25.4	32.5	34.2	32.8	29.4	29.7	44.1	40.2
Infrastructure	-2.7	-4.8	-6.2	-8.4	-11.0	-9.6	-8.6	-9.7	-1.9	-8.1
Service	-5.2	-8.6	-11.8	-15.4	-17.7	-19.8	-22.5	-21.1	-16.3	-16.8
TOTAL	0.0	-0.2	-0.6	-1.0	-1.2	-1.6	-2.0	-2.4	5.5	3.1
Foreign savings (level, tens of millions)										
Historical run	961	579	-1031	-903	-575	-299	1,996	2,412	2,370	2,650
Investment reallocation simulation	905	889	-951	-741	-64	-177	2,153	3,075	3,347	4,075
Terms of trade										
Historical run	0.727	0.702	0.676	0.808	0.732	0.528	0.571	0.684	0.737	0.728
Investment reallocation simulation	0.720	0.735	0.683	0.821	0.763	0.540	0.592	0.732	0.778	0.779

Thus agricultural shocks during the period 1973/4–1983/4 could not have directly accounted for the slowdown of investment and growth in historical perspective. However, it could be argued that, inasmuch as earlier experiences with harvest failures caused deflationary adjustment policies to be triggered, investment and growth might have been higher in the absence of exogenous agricultural shocks. The evidence against this view is as follows. The maintenance of public investment would in practice have called for a less contractionary fiscal stance and, given the extremely close link between budget deficits and borrowing from the central bank in India, for a more accommodating monetary policy. The extent to which this would have failed to arrest inflationary pressures depends on the degree to which supply constraints could be attributed to the shortage of wage goods *per se*, as was clearly true during the 1972/3 and 1974/5 droughts, as opposed to bottlenecks in the transport and distribution system. The former could have been met by imports of wage goods as in simulation 2, a strategy that could have been financed through more export expansion brought about, if necessary, via greater depreciation of the nominal exchange rate. The latter would have been less amenable to short-term solutions. To what degree policy-makers could have protected public investment without losing control over inflation is a question that has less to do with exogenous shock *per se* than with the institutional aspects of separating monetary and fiscal policy in India and the effectiveness of the transport and distribution system.

Simulation 5 Investment reallocation

To what extent could a more appropriate sectoral reallocation of investment in response to exogenous shocks have exerted a favorable impact on GDP and private consumption, i.e., provided efficiency gains comparable in magnitude to those lost as a result of those shocks?

The amount of capital stock in each of the six sectors of the economy is known for 1973/4. These are updated for subsequent years in the historical run using available data on the allocation of investment in agriculture, manufacturing, infrastructure, and services. Investment is distributed within manufacturing – consumer goods, capital goods, and intermediate goods – between sectors 2, 3, and 4 in accordance with capital stock proportions between those sectors in 1973/4.

This simulation, which is to be seen as an exploration of ways of allocating investment across sectors as part of an adjustment program, allows the allocation of investment to the four broad sectors (agriculture, manufacturing, infrastructure, and services) to respond to differences in rates of return earned by capital in those sectors.[15]

Table 6.26 reports the results. The experiment pulls investment out of

Table 6.27 India: investment reallocation simulation: distributional characteristics (percentage deviation from historical run)

Groups	1974/5	1975/6	1976/7	1977/8	1978/9	1979/80	1980/1	1981/2	1982/3	1983/4
Cost-of-living indices										
Urban										
C1	0	6.0	3.0	4.0	6.0	4.0	5.0	8.0	7.5	9.0
C2	0	6.0	3.0	4.0	6.0	4.0	5.0	8.0	7.5	8.9
C3	0	6.0	3.0	4.0	6.0	4.0	5.0	8.0	7.4	8.9
C4	0	6.0	3.0	4.0	6.0	4.0	5.0	8.0	7.5	9.0
C5	0	6.0	3.0	4.0	6.0	5.0	6.0	8.0	7.4	8.9
Rural										
C1	0	6.0	3.0	4.0	6.0	4.0	5.0	8.0	7.6	9.0
C2	0	6.0	3.0	4.0	6.0	4.0	5.0	8.0	7.5	9.0
C3	0	6.0	3.0	4.0	6.0	4.0	5.0	8.0	7.5	8.9
C4	0	6.0	3.0	4.0	6.0	4.0	5.0	8.0	7.5	9.0
C5	0	6.0	3.0	4.0	6.0	5.0	5.0	8.0	7.5	9.0
Gini coefficient										
Urban										
Income	0.4	1.4	0.6	0.6	0.7	0.7	0.7	0.6	1.1	1.2
Consumption	0.4	1.5	0.6	0.7	0.8	0.7	0.7	0.6	1.2	1.2
Rural										
Income	−0.1	0.1	−0.1	−0.1	−0.1	−0.2	−0.2	−0.1	−0.3	−0.3
Consumption	−0.1	0.1	−0.1	−0.1	−0.1	−0.1	−0.2	−0.1	−0.3	−0.3

infrastructure and services (which may broadly be identified as non-tradeables) and into manufacturing and, to a lesser extent, agriculture. The somewhat more efficient allocation of investment raises GDP and private consumption.[16] The balance of payments, however, deteriorates on two counts. First, the intermediate-goods sector, which is one of the beneficiaries of investment reallocation, uses imported intermediates much more intensively than the infrastructure and service sectors (for the share of intermediate imports in gross output (see table 6.9). Second, the extra income generated raises domestic demand, especially for agricultural and consumer goods; this in turn, notwithstanding some increase in domestic production, raises the prices of Indian goods *vis-à-vis* international substitutes. Since consumer goods account for the vast majority of exports (see table 6.9) this leads to a reduction in competitiveness and a noticeable decline in exports.

As a result of differences in depreciation rates across sectors, the economy is left with a capital stock which is 1.7 percent higher at the beginning of 1984/5 than in the historical run. But the foreign debt is 15 percent higher at the beginning of 1983/4 as well. Table 6.27 indicates that the Gini coefficients rise in urban and fall in rural areas, while the cost-of-living indices are uniformly higher for all groups. Thus, no straightforward comparison is possible between the historical run, with its attendant investment allocation, and the policy experiment, in which a seemingly plausible but myopic rule of short-run profitability governs the allocation of investment. It may be noted, however, that the income gains made possible by such reallocation would have placed the economy in an intermediate position between the historical run and the alternative adjustment strategy (simulation 2). Furthermore, this would not have saddled the economy with a debt burden greater than that corresponding to the alternative strategy, so that the remarks at the end of that simulation about the cushion provided by foreign exchange reserves are appropriate here as well. Since the income gains from improved investment reallocation are thus significant, it would be worth examining further the question of introducing greater market orientation in the allocation of investment across different sectors of the economy.

4 Conclusions

During 1973/4 to 1983/4, India recorded an average annual GDP growth rate of 4 percent, surpassing that achieved during the first fifteen years of planning, 1950/1 to 1964/5, and the decade preceding the first oil shock, 1964/5 to 1973/4. The fastest growing component of GDP, however, was the tertiary sector and, in particular, public administration and defense.

Although GDP in the secondary sector accelerated from that achieved in 1964/5 to 1973/4, it did not regain the growth momentum of the first decade and a half. The same was true of the index of industrial production.

The analysis of this chapter, which is mainly based on policy simulations with the model of chapter 4, shows the following.

(1) The stagnation of investment and growth in historical perspective could not be attributed to external shocks and the accommodating borrowing to which they gave rise. Indeed, the opposite seems to be true.

(2) Agricultural output peaks dominated output troughs during the decade 1973/4 to 1983/4. Thus, while exogenous weather-related shocks could not explain comparative stagnation, the deflationary adjustment policies of 1974/5 to which they gave rise contributed to sluggish investment and growth. Those policies appear to have been adopted primarily in response to earlier agricultural shocks and deficit financing rather than the external shocks that are the main focus of the present analysis.

(3) More investment-oriented adjustment starting in 1974/5, combined with supply-side anti-inflationary measures, such as selective imports of wage goods and more vigorous nominal exchange-rate management, would have contributed to growth in the mid 1970s. These could have been more than underwritten by accumulated foreign exchange reserves, but at the cost of adding to the economy's debt burden in the 1980s.

(4) Improved economic management in the form of more profit-guided sectoral allocation of even the historical volume of investment in the face of exogenous shocks could have led to significant efficiency gains for the economy as a whole.

The model could be used to examine questions such as how much domestic resource mobilization would have to be undertaken in order to preserve public investment in the face of exogenous shocks without recourse to the IMF and other sources of external borrowing. The deterioration in public finances in India in recent years makes this a particularly timely policy issue.[17]

Adjustment and income distribution

The model as applied to India is characterized by an elaborate disaggregated treatment of rural and urban households at various levels of income and expenditure.[18] An interesting feature of all the policy simulations is the virtually uniform impact on all groups of households. Indeed, a comparison of the simulations with the historical run reveals hardly any movement in the Gini coefficients of income or consumption inequality. Moreover, the cost-of- living indices do not move significantly differently across the ten groups of households identified by the model.[19] Nor is there any movement in the share of the bottom 40 percent of the population in income and consumption. This is partly due to the "full employment" character of the model, so that returns to all households from different sources roughly offset each other.[20] Thus, while some factors gain and others lose as a result of different policies, these do not, at the level of aggregation used here, make much difference to the relative incomes of households. Moreover, as argued in chapter 4, section 3.2, general equilibrium analysis, by incorporating substitution mechanisms operating through factor markets, tends to dampen movements in the income distribution. Since the assumption of a segmented and fully employed labor market does not appear unreasonable, and, since the data do not permit any further significant disaggregation of households, it seems appropriate to conclude that the distributional impact of adjustment to exogenous shocks in India was not significant. This conclusion would require modification of the range of policies explored to include redistribution of endowments, such as land and capital. Such measures would certainly change the distribution of income and consumption. However, since such redistribution was not an element in discussions of adjustment in India during this period, it is not necessary to consider it further here.

Notes

1 For a discussion of those policies and their consequences, see Bhagwati and Desai (1970), Bhagwati and Srinivasan (1975), and Little, Scitovsky, and Scott (1970).

2 The various hypotheses are surveyed in Ahluwalia (1985).

3 The estimates of annual rates of inflation quoted here and subsequently are based on the chart of annual rates of inflation from April 1971 to October 1983 appearing in Government of India (1984).

4 See Ahluwalia (1985). There was no trend in capital-goods imports in real terms, especially from 1970/1 to 1979/80.

5 These include factors such as grant-financed exports to Bangladesh, administrative decisions such as lifting of the ban on silver exports, unprecedented rise in the international price of sugar, and *ad hoc* increases in exports due to acute scarcity conditions abroad and exports of crude petroleum for processing abroad.

6 For details of the methods used for this derivation, see chapter 4.

7 Here, terms of trade are defined as the ratio of international prices of substitutes for India's exports to prices of imports.

8 These elasticities are based on estimates for developing countries reported in World Bank (1981b).

9 The latter difference is entirely due to the Extended Fund Facility from the IMF.

10 The ratio of investment to GDP at market prices in the historical run appears in table 6.12.

11 The fact that domestic availability can exceed or equal historical run values raises the possibility of multiple solutions. Although the two broad patterns identified here can be expected to characterize other potential equilibria, the precise configuration of exports and imports can be expected to vary across equilibria.

12 Another policy simulation (not reported here) maintained reserves during 1976/7 and 1979/80 at a level equaling six months of imports, and added its difference with actual reserves to foreign savings. Since this is a less aggressive reserves management policy than in simulation 3, its results are a muted version of those in tables 6.21 and 6.22.

13 It would have been possible to have given the factor productivity parameter a "normal" time trend instead of holding it constant in this simulation.

14 Reserve Bank of India (1985).

15 For details of the rule adopted, see chapter 4.

16 The experiment holds the physical volume of investment at its historical run level. However, since prices are different in the simulation, investment at constant prices in the national accounts sense can differ from that in the historical run.

17 For a detailed exploration, see Mitra and Go (1993).

18 For a description, see sections 5.2 and 5.3 of chapter 4.

19 One exception is the significant increase in average rural urban disparities following decumulation of reserves in simulation 3. This is because all extra foreign savings are automatically channeled into investment which boosts predominantly urban factor-intensive capital-goods production. Recall that there is no rural–urban migration which would allow rural workers to benefit from this process.

20 It will be recollected from the discussion in chapter 4 that the "full employment" assumption refers to no open unemployment of laborers. In fact, those who cannot find high-paying employment drift into low-productivity occupations where wages must move to clear the market.

7 Growth without adjustment: Thailand, 1973–82

1 Introduction

Like the other countries in this study, Thailand was adversely affected by the increased oil prices and world-wide recession of the 1970s. Nevertheless, from 1974 to 1981 the Thai economy grew at an annual rate of 7.2 percent, a growth performance exceeded only by Singapore, Korea, and Taiwan among the twenty-four countries adversely affected by external shocks which were analyzed in chapter 2. Population increased at an annual rate of about 2.4 percent, leading to an implied growth in per capita real income of 4.8 percent a year, a figure also among the highest for all middle-income oil-importing countries for 1974–81.

Even more remarkable, this growth rate was achieved with little adjustment to the dramatic change in world market conditions. For example, the controlled domestic price of oil remained unchanged and well below the world price until 1979. And while many other countries slowed down their investment programs, Thailand accelerated hers.

Moreover, some of the policies that were pursued appear with hindsight to have been imprudent. Thailand's export-promotion drive reached its peak in 1975–6 when prices for Thai exports were low and falling. The country borrowed lightly in world capital markets in the early 1970s, when interest rates were low, but heavily after 1975, when rates were high.

Two hypotheses can be advanced to explain Thailand's pattern of development following the first oil shock in 1973–4. The first is that Thailand was effectively insulated from that shock by a series of fortuitous circumstances. The US military presence in southeast Asia enabled Thailand to run a surplus on its foreign transfer account. In addition, Thai export prices rose soon after the oil shock; in fact, the country's terms of trade reached an all-time high in 1974. Thailand was also fortunate in being able to expand the area of land under cultivation during this period, enabling agriculture – the most important sector in the economy – to continue to grow rapidly, as it had in the 1960s.

The second hypothesis is that Thailand simply postponed adjusting to the first oil shock by borrowing from abroad. Indeed, by the early 1980s it became clear that the country could not maintain the high growth rates of the 1970s. External deficits reached almost 8 percent of GDP in 1981, compared with 4 percent in 1975. Commercial lenders were becoming increasingly reluctant to finance those deficits. Reacting to the deteriorating economic outlook, the private sector decreased total fixed capital investment between 1980 and 1982 by 6 percent a year on average. The GDP growth rate slowed to 5.5 percent. In its Fifth Five-Year Plan (1982–6), the Thai government introduced a program of structural adjustment in agriculture, industry, energy, fiscal policy, and public administration. For the first time, the plan explicitly called for reducing current-account deficits.

Which of these two hypotheses more accurately explains Thailand's adjustment experience has important implications for how we view the country's impressive growth rate. If it is the first, then we can say that the Thais were blessed with a certain amount of good fortune and that it would therefore be difficult to transfer lessons learned from their experience to other situations. But if the second hypothesis is correct then the growth enjoyed by the Thais in 1973–82 may have come at the expense of their being saddled with heavy debt-service payments subsequently.

We shall use the model of chapter 4 to help us answer the questions raised by these two hypotheses. To test the first hypothesis, we ask how the economy would have performed without the service payments from US military bases, or with lower export prices, or with limits to the availability of arable land. We also ask how the economy would have evolved in the absence of both these favorable shocks and the unfavorable oil shocks. Turning to the second hypothesis, we look at what the impact would have been if foreign borrowing and investment had taken some other course. For various objective functions, we determine the "optimal" trajectories of borrowing and investment. Since these differ from the actual trajectories, they provide evidence that the borrowing and investment strategy adopted by Thailand was costly in terms of consumption foregone by subsequent generations. Finally, we ask whether changing the composition of investment – as opposed to its level – over the ten-year period would have left the Thais with a stronger economy in 1982.

2 Adjustment experience

Economic performance, 1960–73

Thailand's economic policy since the early 1960s was characterized by a reliance on private economic activity and limited government intervention.

The underlying philosophy was clearly expressed in the First National Development Plan (1961–6):

The key note of the public development program is . . . the encouragement of economic growth in the private sector, and the resources of government will be mainly directed to projects, both in the agricultural and non-agricultural sectors of the economy, which have this objective in view.

The emphasis on private-sector growth, political stability, and a generally favorable investment climate all contributed to the rapid economic growth of the post-war period. Between 1960 and 1973, Thailand's GDP increased on average by 7.8 percent a year. Value added in agriculture rose at an annual rate of 5.2 percent, while the volume of exports rose at 7.2 percent. This growth, in turn, supported growth in the rest of the economy.

In agriculture, the availability of land allowed expansion of traditional subsistence production and helped to absorb a growing labor force. It also facilitated diversification into new cash crops, the mainstay of the rapid growth in agricultural exports. Public investment was restricted to infrastructure and support facilities. This lowered transport and handling costs, and increased the share of output accruing to the farmer. The market system traditionally provided credit, information, and extension services to many farmers in the absence of such services from the public sector (see for example, World Bank, 1980b). This approach contributed importantly toward raising large numbers of the rural population out of poverty.

The manufacturing sector also became an important source of economic growth and employment during this period. A surge in domestic demand, together with import substitution, contributed to an annual growth rate of 8.3 percent. In 1960, the agricultural sector employed 82 percent of the labor force while the manufacturing sector (including mining) employed only 3.6 percent, less than commerce (5.8 percent) and services (4.8 percent). By early 1973, the agricultural sector employed 67.3 percent of the labor force, and the manufacturing sector was second with 10 percent (Government of Thailand, 1960; Government of Thailand, 1973).

External shocks, 1973–81

Like many other developing countries in the 1970s, Thailand relied on imported oil and petroleum products to meet most of its energy requirements. The quadrupling of oil prices in 1973–4 sent Thailand's import bill soaring. The initial balance-of-payments effect was cushioned, however, by a simultaneous rise in export prices. In addition, the high transfer- and service-account earnings from US bases continued through 1975. Inflation was also controlled successfully, falling from 24 percent in 1974 after the oil shock to about 4 percent in 1975.

The terms of trade turned less favorable after 1975. Export prices actually dropped by 2.7 percent in the year 1975–6, but then increased by an average of 8.6 percent a year between 1977 and 1981. Meanwhile, import prices steadily increased, reaching an average rise of 12.1 percent a year for 1977–81. The difference in these growth rates represented a 24 percent deterioration in the terms of trade between 1975 and 1981.

Modes of adjustment

Faced with the need for adjustment, Thailand increased its borrowing from abroad and expanded its exports. Oil-importing countries have pursued three other tools of adjustment as well: import substitution, investment slowdown, and resource mobilization (see chapter 2). Thailand's use of these other modes was light and, in some instances, in the opposite direction.

In an effort to maintain a 7 percent rate of growth in the Fourth Development Plan (1977–81), a level that compares favorably with the performance of the 1960s, consolidated public expenditures, a comprehensive measure of government activity in Thailand, were increased rapidly between FY77 and FY82, tripling in current prices and doubling in constant (1976) prices.[1] The average rate of growth of public expenditures was about 18 percent a year between FY77 and FY81, considerably above the minimum 11.2 percent projected in the Fourth Plan. Notwithstanding the rapid rise in current expenditures, no measures were taken to increase revenues. Energy and other key goods such as cement remained underpriced. It was not until 1979 that a major oil price increase of 40 percent was effected. As long as the domestic price of energy remained low, only a relatively small reduction in energy use occurred. The demand for energy grew 1.8 times faster than GDP in the 1960s, and slowed only to 1.3 times faster in the 1970s. Goverment taxes on energy products were in fact reduced, and subsidies were paid to refiners at various times. As a consequence, most of the impact of rising energy prices was absorbed in the current-account and public-sector deficits. After 1975, total government revenues as a share of GDP stagnated at about 13 percent, and taxes at a little more than 12 percent, both down marginally from their shares in 1970–5. Despite a rapid decline in the relative importance of taxes on international trade, indirect taxes remained the mainstay of Thailand's tax system. In mid 1976 it became evident that the country's balance of payments had improved considerably, that domestic prices had not increased by much, and that public expenditures during the first half of 1976 could not be disbursed as rapidly as planned. The Bank of Thailand switched to an easy money policy to induce credit expansion by financial institutions and thereby encourage more investment by private enterprises.

It bought treasury bills on tender each week at increasingly higher prices, and it reduced the basic annual interest rate charged on loans to commercial banks from 10 percent to 9 percent.

Coupled with the generally favorable economic environment brought about by the policies of the mid 1970s, the expansion of credit led to an increase in investment activities in both the public and private sectors. In 1977 public and private fixed capital investment increased by a record 32.8 percent. The share of fixed investment in GDP also increased, from 21.7 percent in 1976 to 25.3 percent in 1977. The number of investment applications received by the Board of Investment rose from 111 in 1975 and 119 in 1976 to 264 in 1977. At the same time, inflation increased from 4 percent in 1975 and 1976 to 8 percent in 1977.

Between 1977 and 1981, investment activity fluctuated. In 1977 it increased 9.5 percent in real terms, then declined by more than 2 percent in 1979–80, mainly due to a slowdown in the agroprocessing industries, a consequence of bad weather. The average yearly increase of fixed capital investment for 1971–81 was 4.2 percent.

Private saving, typically around 19 percent of GDP, exceeded private investment demand throughout the period 1960–79, and the resulting surpluses were channeled to the public sector through transfers within the Thai banking system. In contrast, the public sector spent more resources than it generated during the 1970s. Except in 1974 and 1975 when the government pursued a restrictive fiscal policy in response to the first oil shock, the gap between public saving and investment approached or exceeded 5 percent of GDP. After 1978, this gap widened. Thus, between 1977 and 1979, public investment remained more or less unchanged as a share of GDP while public saving dropped substantially. Private savings alone could not fill this gap. The government had to resort to foreign borrowing to finance more and more of the growing public-sector deficit. Foreign borrowing increased from 0.5 percent of GDP in FY75 to almost 4 percent in FY80.

The particular time profile of external financing that Thailand followed distinguishes it from most other developing countries. Whereas many developing countries borrowed heavily in the early 1970s – when real interest rates were low and global liquidity high – Thailand borrowed only modestly. One reason for this was the commodity price boom, which cushioned the balance-of-payments effects arising from the increase in oil prices. After 1975, however, many oil-importing countries undertook a major adjustment effort to offset the impact of the first oil shock; among other things, they responded to the substantial rise in interest rates – which began in 1978 – by reducing the rate of growth of their external debt. In contrast, Thailand's external borrowing accelerated during this period, because of marked imbalances between investment and domestic savings, with nominal growth rates of medium- and long-term debt at almost 50 percent in 1979 and 1980, a time of record high nominal and real interest rates. As a result, the ratio of debt to GDP more than doubled from less than 10 percent in 1974 to about 20 percent in 1981. Short-term debt also expanded rapidly after 1975, reaching US$2.78 billion at the end of 1981.

The current-account deficit, which averaged less than 2 percent of GDP for 1960–75, reached more than 8 percent of GDP in 1979. The (total) public-sector deficit surpassed 6 percent of GDP in the same year. In addition to domestic expansionary policies, several other factors contributed to the deterioration of the current account. As mentioned above, export price indices declined in nominal terms while import prices continued to grow after 1975, causing a considerable deterioration in terms of trade. At the same time, surpluses on the saving and transfer accounts suddenly fell by a total of Baht 4.5 billion (US$200 million), largely as a result of the reduced US military presence in the region.[2]

The resurgence in the world-wide demand for exports after the recession of 1973/4 boosted the growth of Thailand's agricultural and manufactured exports. In addition, several domestic policies were adopted to promote exports. Export taxes, which represented 3.7 percent of total exports in 1975, were reduced to an average 1.9 percent of total exports for 1976–81 and to 0.8 percent in 1982. A domestic sales quota on rice that was linked to the amount exported was suspended.[3] Export industries, particularly those such as textiles and sugar facing production problems, received substantial assistance through lending from commercial banks under concessionary terms. Also, the repayment period for concessionary export credits was extended to enable traditional exporters to expand markets by granting longer credit terms to buyers. These policies, together with the increased demand, had a positive effect on Thailand's export performance. During the period 1974–81, the volume of exported goods increased an average of 11.3 percent a year, 1.6 times higher than GDP growth, and 1.7 times higher than merchandise import growth.

The structure of exports underwent considerable change in the 1970s. While agricultural goods still played a major role in the late 1970s (64 percent of merchandise exports), manufactured exports emerged as an important contributor (table 7.1). In 1971 Thailand accounted for 0.4 percent of total manufactured exports by developing countries; in 1979, its share rose to 2 percent. These figures testify to Thailand's positive response to the continuously strong demand for its traditional exports, and its effectiveness in penetrating new markets with manufactured exports.

While levels of protection in Thailand were substantially increased over the period 1974–8,[4] they nevertheless remained relatively low compared

Table 7.1 *Thailand: structure of merchandise exports (percent)*

Type of goods	1970	1982
Primary	86	71
Agricultural	71	64
Non-agricultural	15	7
Manufactures	14	29

Source: National Economic and Social
Development Board and Bank of Thailand.

with those in other developing countries during that period. In the past decade, merchandise imports grew in volume at 6.6 percent a year, slightly lower than GDP and lower than exports. The share of imports in GDP at current prices, however, increased considerably – from 19.5 percent in 1970 to 27.7 percent in 1979 – due to unfavorable developments in the prices of imports, especially oil. Higher oil prices had an effect not only on the volume of imports, but also on their composition. Before the first oil price shock, oil imports accounted for only 10 percent of total import value; after the shock, this increased to about 20 percent.

Some distributional aspects

This broad picture of the Thai economy from 1974 to 1982 would not be complete without description of the distributional aspects of the adjustment experience. In the area of poverty alleviation, too, Thailand has a good record. Household income data indicate that the benefits of rapid growth were enjoyed by large segments of the population. Moreover, the incidence of poverty was cut in half in the 1960s and 1970s: from 57 percent in the early 1960s to 31 percent by the mid 1970s for the whole population, and from 61 percent to 35 percent for those in rural areas.[5]

Agricultural growth had a profound influence on overall economic performance and, therefore, on rural and urban incomes. Although the structure of domestic production changed over time, with manufacturing and financial services gaining a larger share, agriculture remained the single most important sector. In 1980, as table 7.2 indicates, an estimated three-quarters of the labor force remained in agriculture, a larger share than in all but six other middle-income oil-importing countries. Another indicator of agriculture's central role is the effect that a drought-induced slowdown in that sector in 1979 had on other sectors. In 1980, after an impressive growth rate of 10 percent a year during the 1970s, the

Table 7.2 *Labor force and urbanization* (*percent*)

Country	Share of labor force in agriculture		Annual growth of labor force	Share of urban dwellers in total population	
	1960	1980	1970–80	1960	1980
Thailand	84	76	2.9	13	14
Indonesia	75	58	2.1	15	20
Philippines	61	46	2.4	30	36
Korea	66	34	2.8	28	55
Malaysia	63	50	3.0	25	29
All middle-income oil-importing countries	59	42	2.2	37	50

Source: World Bank (1982c).

manufacturing sector saw the slowest growth in fifteen years, mainly because of a slowdown in agroprocessing industries (World Bank, 1981a).[6] Furthermore, agricultural incomes were a major component in domestic demand, an important source of industrial growth. In short, Thailand's good overall performance in poverty alleviation was mainly a reflection of a sustained rise in rural incomes during the years 1963–79.

The rise in rural incomes, in turn, was due to several inter-related factors, the most important of which was the continuous expansion of land under cultivation. This expansion – about 3 percent a year between 1960 and 1979 – absorbed the increase in rural population (3 percent a year in the 1960s, and 2.5 percent a year in the 1970s) and raised the average size of holdings. It was made possible not only by the availability of land but also by the buildup of transport and communications infrastructure, which gave farmers access to new land and to national and international markets. The expansion of land under cultivation was also facilitated by the control of malaria in the north and north east which permitted sedentary settlement of large areas.

Diversification into higher-value crops and a rise in crop prices also contributed to higher rural incomes. Key steps in promoting diversification were improving the linkages with external markets and increasing the share of the wholesale price received by producers. By providing seeds, information, and outlets, the government made it possible for farmers to try out crops with profitable external markets, including sugar, cassava, and maize in the center, maize in the north, and kenaf, maize, and cassava in the northeast. The rise in the price of most agricultural products (except rubber) also explains some of the growth in rural incomes. The agriculture–non-agriculture terms of trade stood at 113 in 1976, compared with 100 in 1962 (World Bank, 1980b).[7]

Still another final factor explaining the rapid rise in rural incomes was the increasing participation of rural households in the modern sector, where incomes were higher. A significant proportion of rural incomes was derived from money wages rather than from self employment. By 1975, 22 percent of the income of agricultural households was earned from non-agricultural activity, such as agroindustries, trade, commerce, construction, and public service (World Bank, 1980b).

Public policies contributed to raising rural incomes primarily by increasing the efficiency of the market system through the provision and maintenance of economic infrastructure such as communications and roads. Specific poverty-alleviation efforts were not considered until the Fourth Development Plan (1977–81), which included explicit anti-poverty objectives as part of its development strategy. The anti-poverty program set out in that plan recognized the leading role of the private sector in reducing poverty and reinforced the government's role in providing support and an appropriate economic framework.

Other government policies had mixed results for economic growth and poverty alleviation. It has been argued, for example, that the policy of maintaining low rice prices for urban consumers through export taxes, reserve requirements, and an export premium acted to the detriment of most rural areas (World Bank, 1980b). Since rice is the main wage good, keeping its price low kept wages in the modern sector low and reduced the real earnings of rural laborers in alternative employment. It has also been argued that public policies promoted regional disparities (World Bank, 1985). The Center and Bangkok were the main beneficiaries of public investment, irrigation works, and subsidized agricultural credit.

At least a quarter of the population, however, did not share sufficiently in the benefits of growth to rise above the absolute poverty level. Poverty remained largely a rural phenomenon in Thailand, and was more pervasive in some regions than others. Most people below the poverty line were farmers engaged in rainfed agriculture, living in the north and northeast (World Bank, 1980b). These regions accounted for 56 percent of Thailand's population in 1980; 45 percent of their GDP was derived from agriculture, compared with a national average of 26 percent.

Rural workers in the south were another exception to the trend of rising rural incomes. Unlike other regions, the south was heavily dependent on a single cash crop, rubber. When rubber prices declined in the late 1960s and early 1970s, the region was less able than others to diversify production.

Despite relatively large areas of unexploited land, agricultural expansion was sluggish. In addition, the south is physically distant from the rest of the country, and the communications network has developed more slowly.[8]

In general, however, Thailand's record on poverty alleviation and income distribution was impressive, all the more so given the emphasis on the private sector and economic growth in the government's policies and the absence of explicit anti-poverty policies. Rather, the general development strategy pursued seems to have contributed to both equity and growth – at a time when other countries were having difficulty making progress toward either goal.

How was this successful pattern of adjustment with development brought about? To try and answer that question, we shall apply the model of chapter 4 to Thailand to assess the importance in quantitative terms of the various factors that seem to have contributed to economic performance in the years 1973–82.

3 Tracking history

Turning to aspects of the model of chapter 4 that reflect the Thai economy, we note two in particular. First, in the agricultural sector, we include land as a separate factor of production. This enables us to perform counterfactual experiments on the availability of land which, as we noted earlier, is thought to have played a major role in Thailand's economic growth. Second, as noted in the discussion surrounding table 4.4, we model the labor markets such that for two categories of labor – urban white-collar and rural workers – the wage is fixed, so that there can be unemployment in these categories. When there is unemployment in the rural labor market, it "spills over" into the informal urban labor market, where a flexible wage equates supply and demand. In this way, we attempt to capture the phenomenon of rural households competing for jobs in the urban sector. Similarly, we allow unemployment of white-collar workers to cascade downward to the urban blue-collar market, which is also cleared by a flexible wage.

This treatment of the labor market requires some justification to which we now turn. Although a detailed examination of wage levels and structures in Thailand is hampered by lack of data, some important features of the labor market can be discerned. The government is a major employer particularly of better-educated employees in higher-status jobs, accounting in 1981 for about 70 percent of all white-collar workers but only 19 percent of blue-collar workers. It is therefore not surprising to find that government wage and employment policies have a substantial impact on the labor market, with the government white-collar wage being the prime determinant of the average white-collar wage.

Another important characteristic is the substantial difference between wages in the formal and informal sectors, suggesting that formal labor markets do not operate competitively. Rather, job rationing may be predominant.[9] If this view is correct, the expansion of the labor force can be absorbed in the informal sector with the wage adjusting to clear the market.

At the same time, there is evidence of high seasonal elasticities of labor supply in rural areas, which may be interpreted to reflect an abundant reserve of "underemployed" labor. Large seasonal fluctuations in agricultural employment are, in turn, caused by changes in the demand for labor over the year.

Taking all these considerations into account, we distinguish in the model among four different types of labor: rural, informal urban, blue-collar, and white-collar. The rural category – which includes all rural workers – is only employed by the agricultural sector. We assume that the rural real wage is fixed and that job rationing exists. The informal urban wage is perfectly flexible and moves to clear the market. This type of labor is employed by all sectors, with all informal urban workers getting the same wage rate. The blue- and white-collar workers are employed by all sectors and by the government. It is assumed that the blue-collar wage is flexible and moves to clear the market. The government and the private sector pay the same wage to blue-collar workers. The real wages of white-collar workers, however, are assumed to be fixed, with job rationing characterizing this type of labor. The government and the private sector also pay the same wage rates to white-collar workers. The absorption of migrant workers into the Bangkok economy is supported by a complex of formal and informal networks to provide job information and placement. According to a labor survey, about 60 percent of the migrants who came to the capital to work either had a job or a promise of a job before moving (Chamratrithirong, 1979). Relatives, friends, and acquaintances were the principal sources of job information, with employment agencies a much smaller but still significant factor. In the model, therefore, we assume that rural versus urban migration is responsive to differentials between the cost-adjusted informal urban real wage and the rural real wage.

We assume that 40 percent of the unemployed white-collar workers find jobs as blue-collar workers, independently of the wage differentials between the two labor categories. This value represents an arbitrary, but we think reasonable estimate, there being no data available to corroborate this figure.

A comparison of actual and model-generated historical values is given in figures 7.1 through 7.5.[10] The model reproduces quite well what happened in Thailand during the period in question. The model's estimate for GDP growth shows basically the same trend as the national accounts estimate. The model-generated path of private consumption was consistently below

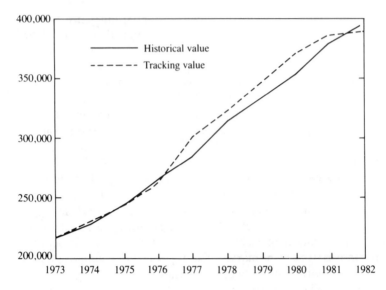

Figure 7.1 Thailand: gross domestic product (millions of 1973 bahts)

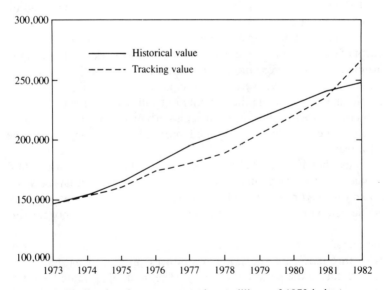

Figure 7.2 Thailand: private consumption (millions of 1973 bahts)

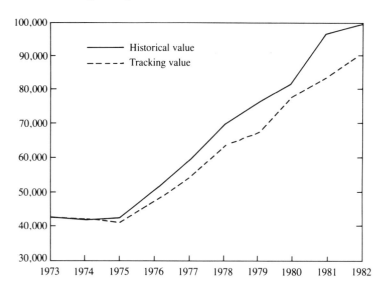

Figure 7.3 Thailand: exports (millions of 1973 bahts)

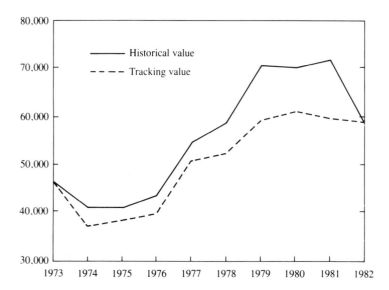

Figure 7.4 Thailand: imports (millions of 1973 bahts)

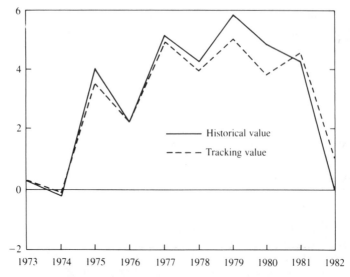

Figure 7.5 Thailand: foreign savings share (percentage of GDP)

the actual one, although the discrepancy is small. The model has difficulty reproducing the export boom of 1977, when the volume of exports grew 40 percent over 1973 levels. This boom was mainly the result of an increase in demand for Thailand's primary exports, such as rice, and of the government's implementation of several export-promotion policies, such as reducing the quotas imposed on rice exporters. These policies are difficult to replicate given the structure of the model. Consequently, exports in the model after 1977 are considerably lower than the actual figures. Nevertheless, the path follows the same basic trend as the historical values. The amount of imports in the model was adjusted so as to have the trade balance follow historical estimates.

4 Policy simulations

Having ascertained that the model reproduces Thailand's actual pattern of development, we shall attempt to assess quantitatively the two hypotheses advanced earlier about Thailand's rapid growth without adjustment to the external shocks of the 1970s. The first is that Thailand was insulated from the shocks by a series of fortuitous circumstances and therefore did not need to adjust; the second is that Thailand borrowed in world capital markets and thereby deferred adjustment.

Table 7.3 *Thailand: transfers from*
US military bases, 1973-6 (millions
of 1973 bahts)

Year	Amount
1973	4,223
1974	2,884
1975	2,165
1976	600

Source: Bank of Thailand.

No favorable or unfavorable shocks

Evidence for the first view is offered by three facts:

(a) Thailand continued to receive service payments from US military bases until 1976.
(b) Export prices peaked in 1974.
(c) Farmers were able to expand the area of land under cultivation without any constraints during the entire period.

To measure the contribution of each of these phenomena to Thai economic growth in the 1970s, we ask: what would Thailand's performance have been if:

(a) there had been no transfers from US bases,
(b) export prices had not peaked in 1974 but instead had followed their historical trend,
(c) there had been no increase in the amount of land under cultivation?

Simulation 1a No transfers from US bases
    The transfers from US military bases in southeast Asia represented a significant, although declining, contribution to foreign inflows into Thailand during 1973-6; see table 7.3. We simulate the effects of eliminating these transfers by reducing foreign transfers and, hence, the current-account deficit sustained in the years 1973-6. The results are recorded in table 7.4. Exports increase and imports decrease with respect to the historical run. The extra exports come at the expense of consumption and investment; GDP is only slightly affected by this loss in foreign transfers. The reason for this is that, with fixed capital stocks and full

Table 7.4 *Simulation 1a: no service payments from US military bases* (*percentage deviation from historical run*)

Economic indicator	1973	1974	1975	1976
Exports	8.0	3.2	2.4	0.6
Imports	−7.3	−3.2	−2.3	−0.6
Consumption	−4.1	−2.1	−1.9	−0.6
Investment	−4.1	−1.5	−1.5	−0.4
GDP	−1.0	−0.6	−0.6	−0.2
Outputs of:				
Agriculture	−1.2	−1.0	−0.8	−0.3
Consumer goods	0.5	−0.4	0.0	0.0
Capital goods	−3.7	−1.7	−1.3	−0.3
Intermediate goods	−0.6	−0.5	−0.5	−0.2
Public infrastructure	−3.0	−1.4	−1.0	−0.3
Services	−1.4	−1.1	−0.9	−0.3

employment in two categories of labor, gross domestic output is essentially supply determined in the model. The effect of a drop in foreign transfers leads mainly to a reallocation of demand from domestic to foreign sources. Moreover, consumption is hurt more than investment because it was assumed that the service payments accrued directly to households. However, the lower household income implies lower savings and therefore less investment in this "savings-driven" model. It is interesting to note that, despite the short-term reduction in investment, the economy's long-term health is not badly affected: by 1977, GDP recovers to its historical level.

Concerning changes in the pattern of output, we note that consumer-goods output is actually higher than in the historical run in the first year of the shortfall in foreign transfers. Declining demand for capital goods and infrastructure releases resources (labor), which are now put to other uses. This leads to an increase in exports, most of which were consumer goods, in 1973. This export boom is sufficient to counteract the loss in domestic demand and results in a net increase in output of consumer goods. Similarly, the intermediate-goods sector suffers less than other sectors because it produces an import substitute. In the wake of declining imports, this sector registers an increase in demand that dampens the effect of an overall decline in economic activity brought about by the elimination of transfers from the military bases.[11]

It is interesting that although output in each sector (except consumer goods) is lower than in the historical run, value added is actually higher in the first year and more or less keeps pace with historical levels subsequently. With a decline in the real wages of two labor groups, all sectors increase employment, thereby increasing value added. However, the reduction in imports, which are mainly intermediate goods, is sufficiently acute that despite the higher value added the net result is a decline in gross output.

Changes in relative prices mirror the changes in the sectoral pattern of output. While the level of domestic prices is lower, the price of non-tradeables falls more than that of tradeables, signaling the real exchange-rate depreciation that is required to sustain a smaller current-account deficit.

Finally, the distributional impact of the loss of foreign transfers can also be explained by the changes in the production mix. Households that rely on employment in the services and capital-goods sectors for their income (mainly blue-collar and casual urban workers) are hurt more than those which depend on the agricultural, consumer-goods, and intermediate-goods sectors (rural and white-collar workers).

To summarize this first simulation: the transfers from US military bases permitted Thailand to sustain a slightly higher growth rate in the early years after the oil shock. They enabled the economy to purchase more imports, which, given their complementary role in production, resulted in a higher level of output. Nevertheless, the lasting effects of this "windfall" appear to be minimal. Although the lower investment levels in the absence of the transfers would have led to lower levels of capital stock, the reduced real wage would have resulted in higher employment (given pools of unemployed labor). Thus value added would have been maintained and the post-1976 economy would have been the same.

Simulation 1b No export price surge

We now address the second question, namely, the impact of the surge in export prices in 1974–5. The international price of Thailand's agricultural exports rose by 30 percent in 1974, by another 6.2 percent in 1975, then fell by 6.2 percent in 1976 before recording steady growth thereafter. We simulate the effects on the economy if the world price had instead followed a smooth path of 8.6 percent annual growth in 1973–6 (the geometric average of the 1973 and 1976 levels). The results, reported in table 7.5, indicate that lower prices for agricultural exports would have had only a slight effect on the economy's performance in 1974 and 1975, and virtually no effect on the long-run path. Not surprisingly, the largest impact is on the volume of exports. Imports are also lower to maintain the same current account as in the historical run (given that the model is savings driven). Reflecting the small drop in overall economic activity, domestic savings and hence investment are lower. Finally, the fall in agricultural prices lowers domestic food prices. This, in turn, permits a decline in wages.

Table 7.5 *Simulation 1b: slower growth in agricultural export prices, 1974–5 (percentage deviation from historical run)*

Economic indicator		1974	1975
Exports		−1.4	−5.0
Imports		−1.4	−3.1
Consumption		−0.5	−1.0
Investment		−0.9	−2.5
GDP		−0.4	−1.8
Exports of:[a]			
Agriculture	(0.05)	−20.7	−16.3
Consumer goods	(0.27)	2.0	4.0
Capital goods	(0.02)	1.0	1.9
Intermediate goods	(0.09)	1.3	2.8
Services	(0.17)	1.1	2.6

[a]Figures in parentheses are share of exports in the output of each sector in 1973.

making other exports more competitive. Thus, while agricultural exports suffer badly in this simulation, all other exports are higher than in the historical run.

Simulation 1c No land growth

The third and final policy simulation in this sequence is the one in which the growth of arable land is halted. Recall that land is modeled as a separate factor of production in the agricultural sector. In the historical run, the supply of this factor is assumed to grow at 4 percent a year; in the simulation, this figure drops to zero. Despite its draconian features, this counterfactual simulation yields very little difference from the historical run. GDP is imperceptibly lower in the first few years. In 1982, the final year, when the cumulative effect of the reduction in land would be most noticeable, GDP is only 1.6 percent lower than in the historical run. The reason is that land is but one factor in agriculture, accounting for less than 6 percent of value added. As its supply shrinks and its price rises, farmers substitute labor and capital for land. Although we assume an elasticity of substitution between land and other factors of 0.9, the ready availability of agricultural labor at a fixed wage induces a fair amount of substitution.[12] In the terminal year, the price of land is 48 percent higher than in the historical run, yet the price of agricultural output is only 2.9 percent higher.

In sum, the three fortuitous events that accompanied the oil price increases made only a minor contribution to Thailand's economic perform-ance in the 1973–82 period. Of the three, the service payments from US

Table 7.6 *Simulation 2: no external shocks (percentage change from historical run)*

Year	Exports	Imports	Consumption	Investment	GDP
1974	16.0	47.0	9.5	23.4	3.0
1975	4.0	41.3	9.5	19.8	5.2
1976	1.5	41.5	4.5	12.1	0.9
1977	3.0	41.5	7.9	13.5	4.1
1978	5.6	40.4	10.6	18.3	6.9
1979	8.9	49.7	14.1	24.6	9.9
1980	13.2	68.0	17.7	31.8	12.1
1981	13.8	70.1	20.5	34.5	15.1
1982	13.4	55.6	17.9	29.9	17.9

military bases seem to have been the most important, with the 1973–4 export price boom next, and the expansion of arable land the least significant.

Simulation 2 No external shocks

It is reasonable to ask, however, whether the negative shocks had an equally mild impact. That is, was the effect of the oil price rise on Thailand also so slight that it was, in fact, counteracted by these positive shocks? The answer is no. An experiment in which import prices grew at pre-1973 rates (9 percent instead of 15 percent a year) and all three favorable events were eliminated reveals that the net effect on Thailand was negative, as recorded in table 7.6.[13] In the absence of both types of shocks, the Thai economy would have grown considerably faster, with real GDP in 1982 being almost 14 percent higher than its actual value. The lower import prices permitted more imports to enter the economy which, given their complementary role in production, enhanced output. In addition, higher imports raised tariff revenues which, in turn, gave a boost to government savings and investment. Thus, it cannot be concluded that Thailand's combination of positive and negative shocks canceled each other out, making adjustment unnecessary. We turn, therefore, to the second hypothesis for Thailand's adjustment-free growth path.

Alternative borrowing and investment strategies

There are many ways to test this second hypothesis, namely that Thailand deferred the necessary adjustment by borrowing abroad. Lower levels of borrowing would have led, of course, to lower growth rates in the 1973–82 period and a lower debt in 1982. However, this does not mean that the borrowing was imprudent. The Thais may simply have been exploiting intertemporal arbitrage possibilities offered by international capital markets. The optimal level of borrowing depends, among other things, on the rate of return to capital in Thailand, world market interest rates, and the social rate of time preference. Here we attempt a particular test of the proposition that Thailand "overborrowed" in the 1973–82 period.[14] We ask: could the actual capital stock in 1982 have been achieved with a lower debt? Specifically, we adjust the time profile of investment and borrowing to minimize the post-1982 debt-service obligations, keeping the terminal capital stock fixed at its 1982 level.

The computational costs of optimizing our six-sector non-linear model over nine time periods would be prohibitive. Therefore, we employ an approximation technique developed by Sierra and Condon, 1987. This technique begins with the observation that the two variables that drive an optimal borrowing strategy are investment and foreign savings. Of course these two variables are connected, their connection being expressed by the model. Thus, for a given external and policy environment, there exists a unique relationship between different levels of investment and of foreign savings. Sierra and Condon (1987) estimate this relationship using a polynomial approximation. They "shock" the general equilibrium model with different values of foreign savings and fit a fourth-order polynomial to the resulting values of investment. This equation is then grafted onto the debt module. This smaller model can be optimized over nine years at very low cost. Moreover, as Sierra and Condon show, the approximation is a good one and the resulting optimal path does not deviate significantly from the "true" optimum.

Simulation 3a Minimizing post-1982 debt service

Simulation 3a reveals that the investment path that minimizes post-1982 debt-service obligations differs substantially from the historical run, as shown by a comparison between the dashed and solid lines in figure 7.6. The optimal profile also squares with intuition: Thailand should have invested and borrowed more than it did in the early years, when interest rates were low, and much less in the later years, when rates were at an all-time high. The terminal debt, under the experiment, is 28 percent lower than its historical value. Clearly, the 1982 capital stock could have been achieved with a much lower debt burden by shifting the profile of investment and borrowing.

This simulation determines the optimal borrowing path when there is perfect foresight of the trajectory of interest rates. But few people in 1973

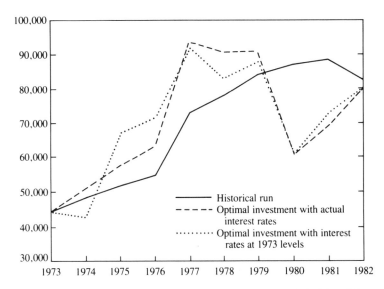

Figure 7.6 Thailand: simulation 3a: optimal investment (minimizing debt service –
millions of 1973 bahts)

could have predicted the erratic behavior of interest rates in the second half
of the 1970s. The deviation of the investment path from the optimal one
could have been due to poor prediction of interest rates as well as to
suboptimal borrowing. To distinguish between these two, we also compute
the optimal path if interest rates had stayed at their 1973 levels. This myopic
path, given by the dotted line in figure 7.6, also differs substantially from the
historical one. Thus, even if Thai policy-makers had expected the low
interest rates of 1973 to persist, they should have been following a different
path than they did. Indeed, the myopic path rather closely resembles the
perfect foresight one. This gives rise to the conjecture that to achieve a given
capital stock, if minimizing debt-service obligations is the objective, then a
period of rapid borrowing should be followed by one of lower borrowing. It
has been shown that foreign borrowing is associated with appreciation of
the real exchange rate in developing countries (Ghanem and Kharas, 1985).
A higher real exchange rate makes it more difficult to meet debt-service
obligations. Thus, the slowdown in borrowing is needed to enable relative
prices to adjust to meet debt-service payments.

Simulation 3b Maximizing 1982 capital stock

An alternative question is: Given its debt in 1982, could Thailand
have altered its profile of borrowing and investment to achieve a higher

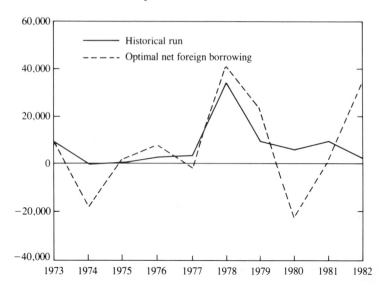

Figure 7.7 Thailand: simulation 3b: optimal net foreign borrowing (capital stock maximizing – millions of 1973 bahts)

capital stock in 1982? As figure 7.7 shows, the optimal borrowing path would differ from the historical one. The resulting pattern reflects the optimizing model's attempt to tradeoff depreciation (which tries to push investment into the later years) with high interest rates in 1979–82 (which would push investment into the early years). The resulting terminal capital stock, however, is only slightly higher. Thus, for a given volume of terminal debt, Thailand could not have done much better by adjusting its profile of foreign borrowing. This strengthens the notion that it was the country's investment and borrowing strategies taken together, rather than its investment strategy given its borrowing strategy, that was suboptimal.

Simulation 4 Utility-maximizing borrowing-cum-investment

Simulations 3a and 3b show, then, that Thailand could have achieved its impressive 1973–82 growth rate with lower debt by changing its time profile of investment and foreign borrowing. To the extent that foreign borrowing is a substitute for domestic savings, this lower debt would have come at the expense of domestic consumption. We cannot conclude, therefore, that the Thais would have been unambiguously better off with this alternative investment and borrowing pattern. Hence, we next perform a simulation in which the intertemporal utility of consumption is maxi-

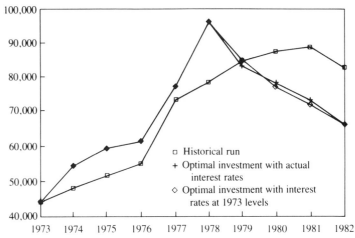

Figure 7.8 Thailand: simulation 4: optimal investment (utility maximization – millions of 1973 bahts)

mized. In this way, we explicitly incorporate the tradeoff between foreign borrowing, which permits current consumption, and domestic savings, which increases future consumption thanks to lower debt-service payments. The intertemporal utility fuction is:

$$V = \sum_{t=0}^{T} \left(\frac{U_t^{1-\beta}}{1-\beta} \right) \left(\frac{1}{1+\delta} \right)^t$$

where

δ = pure rate of time preference (set equal to 0.05),
β = elasticity of marginal utility (set equal to 0.8), and
U_t = instantaneous utility of consumption in year t.

The functional form of U_t represents our consumer demand system, which was taken to be a linear expenditure system (see the discussion on p. 118). We maximize this utility function over the 1973–82 period subject to the constraint that the terminal debt and capital stock conform to their historical levels. We then ask: could economic welfare have been improved during the 1973–82 period by pursuing a different borrowing-cum-investment strategy while leaving the post-1982 condition of the economy unchanged? The answer, as shown by figure 7.8, is yes. The optimal strategy calls for higher investment (and borrowing) in the early years and much lower levels of each in the later years. Note that this is not due to the interest-rate "shock" of the early 1980s. Even if 1973 rates had prevailed throughout the decade, a shift in the investment-cum-borrowing profile

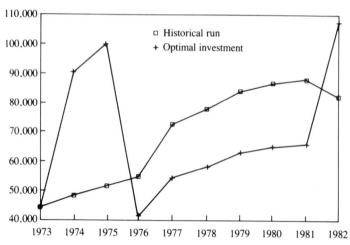

Figure 7.9 Thailand: simulation 4: optimal investment (minimizing debt service – millions of 1973 bahts)

would have been called for as shown in figure 7.8. A symmetric experiment which minimizes post-1982 debt-service payments subject to utility being at historical-run levels yields the same pattern of optimal investment: higher in the early years, lower in the later ones (see figure 7.9). This confirms the intuition, developed from the earlier results, that, even if it bought Thailand a high growth rate in the 1970s, the investment and borrowing path followed was by no means optimal. Although Thailand's foreign borrowing conferred certain consumption and savings benefits, these benefits would have been better allocated over time with a different investment strategy. Finally, the optimality of the investment path in figure 7.9 is due not to the largely unanticipated interest-rate hike at the end of the period, but rather to the structure and historical evolution of the Thai economy.

Simulation 5 Reallocating investment among four sectors

In the simulations just discussed, we have attempted to alter the intertemporal allocation of borrowing and investment, while, however, keeping the intersectoral allocation of investment resources constant at their 1973 levels. That is, while letting the volume of investment vary, we assume that the share going to each sector is the same every year as it was in 1973. To perform the next simulation, we keep the same volume of investment each year but allow its intersectoral allocation to be determined with reference to sectoral rates of return. What we are thereby asking is: how would the economy have behaved if investible resources were allowed to flow to where capital was scarcest?[15]

A comparison of outcomes under this rule with a situation where the

Table 7.7 *Thailand: composition of capital stock*

Sector	1975	1980
Agriculture	11.5	8.0
Manufacturing[a]	26.4	26.7
Public infrastructure	21.1	20.1
Services	40.2	44.2

Note:
[a] Includes consumer-, capital-, and
intermediate-goods sectors.
Source: Bank of Thailand.

Table 7.8 *Simulation 5: change in
allocation of investment among
four sectors (percentage deviation
from historical run)*

Year	Exports	Imports
1974	0.0	0.0
1975	0.0	0.2
1976	1.4	0.4
1977	2.7	0.4
1978	4.2	0.1
1979	6.1	−0.3
1980	8.6	−0.8
1981	10.9	−0.8
1982	13.9	−1.3

shares of investment going to various sectors are kept constant at their 1973 values, as in the historical run, may be thought to be extreme. However, some more recently available data at the four-sector level – agriculture, manufacturing (including consumer, capital, and intermediate goods), public infrastructure, and services – indicate that the composition of the capital stock across the four sectors did not in fact change significantly between 1975 and 1980 (see table 7.7). In the simulation we allow investments in these four sectors to respond to differences in profitability. That is, the share of manufacturing as a whole could vary according to differences in sectoral rates of return, as could the shares of agriculture, public infrastructure, and services. However, within manufacturing, the shares of investment accruing to the consumer, capital- and intermediate-goods sectors were kept at their 1973 levels. The results of this simulation, found in tables 7.8 and 7.9, yield a pattern where exports are higher and

Table 7.9 *Simulation 5: change in allocation of investment among four sectors (percentage deviation from historical run)*

Sector	Output in terminal year (1982)
Agriculture	12.2
Consumer goods	6.8
Capital goods	1.8
Intermediate goods	4.0
Public infrastructure	2.7
Services	−1.7

Household group	Utility in terminal year (1982)
Own-account rural	8.7
Own-account urban	4.7
Casual rural	6.3
Casual urban	7.9
Blue-collar	6.1
White-collar	−2.8

imports are lower than in the historical run and where there is a clear and significant shift of resources toward the tradeable sectors, particularly agriculture and consumer goods. Except for the services sector, output in the terminal year is higher than in the historical run across the board, and utility is higher for all groups, particularly the rural and poor households, save the richest segments of the population – white-collar workers – who derive most of their income from the services sector. The need for foreign borrowing is also reduced, with the public debt in the terminal year lower than its historical level.

Thus, by changing the mix of investments, Thailand could have improved the distribution of income and lowered its foreign debt without affecting the overall volume of investment. This would have increased welfare in the country. The direction in which the mix should have been altered does not have to be determined by solving some complicated intertemporal optimizing problem. Rather, it is signaled by the current return to capital services in the various sectors.

5 Conclusions

Thailand's experience during the decade 1973–82 was characterized by rapid economic growth without much adjustment to the 1973 oil price increase or to the ensuing world-wide recession. Looking more closely, we find that the country benefited from several favorable "shocks" and that it borrowed heavily in world capital markets. Using a six-sector general equilibrium model of the Thai economy (which tracked the behavior of several key variables reasonably well), we have shown that the favorable external circumstances contributed little to Thailand's economic growth in this period. Moreover, they did not mitigate the need for adjustment. The harmful effects of higher import prices in the 1970s outweighed the beneficial effects of these favorable shocks. Turning to foreign borrowing, we found considerable evidence that Thailand's borrowing strategy was not optimal. The country could have achieved the same 1982 capital stock with less debt had it adjusted its profile of borrowing over the decade. Finally, taking the level of investment as given, we have seen that significant gains could have been achieved had the composition of investment been allowed to respond to the profitability of capital in each sector. This would have resulted in a shift of resources toward the tradeable sectors, a lower foreign debt, and a more equitable distribution.

What lessons can be drawn from this exercise for adjustment in other oil-importing countries? First, favorable temporary shocks are likely to do little to counteract the need for adjustment to a permanent change in the external environment. Second, while borrowing abroad does postpone adjustment, the tendency to overborrow can be quite costly. In general, it appears as if a period of rapid increase in foreign debt should be followed by a period of decreased borrowing to facilitate debt-service payments. Third, an ambitious investment program may not be inconsistent with adjustment. As we demonstrated, the mix of investments, rather than the volume, can play a crucial role in determining the outcome for the economy.

As for implications for Thai economic policy, there is no question that the economy registered an impressive performance during the 1970s. However, this was at a cost of sizeable debt-service payments and slower growth in the following decade. The economy would have been better off with a different time profile of foreign borrowing and a different sectoral allocation of investment. The signals for a better investment allocation were given by the intersectoral returns to capital. Thus, policy-makers in Thailand would be well advised to promote an environment in which investible resources can flow easily to sectors where their profitability is highest. This leads not only to faster growth but also – because it is the tradeable sectors that will attract this investment – to lower borrowing and improved income distribution.

Notes

1 Consolidated public expenditure in Thailand consists of recurrent and capital expenditures of both central government and state enterprises. This differs from the conventional national accounts approach, which does not include the recurrent expenditures of state enterprises. FY77 covers the period October 1, 1976 to September 30, 1977.
2 A phased withdrawal of the American presence began in 1969, as conditions in southeast Asia began to change. By late July 1976, the last of the American air and naval units had departed from the region.
3 This policy had to be replaced by other measures to slow down rice shipments abroad after the country was badly hit by a drought (Bank of Thailand, 1977).
4 Protection increased from an average nominal level of 35 percent in 1974 to 51 percent in 1978 for products with little competition from imports (less than 10 percent of domestic production) and from 25 percent to 36 percent for goods competing with imports. Effective tariff rates increased from 39.7 percent in 1974 to 99.6 percent in 1978 for non-import-competing goods, and from 44.8 percent to 85.9 percent for import-competing goods.
5 Some of the data in this section come from World Bank (1980b) and from World Bank (1982c).
6 Manufacturing production growth recovered in 1981 (6.4 percent) but remained below earlier levels.
7 Access to external markets for several crops, however, allowed farmers to switch among upland crops in response to relative price changes, so they probably did better than indicated by the terms-of-trade index.
8 Not surprisingly, there is a concentration of wealth in central Thailand and in the capital, Bangkok. Bangkok's population rose from 3.2 million in 1970 to 4 million in 1978. Migration into Bangkok was 70,000 in 1973; 60,000 in 1974, 67,000 in 1975, and 92,000 in 1976. The 1970 census indicates that some 35 percent of Bangkok's population was born outside Bangkok (National Statistical Office, *Survey of Migration in Bangkok Metropolis*, annual publication, 1974–7).
9 This view is supported by several studies. See, for example, Sussangkarn (1983), from which many of the observations in this discussion are taken.
10 For a description of the methods used to track history, see chapter 4.
11 In fact, the goods that compete with imports as intermediate inputs are an aggregate of several sectors' output, but the weight of the intermediate-goods sector is by far the largest.
12 Sensitivity analysis in which this figure was reduced to 0.2 reveals that the result is quite robust. While the effect of reduction in land availability is about 50 percent greater, the deviation from the historical run is still miniscule. This is because the share of land in value added in agriculture is only about 6 percent.
13 Except for the elimination of transfers from US bases, we assume the foreign capital inflow remains unchanged in this experiment. In other words, we assume that Thailand's foreign borrowing would have been the same in the absence of

the two oil shocks. Since Thailand did not borrow from special oil facilities, this is not an unreasonable assumption.

14 For an alternative test, which reaches the same conclusion, see Kharas and Shishido (1986).

15 Note that the "closure rule" in this simulation is different from that in all other simulations reported in this chapter. By fixing total investment, we allow foreign savings to be endogenous. For details of the investment allocation rule adopted, see chapter 4.

8 "Overshooting" adjustment in a primary producing country: Kenya, 1973–82

1 Adjustment experience

Balance of payments

At the time of the first oil crisis Kenya's balance-of-payments situation was relatively weak. Small current-account deficits in the late 1960s had grown to over 5 percent of GDP by 1973 following a rapid expansion in government spending.[1] The private long-term capital flows of these years were inadequate to finance such deficits so the government, for the first time, had to borrow heavily from abroad. This crisis, as well as being associated with the end of price stability, also accelerated the process – already evident in the 1960s – of steadily expanding the range of commodities subject to import licensing, as well as of provoking the more stringent enforcement of exchange controls.

Since 1973, Kenya's balance-of-payments performance has been dominated by dramatic movements in the external terms of trade shown in figure 8.1a.[2] There was a 20 percent overall terms-of-trade deterioration between 1973 and 1975 largely associated with a doubling of overall import prices (mainly fuel); a 53 percent overall improvement between 1975 and 1977 largely associated with a 93 percent overall increase in export prices (mainly coffee); a 32 percent overall deterioration between 1977 and 1980 largely associated with a further 60 percent increase in import prices (again mainly fuel);[3] and a further but smaller deterioration thereafter. These movements were associated with correspondingly large swings in import quantities partly because of the quantity responses to varying import prices but, probably more important, because of the varying use of quantitative restrictions on imports. This result is evident from figure 8.1b, which also shows how relatively little movement there was in export quantities. It is also apparent from this figure that the "shock" associated with the 1976–7 coffee boom was at least as great as those shocks associated with the 1973–4 and 1979–80 rises in the price of imported fuels. The disaggregated analysis

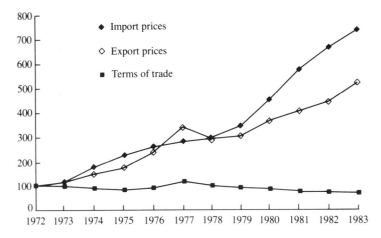

Figure 8.1a Terms of trade, 1972–83

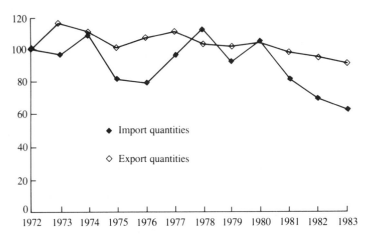

Figure 8.1b Trade quantities, 1972–83

of this phenomenon presented in chapter 3 suggested that it would probably have been difficult for the economy to sustain a coherent program of adjustment to the first oil crisis through the 1976–8 period even though the foreign exchange situation was clearly much easier.

The impact of these fluctuations on the balance of payments was to produce a further sharp deterioration of the current account in 1974, a recovery into modest surplus by 1977, a dramatic slide back into massive deficits in 1978–80 (averaging more than $500 million a year),[4] and the continuation of these through 1983. This period also witnessed a steady buildup of public borrowing from overseas, even during the coffee boom. This buildup accelerated alarmingly in 1978–80 (when net long-term borrowing reached nearly $300 million a year) as did short-term borrowing, which had previously been relatively moderate. External public debt (including undisbursed debt) stood at $3 billion by the end of 1980 and at $3.8 billion by the end of 1982; the debt-service ratio stood at 12 percent as compared with only 3 percent in 1973; and international reserves, in spite of the heavy borrowing, represented only two months of imports. In short, while sharp procyclical swings of import quantities in 1973–80 were one response to the external shocks, they were not adequate to achieve a full balance-of-payments adjustment. On the contrary, the current-account deficit as well as the rate of growth of dependence on external debt both reached levels that confronted Kenyan policy-makers with very serious problems in the 1980s.

Fiscal policy

Kenya's fiscal policy was generally expansionary but with substantial year-to-year variability.[5] Much of the instability can be traced to tax revenues, which benefited from increases in the prices of both exports and imports. In spite of an inelastic tax system, a series of discretionary tax adjustments (including the limited use of export duties to siphon off revenues from coffee and tea growers in 1977–8) served to maintain tax revenues as a high and rising share of GDP. The main vagaries were a 37 percent increase in nominal tax revenues in FY 1974 (July 1, 1973 through June 30, 1974), a 50 percent increase in FY 1978, and increases of about 20 percent in both FY 1980 and in FY 1981. Non-tax revenues also fluctuated. In most periods the movement of current expenditures followed that of revenues, albeit with a degree of dampening, and the consequence was the maintenance of a small but variable current budgetary surplus[6] at least until 1982, when rising interest charges pushed the account into deficit. However, with capital expenditures rising rapidly (although with occasional flat periods), the overall deficit on the budget became large. By the late 1970s it was averaging about 6 percent of GDP, compared with less than 4 percent in the 1960s. In the early 1980s the average was closer to 10 percent, as figure 8.2 shows.

The various pressures on the government that accounted for the inexorable rise in spending largely ruled out the active use of fiscal policy to help achieve macroeconomic stability.[7] These pressures included a massive increase in the needs of the defense budget (more than 4 percent of GDP in the mid 1980s compared with 1.5 percent in the mid 1970s),[8] large budgetary outlays associated with the establishment of independent Kenyan corporations following the disintegration of the East African

Table 8.1 *Final demand relative to 1976 levels (in 1976 prices)*

	1973	1976	1978	1980	1982
Private consumption	0.972	1.0	1.21	1.26	1.32
Public consumption	0.770	1.0	1.30	1.38	1.38
Export of goods and non-factor					
services	0.96	1.0	1.05	1.05	1.01
Gross fixed capital formation	1.1	1.0	1.40	1.36	1.16

Source: World Bank (1982a), table 2.4.

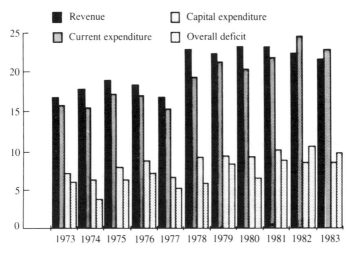

Figure 8.2 Government finances (percentage of nominal GDP)

Community in 1977; a rapid growth in spending for education (a fifth of the total budget), associated with substantial progress in raising school enrollment rates and eliminating school fees; and significant nominal and real increases in the costs of general public administration. In spite of these increases, however, there was still widespread concern that recurrent funds were not adequate for the full and efficient use of public investment projects (such as roads, water services, and agricultural services).

There is no evidence that the government used expenditure policy as a tool for managing short-term aggregate demand. However, government policies impinged upon levels of private-sector demand in several ways. Two of particular importance were monetary policy and wage policy. Before considering these, however, we review the shifts in the structure of aggregate demand as set out in table 8.1.

The contrasts here are very clear. Public consumption grew rapidly between 1973 and 1976 and then again between 1976 and 1978 but leveled off thereafter. Private consumption also grew rapidly from 1973 to 1978, although less so than public consumption; it became a more dynamic element in demand growth after 1978. In sharp contrast, fixed capital formation fell by almost 10 percent between 1973 and 1976, then rose extremely strongly to 1978 only to decline again. Stock building, not shown in the table, fell sharply in the period after the first oil crisis, but then rose even more sharply in the period of the coffee boom up to 1978 and again after 1979. It thus followed the movement of import quantities set out in figure 8.1b.

Monetary policy

Several factors help to explain the influence of monetary policy on the economy. First, the movements of the Kenyan money supply aggregates in the 1970s were dominated by large changes in foreign reserves associated with the volatile balance-of-payments situation already described. Since, in general, the authorities did not seek to sterilize these changes, money supply movements were extremely erratic,[9] yet they convey little information about the underlying stance of monetary policy. Second, the rate of growth of domestic credit, which is a sounder indication of monetary tightness or ease than the money supply in these circumstances, was managed in an expansionary fashion, but in most years the expansion was not excessive.[10] Only in three years (1975, 1978, and 1981), was the growth of domestic credit significantly higher than could be justified by the underlying growth of the economy and the world inflation rate. In each case this was associated with a rapid growth of lending to the public sector.[11] Thus only in these years can monetary policy as such be identified as a key influence on monetary growth. Third, monetary growth itself demonstrates a close, albeit lagged, relationship with private spending. For example, the fall in the rate of monetary expansion during 1973–4 (associated with reserve losses) was associated with a significant fall in aggregate private demand one year later. Similarly, the large rise in monetary growth between 1974 and 1977 (associated with reserve gains as well as with rapid credit growth in 1975) followed by a fall in that growth between 1977 and 1980 mostly associated with reserve losses seem to have contributed respectively to a sharp rise in private spending between 1975 and 1978 and a drop in private spending in 1977–9.

As Ahamed and Branson (1983) point out, a change in the money supply in Kenya may appear to have had somewhat unusual effects on prices and inflation. This is because a loss of reserves resulted in lower monetary growth, which in turn reduced excess demand and inflationary pressures. But to the extent that the standard trade policy response to the loss of reserves was a tightening of the availability of import licenses, inflationary pressures were increased from the cost side. Depending on the relative strength of these two opposing forces, slower monetary growth may be accompanied by higher or lower inflation. Obviously in those three years when credit was the main influence on monetary expansion, a more traditional link between money and inflation is to be expected.

Two principal conclusions emerge from this analysis. First, in the majority of years when domestic credit policy was largely neutral, monetary movements and their apparent "effects" on private spending can probably be regarded as merely a manifestation of the effects of the varying availability of foreign exchange and imports on those expenditures; that is to say, monetary policy as such was not exerting an analytically separate effect. Second, in the three years when credit policy deviated from its largely neutral stance, it spurred expansion and thereby exacerbated the effects coming from expansionary fiscal policy. In none of the years between 1973 and 1980 did the authorities appear to have attempted to impose significant credit crunches on the private sector in terms of either the availability of credit or its price. Most interest rates were kept low, and it was only in 1983 that the real interest rates on deposits generally became positive.

Wage policy

The authorities relied much more significantly for their management of private demand on wages policy. It is already well documented (see Ahamed and Branson, 1983) that after 1973 Kenya was unusually successful in engineering a significant fall in real wages as the demand for labor fell in response to the supply effects coming from more expensive oil. This in turn was attributable to a system of collective bargaining that, until 1979, established relatively long-term employment contracts with no provision for indexation. Thus, as inflation accelerated (from 9 percent in $1972-3^{12}$ to 18 percent in 1973–4), the nominal rigidity of wages generated large reductions in real product wages – this is, nominal wages deflated by an output deflator. This decline was stabilized but not reversed during the subsequent boom in coffee and tea prices after 1976. The consequence was that formal sector employment, a considerable part of which would have been subject to government policies on fixing wage guidelines, grew at a significant albeit decelerating rate through the second half of the 1970s and into the 1980s. Jobs in the modern sector (admittedly only 14 percent of total employment in Kenya) were consequently not a major victim of the various oil crises.

Two additional factors may have played a role in permitting the acceptance of the major decline in real wages and the associated growth in employment. First, it seems probable that, at the outset of the period, wages in the formal sector significantly exceeded the effective supply price of labor. Second, the movement of the internal terms of trade against agriculture as a result of exchange-rate policies and the increased protection of manufactures helped to hold down consumer prices and ensure that wages, deflated by the consumption price index, fell less rapidly than real product wages. It seems clear, however, that the inability of these trends to continue in the long run, as well as a more assured indexation of wages since 1979, was likely to have resulted in significant changes in labor-market responses to disturbances in the 1980s.

Exchange-rate policy

A final element of the policy package concerns the exchange rate. Until 1974 when the Kenyan shilling was pegged to the dollar, the variations in the exchange value of the dollar caused some large unplanned variations in the effective exchange rate against the currencies of trading partners. After the 1974 devaluation, this problem was partly avoided by the pegging to the SDR. Between 1974 and 1980, the nominal exchange rate against a trade-weighted basket of currencies drifted down by about 14 percent – a trend accelerated by a further discrete devaluation in 1981. Relative to the US dollar (the relevant currency from the viewpoint of assessing the effects of variations in oil prices), the movement of the nominal exchange rate was much more erratic. Depreciation between 1974 and 1976 gave way to a 12 percent appreciation between 1976 and 1980 and then to a depreciation of approximately 17 percent in 1981. In real terms the exchange rate appreciated for much of the 1970s even when calculated against a trade-weighted basket of other currencies. Between 1973 and 1976, for example, there was an appreciation of over 7 percent; there was also a small appreciation after 1979. Not all of these movements were appropriate to the circumstances, and some of them help to explain why export quantity growth was so poor during the 1970s. However, the discrete adjustments of the rate in 1974 and again in 1983 did move in the right direction.

Summary

At the risk of some oversimplification, we conclude this section by briefly summarizing the Kenyan policy approach to adjustment. The main response to the considerable terms-of-trade volatility of the 1970s was a variation in quantitative controls on imports which, together with certain other influences, generated considerable variability in import quantities during this period. As the application of the model of chapter 4 to the Kenyan experience will show, this also resulted in major variability in the supply price of imports. The adjustments to aggregate demand, which were associated with variations in the terms of trade and in disposable income, were mostly borne by private demand and especially by investment. Government expenditures by contrast exerted a consistently expansionary influence on the economy and, therefore, accounted for an increasingly large part of total aggregate demand. This was achieved partly through a series of discretionary tax adjustments, which injected considerable buoyancy into tax revenues. With a few notable exceptions, monetary expansion was not a dominant source of public-sector financing. Instead, residual financing was achieved through a rapid buildup of external public debt, which became less and less sustainable.

The policy influences affecting levels of aggregate demand in the private sector were relatively few. Although there is evidence of a statistical relationship between rates of monetary expansion and levels of private expenditure, this does not reflect any real attempt on the part of the monetary authorities to influence demand through active use of monetary policy. On the contrary, most of the movements of the monetary aggregates during this period arose from the authorities' passive response to large changes in foreign reserves. A more significant policy influence on demand was exerted by wage policy. But here too the results which we have observed can be construed to have derived from a relatively passive response on the part of the authorities. The juxtaposition of a sharp acceleration of inflation at the time of the first oil crisis with an existing institutional mechanism for wage fixing designed for non-inflationary circumstances, permitted a sharp once-and-for-all reduction in real product wages between 1973 and 1976. This was extremely useful in permitting the maintenance and expansion of modern-sector employment. But it is not a device which could have been expected to achieve similar results in the future, although substantial further falls in real wages, in both the private and public sectors, did occur after 1981.

2 Tracking history

Results

The results of tracking the model of chapter 4 over the years 1973 to 1982 are set out in figures 8.3–8.7, one for each of the five tracking variables for which data were readily available: total value added (GDP at factor cost), private consumption, total exports, total imports, and, for some runs of the

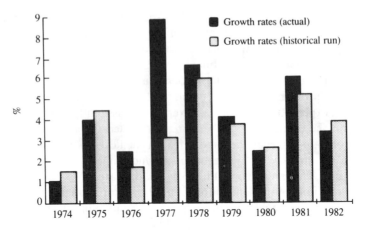

Figure 8.3 Historical run: value added

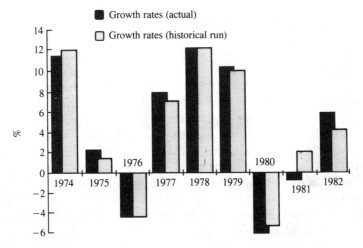

Figure 8.4 Historical run: private consumption

model, wage employment.[13] It will be seen that the model is successful at tracking the general movement of total value added (figure 8.3) and succeeds in picking up most of the big swings during the period (for example, 1976 compared with 1975 and 1981 compared with 1980). But it does not capture the extremely large rise in the growth rate in the coffee boom year of 1977. By contrast the tracking of private consumption (figure 8.4) is extremely close, with all the sharp changes in 1975, 1976, 1977, 1978, 1980, and 1982 captured remarkably well. This is also true of the import series (figure 8.5), which tracks the extremely volatile movements over the

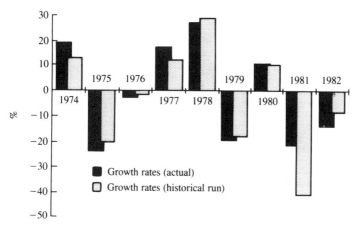

Figure 8.5 Historical run: imports

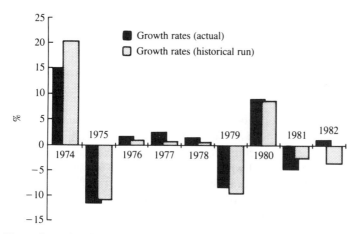

Figure 8.6 Historical run: exports

period 1973–80. The sharp downward movement in imports after the first oil price hike in 1975 is captured quite clearly, as is the downward movement caused by the second oil price hike in 1981, the rise caused by the coffee and tea boom in 1977/8, and the further rise associated with the 1979/80 drought. The historical run also captures the downturn of imports in 1981 and 1982, although it does not track the magnitude of the dip particularly closely.

The export series, as we noted earlier, is far less volatile than the import series. Nonetheless, the performance of the model in capturing the flatness of the export series in 1976–8 as well as the occasional big movements such as that in 1975 is encouraging (see figure 8.6). The errors in imports and

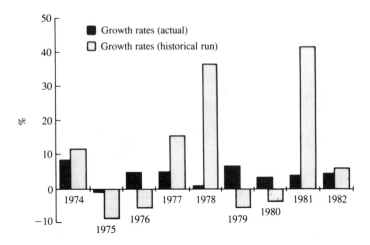

Figure 8.7 Historical run: wage employment

exports are of course linked since an underprediction of exports will generate some boost in the domestic cost of imports (through a higher premium on import licenses) and so push down the predicted level of imports. This factor seems to have been of some significance in both 1981 and 1982.

It will be recollected (for details, see chapter 4) that urban wage rates are indexed to the consumer price index, leading to a one-for-one spillover into the market for the urban self employed and a flexible wage to clear the latter market. The returns to rural wage and self-employed labor relate to the corresponding urban rates by way of fixed differentials; unlike in the urban areas, rural labor is not assumed to be fully employed. In early runs of the model a small weight was given to wage employment in the objective function used to solve for the tracking parameter. It proved extremely difficult, however, to achieve the convergence of the model for the years around 1979 so, for most purposes, wage employment was abandoned as a tracking variable. This partly accounts for the poor tracking performance of this variable indicated in figure 8.7. It should also be noted, however, that the year-by-year data on wage employment are probably not very reliable. In addition, since wage employment represents only a small part of total employment, the percentage changes shown in figure 8.7 are necessarily very sensitive to changes elsewhere.

Import substitution in the historical run

Chapter 3 established that there was a significant restraint on imports between 1973 and 1976 and again between 1978 and 1980 without,

Table 8.2 *Value of import licensing premium, 1973–82*

Year	Percent
1973	25.00
1974	none
1975	5.29
1976 (base year)	none
1977	none
1978	1.72
1979	22.37
1980	none
1981	none
1982	25.00

however, identifying the mechanism that brought this about. Since the general equilibrium model explicitly incorporates premium rationing of fuel imports, it is useful to look at the premium on import licenses generated by the model, the value of which fluctuates in the manner shown in table 8.2.

The main features of this series are the significant value of the premium in 1973, the absence of any premium rationing in 1976 and 1977, and the considerable fluctuations between 1978 and 1982, with high premia in both 1979 and 1982. Although 1974 was a year when the impact of the oil price increase might have been expected to show up most dramatically, this effect was in reality muted by a large increase in external borrowing and by some increase in export prices. Thus adjustment in this narrow short-term sense was successful, and the economy sustained no serious decline in either imports or consumption. A far larger increase in the premium, and an associated fall in imports (figure 8.5), was sustained in 1975 when both foreign borrowing and export prices declined slightly relative to their 1974 level. Similarly, although the larger part of the coffee and tea price boom occurred in 1977, this effect was muted by an actual fall in external borrowing that year. So, although imports rose strongly in 1977, this was more a consequence of an income effect than of any marked drop in the relative prices of imports. They rose more markedly in 1978, when external borrowing also rose to over $240 million – indeed, so much so that, in spite of the large borrowing, a small licensing premium on imports emerged. The subsequent severe tightening for foreign exchange availability in 1979 was associated with some decline in export volumes, a lower level of external borrowing, and some increase in import prices. These conspired to push up the licensing premium quite sharply. However, the very large increase in

Table 8.3 *The evolution of cost structures in consumer-goods production, 1973–82 (share of total output)*

Year	Value added	Wage labor	Self-employed labor	Capital	Domestic intermediate goods	Imported intermediate goods
1973	0.188	0.073	0.013	0.102	0.671	0.141
1974	0.180	0.075	0.011	0.103	0.663	0.147
1975	0.187	0.075	0.013	0.099	0.676	0.138
1976	0.187	0.075	0.012	0.100	0.680	0.121
1977	0.188	0.075	0.011	0.102	0.669	0.143
1978	0.189	0.072	0.016	0.101	0.674	0.138
1979	0.189	0.072	0.016	0.100	0.685	0.127
1980	0.191	0.076	0.011	0.104	0.673	0.136
1981	0.197	0.075	0.012	0.110	0.680	0.121
1982	0.198	0.075	0.013	0.110	0.680	0.121

import prices in 1980 was associated with an actual fall in the licensing premium because once again it was matched by large external borrowing ($280 million) and continued favorable export prices. The consequences of higher oil prices really made themselves felt only in 1981 and 1982, when they were complemented by lower export prices as well as by lower external borrowing. Hence in both of these years imports fell sharply (see figure 8.5).

The sectoral implications of import substitution may be illustrated with reference to the manufacturing subsectors. The results in table 8.3 and 8.4 show a degree of stability in the coefficients which, given the volatility of relative prices characterizing the period, reflects assumptions about elasticities of substitution chosen in the model *a priori*. Nonetheless, certain trends are obvious. In particular, both sectors show a significant trend toward import substitution, with the ratio of imported intermediates to output falling from 0.141 to 0.121 in the case of consumer goods and from 0.258 to 0.226 in the case of intermediate goods. This is matched mainly by a large rise in the share of domestic intermediate inputs. The evidence from the two tables is that relative price movements, including those coming from the licensing premium, were adequate to reduce substantially the value of imports relative to output as well as their volumes. However, as the partial equilibrium results of chapter 3 indicated, this effect was far from being evenly sustained over time. In the case of consumer-goods production in particular, it is clear that during the coffee and tea boom there was substantial negative import substitution, which raised the share of

Table 8.4 *The evolution of cost structures in intermediate-goods production (share of total output)*

Year	Value added	Wage labor	Self-employed labor	Capital	Domestic intermediate goods	Imported intermediate goods
1973	0.326	0.150	0.013	0.162	0.416	0.258
1974	0.325	0.157	0.012	0.156	0.424	0.250
1975	0.325	0.156	0.014	0.155	0.425	0.250
1976	0.325	0.152	0.012	0.160	0.425	0.227
1977	0.325	0.154	0.011	0.159	0.421	0.254
1978	0.324	0.140	0.016	0.169	0.419	0.257
1979	0.328	0.146	0.017	0.166	0.431	0.241
1980	0.327	0.150	0.011	0.166	0.426	0.247
1981	0.334	0.151	0.012	0.171	0.439	0.227
1982	0.336	0.143	0.012	0.181	0.437	0.226

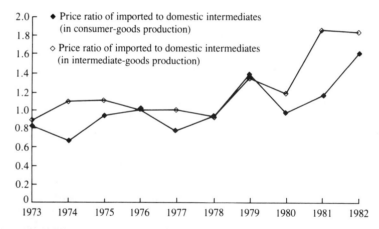

Figure 8.8 Relative prices of imported and domestic intermediates

imported intermediates to a level higher than that before the 1974 oil shock (table 8.3). In the case of intermediate goods, this effect is also apparent (table 8.4). The underlying relative price movements, i.e., of imported intermediate goods to domestic intermediate goods are shown in figure 8.8. The rise in the relative price of imported intermediates for consumer goods that occurred after 1974 was substantially reversed by 1977. But in 1979 and again in 1981 and 1982, price movements once more signaled the need

Table 8.5 *The evolution of cost structures in capital goods production, 1973–82 (shares of total output)*

Year	Imported element	Domestic element
1973	0.274	0.726
1974	0.297	0.703
1975	0.270	0.730
1976	0.268	0.732
1977	0.284	0.716
1978	0.247	0.753
1979	0.227	0.773
1980	0.225	0.775
1981	0.276	0.724
1982	0.291	0.709

to shift away from imported supplies. In the case of intermediate-goods production, the rise in the relative price of imported supplies was rather more consistent from 1976 onwards.

Finally, the clear-cut trend of import substitution for intermediate goods is not matched by a similar trend in final capital goods (the only category of final imports modeled as an endogenous variable). Table 8.5 shows that, although there were periods when the import share of the total value of capital goods delivered declined (as in 1977 to 1980), these drops have been matched by equally large increases in subsequent periods, so that overall there is a greater import intensity of capital investment at the end of the period than at the beginning. In this case, the assumed low elasticity of substitution between domestically produced and imported capital goods has significantly restricted the ability of the economy to side-step the effects of fluctuating world prices by means of import substitution.

The variability of the import licensing premium suggested by the model also gets manifested in significant variation in both total incomes and in the factorial distribution of incomes. For example, in 1973 the income from the premium was equivalent to 7.2 percent of value added as compared to zero and 2.2 percent in 1974 and 1975, respectively. By 1979 it was the equivalent of almost 14 percent of value added. Since the model attributes all such income to capital, swings of this order of magnitude have a profound effect on income distribution. In 1979, for example, the factorial distribution of income gave capital a 28.2 percent share as against 20.6 percent in the base year and 19.5 percent in the preceding year.

As an interim conclusion we can note that, although the Kenyan authorities seem to have had some success in neutralizing the immediate domestic price impact of the more severe terms-of-trade shocks (oil in 1974 and 1980 and coffee and tea in 1977), these successes are distinctly qualified for three reasons. First, in some years such as 1974, Kenya seems to have seriously overcompensated for the disturbance by borrowing far more than was required and allowing very large increases in consumption and imports (see figures 8.4 and 8.5). Second, those influences which are partly under government control (such as foreign borrowing) seem, in general, to have delayed the effects of the shocks in time rather than helped adjust to them: the experiences of 1974/5 and 1980/1 are examples. Third, exogenous export price movements helped neutralize or exacerbated the shocks in certain years.

3 Policy simulations

This section turns to some counterfactual policy simulations designed to explore the implications of different external conditions and policy responses. Specifically, the model is used to answer the following questions.

(1) How would the economy have evolved during the period 1976–82 in the absence of (i) the 1979–80 oil price shock and (ii) the coffee boom of 1977–8, and with a "normal" volume of foreign borrowing in the 1970s?
(2) What would have been the impact of allocating the economy's actual volume of investment across sectors in response to considerations of short-run profitability?
(3) What contribution would domestic resource mobilization need to have made in order to support historical levels of investment with a more conservative borrowing strategy?
(4) What improvements in economic performance would have resulted from a more rapid expansion of land available for agricultural purposes?

Simulation 1 Reducing terms-of-trade disturbances
The first simulation, which is run for 1976–82, is designed to assess how much of the variability in Kenya's economic performance during that period can be ascribed directly to the two major external shocks that occurred – the coffee and tea boom in 1977–8 and the second oil shock in 1979–80.[14] To remove these shocks two assumptions are made:

That the prices of intermediate imports maintain the same trend of growth in 1976–82 as in 1972–5. This has the effect of knocking out the oil shock;

That agricultural export prices change over 1976–82 at the same rate as do the prices of intermediate imports. This has the effect of knocking out the coffee and tea boom.

The prices of minority items of exports and final imports are allowed to evolve at the same rate as in the historical run. Government expenditure and tax rates are also held at their historical run levels so that, in these areas, the simulation reflects an unchanged policy package. However, in recognition of the fact that variations in Kenya's external borrowing after 1975 were probably strongly conditioned by terms-of-trade movements (with the coffee and tea boom increasing the potential supply of new borrowing and the oil price hike increasing the potential demand), the net volume of borrowing was set constant at $90 million, which is a crude estimate of Kenya's "normal" annual foreign borrowing for the 1970s. The model was also run with investment determined endogenously so as to abstract from the large swings caused by the external shocks.

The main result of the simulation is that fixed capital formation increases over the historical year value in every year but one by an average of 14 percent. The exception is 1978, which was in any case the peak year for investment in the historical run. The generally improved level of investment means that the economy ends the period with a substantially higher productive potential and that the output generated during the period of the simulation is also significantly higher than in the historical run. It is the higher output potential as well as the higher level of actual output that represent the major gains from eliminating the terms-of-trade shocks.

These gains, however, are not evenly distributed. Insofar as sectoral output is concerned, the capital-goods sector easily enjoys the largest gain in production – an average of 11 percent a year – while the agricultural and service sectors enjoy much smaller gains – an average of 0.8 percent and minus 3.2 percent, respectively. This is the consequence of the substantial rises in investment relative to other categories of demand in most periods (see figure 8.9). This might be interpreted as a degree of urban bias in the gains that arise, but in fact that is not the case. In all years, other than 1978, the results of the simulation suggest a fall in the share of urban households in the total of household income by 3.5 percent, for example, in 1982. This is explained by the fact that the share of capital-goods industries in total value added is quite small (5.2 percent in 1976) while several of the sectors benefiting least from the increased growth of output, such as infrastructural goods, are also urban based.

As for the pattern of demand, it is noteworthy that the absence of external shocks makes possible substantial increases in imports relative to the historical run in several years, especially 1979, 1981, and 1982. This is

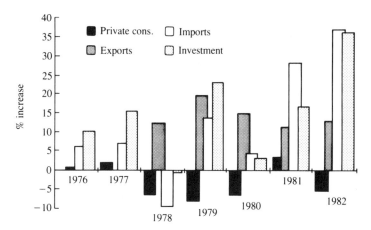

Figure 8.9 Simulation 1: increases in elements of demand relative to historical run

clearly indicated in figure 8.9. The peaked pattern to imports in 1977–80 is not eliminated, but it is flattened out substantially while the severity of the import cutbacks in both 1981 and 1982 is very much moderated. This flattening process is further helped by a 9 percent fall in import volumes relative to the historical run in 1978, the peak year for imports. While the volume changes of imports are partly induced by quantity changes associated with generally higher output, more important are the relative price changes which, in simulation 1, are generally in favor of imports. This has generated quite a substantial increase in the relative dependence on those imports which the model specifies as price sensitive. For example, in 1982 the share of imported intermediate goods used in producing consumer and agricultural goods is 18 percent and 20 percent respectively, compared with 10 percent and 13 percent in the historical run. Similar increases are observed for the other four sectors.

The increased import capacity of the economy, in spite of lower borrowing in some years, is also partly attributable to increased export volumes. As figure 8.9 indicates, there were substantial percentage increases in export volumes relative to the historical run in all years from 1978 through 1982, averaging about 14 percent a year. These improvements are attributable in turn to the downward-sloping demand schedule for exports assumed in the model and to the relative drop in export selling prices.

Finally, the combination of increased GDP in most periods, the other demand changes that have been described, and the assumed constancy of government consumption at historical levels causes private consumption to follow a somewhat uneven path over the period. As figure 8.9 indicates, it

240 Adjustment in a primary producing country: Kenya

falls relative to its historical run level in four of the eight years covered by
the simulation. Yet private consumption grows at a satisfactory rate of
between 3 and 13 percent in all but two years, with the drops occurring the
same two years, 1980 and 1982, when GDP fell relative to the historical run.
The first of these was a year of exceptionally high external borrowing ($280
million), and the dip to the assumed level of $90 million appears to be rather
more than the economy can tolerate. In contrast, in 1978 when borrowing
was also high ($240 million), private consumption, although below its
peak, still grows more than 3 percent over the previous year.

The main conclusion to be drawn from simulation 1 is that the Kenyan
economy would have benefited in several respects if neither the coffee and
tea boom nor the 1979–80 oil shock had ever happened. The aggregate of
production over the period would certainly have been higher; the terminal
capital stock to produce output growth in the future would also have been
enhanced. In spite of gross external borrowing of $540 million spread
evenly over the six years of the simulation, compared with some $1 billion
in reality, the import capacity of the economy would have been higher in
every year except 1978. Export volumes would also have been higher in all
the later years. No obvious deterioration in the distribution of income
undercuts this catalogue of benefits and, although private consumption
would have been lower in several years, it would nonetheless have
manifested a satisfactory rate of increase. Furthermore, it seems likely that
a marginal upward adjustment in external borrowing or a marginal
downward adjustment in government consumption (both of which variables are fixed exogenously for the purposes of this simulation) could have
ensured a somewhat more favorable outcome for private consumption.

Finally, in spite of the generally more placid external environment
assumed by simulation 1, the economy itself continues to manifest a
considerable degree of volatility. This is clear from figures 8.10 through
8.13, which show the evolution of the four main tracking variables of the
model. The volatility of value added as indicated by the standard deviation
(3.44) is higher than in the historical run (1.45). This is most probably
explained by the volatility of exogenous variables not amended as a part of
the simulation – especially government consumption, stock changes,
certain categories of exports and imports, and non-capital transfers from
abroad. In the case of private consumption, the simulation produces some
slight moderation of the extreme movements otherwise observed around
the coffee boom years but, if anything, it accentuates the swings thereafter.
Imports do reflect the more placid external environment to a far greater
extent, the dramatic swings of 1978 and 1981 both being substantially
moderated by the simulation. This effect is less marked in the case of

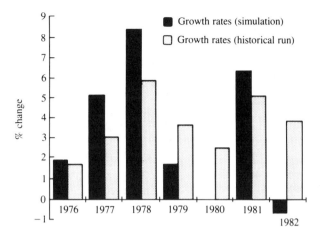

Figure 8.10 Simulation 1: value added

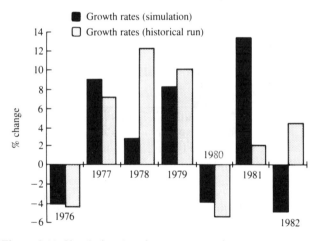

Figure 8.11 Simulation 1: private consumption

exports because the historical run series is itself extremely flat. However, the radical improvement in export volumes in 1978, as shown in figure 8.13, is particularly striking. The results overall certainly indicate that there were many other influences on the volatility of the economy besides the terms-of-trade shocks which simulation 1 removes.

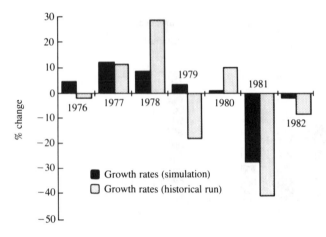

Figure 8.12 Simulation 1: imports

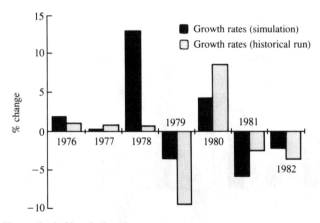

Figure 8.13 Simulation 1: exports

Simulation 2 Reallocating investment

Reflecting rigidities in the system actually used in Kenya, the historical run allocates values of total fixed investment in each year to sectors proportionally to the 1976 sectoral shares of total capital. The figures in table 8.6, which provide simple average sectoral rates of return for the first four and the last four years of the study period, show a significant relative tightening in the availability of capital but not in a manner that was spread evenly across sectors.[15] The most serious tightening in the availability of capital is in relation to capital goods, with a rate of return 3.3

Table 8.6 *Sectoral rates of return on capital 1973–6 and 1979–82*
(*percent*)

	Average 1973–6	Base year 1976	Average 1979–82
Consumer goods	22.2	21.4	30.9
Capital goods	6.3	7.7	21.1
Intermediate goods	17.1	19.7	34.1
Infrastructure goods	7.7	7.3	11.3
Services	10.5	11.0	9.0

times higher in the second period than in the first, and intermediate goods, where it is almost twice as high. It is noteworthy that the relative position of consumer goods eases considerably. The rates of return, in the case of capital-goods production, were strongly correlated with swings in aggregate investment; these cause far larger changes in that sector's derived demand for capital than in the supply made available to it. So, when fixed investment slumped in 1974–6, the rate of return for capital-goods production fell to an average of only 6.3 percent, implying a substantial relative price fall. By contrast, when investment was booming in 1978–9 the average rose to well over 20 percent, implying a substantial relative price rise. Although the variability in other capital-using sectors is less than this, there was a major upsurge in the rate of return in the intermediate-goods sector in 1978–80 to an average of about 35 percent.

Simulation 2 attempts to analyze these tendencies further by replacing the constant proportions method of allocating investment sectorally, which is used in the historical run, by an allocation scheme related to sectoral rates of return. This also provides a better approximation to a market basis of allocation.[16]

The results are summarized in table 8.7. The standard deviations of rates of return shown in the last column indicate two things. First, the counterfactual policy simulation consistently finds solutions involving a lower variance of rates of return than does the historical run. Second, the tendency for the variance of rates of return to increase over time in the historical run contrasts with a tendency for the variance to lessen in the simulation. The results are particularly striking in 1979 when the standard deviation of rates of return is only 2.9 in the simulation but almost 10 in the historical run. Of particular interest is the ability of the new solution to take the pressure off capital availability in intermediate-goods production, where the rate of return on capital falls from over 40 percent to 21.2 percent

Table 8.7 Simulation 2: Sectoral rates of return on capital (percent)

	Consumer goods	Capital goods	Intermediate goods	Infrastructure	Services	Standard deviation
1976-HR	21.4	7.7	19.7	7.3	11.0	6.69
-Simulation	13.6	4.5	11.8	7.3	12.9	3.94
1977-HR	30.7	8.7	22.5	8.0	13.2	9.77
-Simulation	18.8	4.9	12.9	8.4	16.6	5.72
1978-HR	24.4	18.8	36.3	12.0	9.7	10.91
-Simulation	14.5	9.9	19.8	14.5	14.2	3.51
1979-HR	26.0	29.2	30.6	11.1	10.5	9.85
-Simulation	14.6	11.4	19.1	16.2	13.7	2.87
1980-HR	38.4	25.8	40.3	14.6	11.9	13.10
-Simulation	18.0	10.3	21.2	20.8	19.4	4.45
1981-HR	34.8	15.4	29.3	8.8	8.6	12.04
-Simulation	15.5	7.7	15.7	14.9	18.1	3.93
1982-HR	24.3	14.1	36.4	10.7	5.0	12.41
-Simulation	12.2	6.4	14.9	15.1	12.6	3.52

Note: HR = historical run.

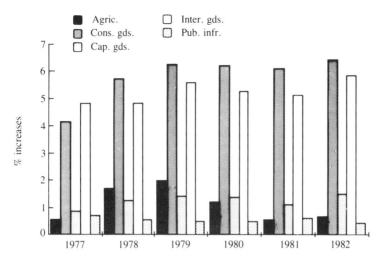

Figure 8.14 Simulation 2 – increases in gross output relative to historical run

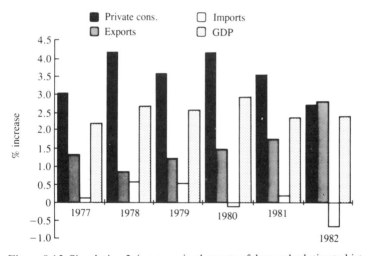

Figure 8.15 Simulation 2: increases in elements of demand relative to historical run

in 1980. Since sectors 2, 3, and 4 are combined in the simulation, similar beneficial effects also apply to consumer-goods and capital-goods production.

Considerable benefits also arise from the improved investment allocation in terms of the economy's generation of output and income. These benefits are summarized for the period 1976–82 in figures 8.14 and 8.15. The first of these shows that, while all sectors receive some benefit, it is most marked for consumer and intermediate goods, sectors in which the problem of inadequate capital was earlier noted to be most acute. In these two sectors the gross output gains average 5.8 percent and 5.3 percent, respectively. In the other sectors including services, which is not shown in the figures, the gains average between 0.6 percent and 1.3 percent.

In the case of GDP and the elements of aggregate demand, figure 8.15 shows especially substantial gains relative to the historical run for private consumption (3.5 percent on average). Exports also benefit significantly from some reduction of prices, which results from the more efficient reallocation of investment; the average improvement compared with the historical run is 1.6 percent. By contrast, the simulation generates only minimal perturbations of the ratio of import to domestic prices and hence generates a negligible price stimulus to imports. The small increases in import volume which are observed come mainly from the effects of the general expansion of production. Aggregate foreign savings are 4.4 percent lower than in the historical run.

Simulation 2 differs from simulation 1 in that it holds investment constant at its historical run level. It thereby demonstrates the advantages that could have obtained solely from the reallocation of investment, without any increase in its total. Thus, although the future production potential of the economy is not enhanced in simulation 2 as in simulation 1, comparably large gains are available in the years covered by the simulation. In terms of gross output the average gain in simulation 2 relative to the historical run is 2.2 percent, compared with 2.3 percent in simulation 1. For value added the gains are 3.1 percent and 1.24 percent, respectively. The conclusions indicate that, in relation to the output variable, avoidance of inefficiency in investment allocation would have been as beneficial to the economy as the avoidance of the terms-of-trade disturbances which characterized the period. It seems that there are no adverse distributional effects to set against this. In 1982, for example, the income share of rural smallholders is 40.6 percent in the simulation as against 40.2 in the historical run. The income share of rural households as a whole stands at 60.7 percent in the simulation as against 60.5 in the historical run.

Simulation 3 Improving resource mobilization
The third simulation examines the consequences for the economy of allowing flexibility in tax rates and government expenditures designed to promote a more stable evolution of fixed investment and external borrowing. It explores whether by some alteration of its fiscal position, the government could have made some adjustment to external shocks while at

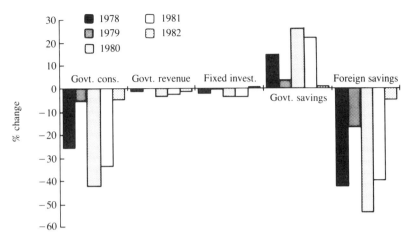

Figure 8.16 Simulation 3: changes in resource mobilization relative to historical run

the same time protecting fixed investment at its historical run level and restricting external borrowing to some "normal" level relative to fixed investment. More specifically, the ratio of fixed investment to GDP in this simulation is held constant at its historical run level while the ratio of external borrowing to investment is fixed at 35 percent, a crude approximation to its normal long-term level. To accommodate these constraints the model solves endogenously for a single parameter which represents the proportionate degree of adjustment applied to both government consumption and tax rates.

Results for this simulation have been obtained only for the period 1978 to 1982. The broad movements in the various elements of the resource allocation of the economy are summarized in figure 8.16. A large percentage decline in foreign borrowing is easily the major element of change in every year. This is accompanied by relatively large increases in government savings in most years. The main exception is 1982, when foreign borrowing decreased by less than 5 percent relative to the historical run and government saving increased only very slightly. The increases in government savings are less than might have been anticipated, since the simulation also indicates that GDP and, hence, fixed investment are generally lower than in the historical run. The fall in GDP and other elements of the tax base also means that, in spite of a tax rate increase every year, total government revenue falls relative to the historical run. Thus, all the burden of providing increased government savings falls on government consumption, which drops by an average of 22 percent a year relative to the

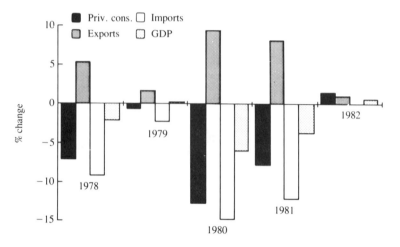

Figure 8.17 Simulation 3: changes in elements of demand relative to historical run

historical run. The dips are particularly large in 1978 and 1980, which were the years of greatest external borrowing in this period.

Figure 8.17 shows, among other things, that the combined effect of the various assumptions of the simulation is such as to reduce GDP, relative to the historical run, in most years: the main exception is 1982, where there is an increase of less than 1 percent. Apart from the deflationary effects of lower government expenditure, household incomes and thus private consumption are quite severely affected in some years. In the boom year of 1978, for example, private consumption is 7 percent lower than in the historical run, although it still shows a growth rate over the previous year of 4.4 percent. More serious, the years 1980 and 1981 – which were already poor years in terms of consumption growth – suffer further reductions of consumption of 12 percent and 7 percent, respectively. Clearly for 1978 the assumptions underlying the simulation make good sense and would not have caused undue hardship for the economy: growth rates of income and consumption would still have been high. In the oil shock years of 1980 and 1981, however, the reduced external borrowing which the simulation assumes and the increased efforts at public saving would have made little sense and would have inflicted considerable hardship. Recall, however, that total investment is maintained at historical run levels throughout the simulation.

In relation to foreign trade, the simulation suggests a substantial drop in imports in most years. This is the consequence largely of the quantity changes already discussed, since the relative prices of imports and import shares are affected only slightly in spite of some changes in the premium on import licenses: they are lower in 1978, 1979, and 1982 but marginally higher in 1980. Exports, by contrast, rise quite markedly in the three years when the effects of the simulation are most substantial – namely 1978, 1980, and 1981. This is as a result of lower domestic relative to world prices.

Simulation 4 Improving land availability[17]

The fourth simulation attempts to identify the improvements in economic performance associated with a far more rapid expansion of land available for agricultural purposes than is assumed in the historical run of the model. It sets the growth of land supply at 3 percent a year – close to the rate of population growth – as compared with the 0.5 percent a year assumed in the historical run. Since the data available to us on the actual increase in land for cultivation are limited, this experiment also provides some indication of the correctness or otherwise of the historical run assumption about land supply.

As was to be expected, a main result of this simulation is a somewhat faster trend rate of growth of output. By 1982, this faster growth produces a level of total GDP which is approximately 2.5 percent higher than in the historical run. Most of the improvement is associated with agricultural value added, which is almost 5 percent higher than in the historical run, but other sectors show modest induced increases as well. The lowering of the rate of return on land is very substantial but still not enough to balance the supply and demand of land at a price as low as in the base year.

The lowering of input prices consequent upon the greater availability of land results in only a very limited amount of substitution. Exports by 1982 are less than 1 percent higher than in the historical run, so there is very little scope for an enhanced level of imports; indeed, in several years, imports are slightly lower than in the historical run. However, the foreign exchange balance is achieved with somewhat different values of the import licensing premium, which means that changes in income and income distribution occur. In particular, in 1979 and 1981 – both years of considerable foreign exchange tightness – the situation, while remaining difficult, is nevertheless substantially eased by the greater availability of land. Similarly, in both 1978 and 1980 the relatively easy foreign exchange position is eased further.

As regards the distribution of income and consumption, the consequences of the greater availability of land, while of a significant order of magnitude in a few cases, are generally not sufficient to overturn the broad movements which are observable in the historical run. In the latter, for example, there is a substantial rise in the late 1970s in the income shares of both the urban poor and the urban rich. This rise continues to 1980 in the case of the former group and to 1979 in the case of the latter group, but thereafter the income share of the urban poor declines quite sharply – to a share below that established in the 1976 base year – while that of the urban rich rises further. The new assumption about land availability results in a modest slowing of the rise of both these income shares to the end of the 1970s; a significant further decline in the share of the urban poor (to 22.5 percent in 1982 as against 25.2 percent in the historical run); but to almost no further change in the income share of the urban rich.

By contrast, the historical run results for both rural household groups (smallholders plus landless and larger landholders) indicate a falling income share for the first group to 1979 and a rise thereafter, and the exact opposite movement for the larger landholders. Improving land availability substantially moderates the fall in the income share of smaller landholders to 1979 and intensifies the increase to a modest extent thereafter (in 1982 their share is 35.6 percent as against 35.4 percent in the historical run). However, the income share of the smallholders and the landless is still lower in 1982 than in the 1976 base year.

4 Conclusions

What can the policy simulations of this chapter reveal to us about Kenya's performance? First, the volatility of the country's experience over time as reflected in the solution values of, for example, the import licensing premium (see table 8.2) is explained as much by the responses to terms-of-trade disturbance as by the disturbances themselves. In particular, the timing of external borrowing seems to have delayed the effects of these shocks but, in some cases, with a degree of overcompensation. Certainly 1974 and 1980 were far less difficult years for the economy than might have been predicted simply on the basis of the large movements in import prices. In both cases, the increase in external borrowing and its subsequent reduction one year later were sufficient to shift the main effects of the oil shocks to 1975 and 1981, respectively (see also figure 8.5). While this may appear to be a criticism of the policies adopted by the authorities, the inherent difficulties in "getting it right" are readily confirmed by the counterfactual policy simulations. Even if the economy had not been subject to terms-of-trade shocks after 1976, it would nonetheless have manifested considerable year-to-year instability (see figures 8.10 to 8.13). In addition, any real pressures to adjust to the first oil price shock must have been substantially diluted by the pattern of circumstances which occurred between 1976 and 1980.

The results from simulation 1 indicate that the combination of import price and export price shocks imposed very considerable costs on the economy. In the absence of those shocks not only would the aggregate of production over the period studied have been higher, but the potential for future growth would also have been greater because of an increased volume of capital formation. Furthermore, all this would have been achieved with gross external borrowing of approximately half the actual magnitude and so with a very much lower debt-service burden at the end of the period. Admittedly consumption levels would have been reduced during four of the seven years studied, but, since these include the coffee boom years, when actual consumption growth was high, consumption would still have manifested satisfactory growth in most periods.

Although the problems facing the economy arose partly from external shocks and in this respect were beyond Kenya's control, the results indicate the potential benefits to be derived from sound economic management. In particular, the consequences of a more market-based process of investment allocation, as opposed to a rigid fixed approach based on proportions as assumed in the historical run, clearly demonstrates the superiority of the former. It is true that, in the absence of the necessary detailed research, the historical run assumptions about investment allocation in simulation 2 are rather stylized descriptions of the allocation process. Furthermore the experiment adopts but one of a variety of approaches to the reallocation of investment in response to differences in sectoral returns. However, since we do know that there were elements of rigidity in the approach actually used in Kenya, the results from simulation 2 are of considerable interest. They show that the output of most sectors, but especially consumer goods and intermediate goods, would have been substantially improved by a market-based approach to allocation with gains of 5–6 percent relative to the historical run. It is also of interest that both gross output and total value added would have been increased by a larger order of magnitude by adopting such an allocation than they would have been had the terms-of-trade shocks been removed. Furthermore, this could have happened without generating any obvious distributional problems.

Finally, while there are policies which, had they been employed, could have improved the performance of the economy, the results also indicate the limitations on such improvement. Simulation 3, which identifies a solution to the model in which fiscal adjustment is used to reduce external borrowing while at the same time insulating fixed investment from the effects of external shocks, shows that such an approach would involve considerable costs. In particular, the increase in public saving required by this alternative solution generates large reductions not only in government consumption but also in private consumption and total GDP. In some years, such as 1978 these reductions can be construed as sound countercyclical adjustments to what is otherwise a boom situation; this cannot be said, however, of the reductions brought about in 1980 and 1981. So a rigid investment and borrowing policy such as that invoked for simulation 3 is not to be recommended in general although it certainly would have been preferable to the policies actually followed in some years. In particular, the much expanded external borrowing in the boom year of 1978 seems to have made very little sense.

Notes

1 Ahamed and Branson (1983) emphasize the rise in public investment from 6.2 percent of GDP in 1970 to 9.0 percent in 1971 as one major cause of this deterioration.

2 The impact of weather conditions on agricultural production has also been important in some years. Ansu (1985) identifies the terms of trade as easily the most important of several balance-of-payments shocks.

3 All data are from World Bank (1982a).

4 Exogenous terms-of-trade changes are not a complete explanation of balance-of-payments movements. Killick et al. (1984) discuss alternative monetarist and structural explanations at some length.

5 Significant improvements in the budgetary balance after independence were associated with the conservative stance of James Gichuru, Finance Minister between 1962 and 1969. This conservatism was largely absent in the 1970s. See Killick et al. (1984).

6 Data from World Bank 1982, table 5.1. A temporary influence was the IMF Extended Facility negotiated in 1975.

7 A major policy statement of the government in 1975 (Sessional Paper No. 4 for 1975) indicated a serious intention to use fiscal policy as an instrument of stabilization. However, the intention was largely unfulfilled during the 1970s.

8 Ansu (1985) notes that half the increase in total government expenditure as a share of GDP from 1973 to 1982 was attributable to general administration and defense alone.

9 The annual change ranges from +47 percent in 1977 to −1.2 percent in 1980. We make no attempt here to explore the interesting question of the extent to which the structure of the Kenyan financial system would have permitted a more active use of monetary policy. However, the analysis in Killick et al. (1984) suggests only a very limited scope for this.

10 This statement is based on the simple model used by Ahmed and Branson (1983), namely "excess" $DCE = rc - p^* - y$, where DCE is domestic credit, c is the rate of growth of nominal domestic credit, r is the ratio of domestic credit to the money stock, p^* is the inflation rate in trading partners, y is the rate of growth of domestic output.

11 This conforms with the conclusion of Killick et al. (1984) that the fiscal years 1974/5, 1978/9, and 1980/1 were the only ones where deficit financing was large.

12 Data from the IMF's *International Financial Statistics*.

13 For a description of the methods used for tracking, see chapter 4. The key element of the underlying data base for the model is the social accounting matrix for 1976. See Allen and Hayden (1980).

14 Aspects of the coffee boom are analyzed in detail in Bevan, Collier, and Gunning (1987, 1989).

15 It may be noted that no significance attaches to the absolute values of any rate of return in any year and that only the movement of these values relative to some other price conveys information.

16 For details of the rule adopted, see chapter 4. The rule is applied to agriculture (sector 1), manufacturing (sectors 2–4), public infrastructure (sector 5), and services (sector 6). Investment continues to be allocated within manufacturing in the proportions corresponding to the historical run.

17 For this simulation only, the comparison between the tracking and counterfactual results relates to a slightly different version of the model from the one described before. This is not expected to influence the results very much.

9 Adjustment in an inward-oriented economy: Turkey, 1973–81

1 Introduction

The Turkish economy appeared to weather the first round of oil price increases successfully, and GDP growth averaged 7.6 percent in 1973–7 as compared to 6.0 percent in the decade 1963–73. However, this growth was achieved largely through increased foreign borrowing, and the current account swung from a surplus of 2.8 percent of GDP in 1973 – generated by a devaluation-induced export expansion and workers' remittance inflow – to a deficit of 6.1 percent in 1977. The second round of oil price increases found the economy far more vulnerable to external shocks: both the remittances and the markets for Turkish exports shrank, the increasing overvaluation of the lira exacerbated the foreign exchange shortage, and foreign lenders, concerned about default, were unwilling to increase their exposure. In 1978–81, Turkey was thus forced not only to adjust to current changes in world conditions, but also to undertake those adjustments that were called for by the first abrupt rise in oil prices but were then postponed by increasing external borrowing. GDP growth averaged less than 1 percent during these years and the economy underwent its most severe foreign exchange and economic crisis in the post-war period.

Turkey's performance raises a number of questions. Was the attempt to postpone adjustment by increasing its external borrowing doomed to failure, or was it a potentially successful strategy that was derailed by the second round of oil price increases and other exogenous events? Would more sensible economic policies in the first half of the 1970s have permitted Turkey to maintain its high rate of growth during the second half of the decade even with the external shocks? What were the implications of the drastic annual changes in real capital inflows? In what follows, we use the model of chapter 4 to shed light on these and related questions.

254

2 Adjustment experience

The legacy of a closed economy

An understanding of Turkey's response to the external shocks of the 1970s requires one to look at the broad outline of the country's development stategy in earlier decades. Throughout most of the post-war period, Turkey pursued an industrialization strategy emphasizing domestic production for domestic markets. This implied a habitual reliance on protective trade barriers to restrict the inflow of imports and to foster domestic, often state-owned, import-substituting industries.

Prior to 1973, the Turkish economy was less "open" than that of nearly every other middle-income country. In 1960, exports represented just 4.2 percent of GDP in Turkey; by 1977, this proportion had risen only to 5.6 percent. The corresponding averages for a group of a dozen other middle-income countries were 11.6 percent in 1960 and 18.5 percent in 1977 (Lewis and Urata, 1983). Imports were low as well, with the share of imports in GDP only 6.5 percent in 1960, 8.0 percent in 1970, and 12.3 percent in 1977, in comparison with middle-income country averages nearly twice as large.[1]

One legacy of this autarkic strategy was a pattern of boom-and-bust cyclical growth. Typically, a period of rapid inward-oriented industrial growth increased import demand, leading to a foreign exchange crisis, followed by a major devaluation and slowdown in growth. Three such episodes can be identified in the post-war period; they led to major devaluations in 1958, 1970, and 1979–80. In each case, the devaluations served to reduce the pronounced anti-export bias inherent in the import-substitution strategy. Although exports did respond favorably, the effects in 1958 and 1970 were only transitory. The government's subsequent exchange-rate policy failed to maintain the real depreciation that occurred, and incentives again moved against exports.

Turkey in 1973 was still benefiting from the 1970 devaluation. Exports had responded with a 30 percent annual growth (in dollar terms) over the 1970–3 period. An additional windfall accruing to the economy was the growth of workers' remittances, which rose from $273 million in 1970 to $1.2 billion in 1973. This unprecedented growth in foreign exchange earnings permitted increased imports as well as the accumulation of around $1.8 billion in foreign exchange reserves during 1970–3. As the pre-OPEC era ended, Turkey's prospects for continued rapid growth appeared good.

Postponing adjustment: 1973–7

In keeping with its traditional autarky, Turkey's response to the first oil price shock centered on policies designed to maintain growth and insulate

Table 9.1 *Turkey: structure and growth of GDP, 1973–81*

Economic indicator	Percentage composition			Growth rates		
	1973	1977	1981	1973–7	1977–81	1973–81
Total consumption	83.5	82.9	83.8	8.5	−1.6	3.3
Government	12.5	13.5	10.9	9.5	5.1	7.3
Private	71.0	69.4	72.9	8.4	−2.4	2.8
Total investment	20.0	24.4	19.4	14.0	−5.6	3.7
Government	7.9	12.5	12.0	19.8	−1.2	8.8
Private	12.1	11.9	7.4	9.1	−11.0	−1.5
Stock changes	−1.1	0.8	2.6	—	7.8	—
Exports	8.5	5.3	11.9	−3.7	n.a.	n.a.
Imports	−11.1	−13.5	−17.7	9.0	n.a.	n.a.
GDP	100.0	100.0	100.0	7.6	1.4	4.4
Value added in:						
Agriculture	21.5	20.9	21.3	6.8	1.8	4.3
Consumer goods	7.3	7.4	7.0	8.0	0.1	4.0
Capital goods	8.2	8.2	8.3	7.4	1.7	4.5
Intermediate goods and oil	9.3	10.1	9.6	9.9	−0.1	4.8
Infrastructure and services	43.4	44.0	45.7	8.0	2.3	5.1

Notes: n.a. = not available in sources.
Percentage composition figures are nominal shares; growth rates are in real terms.
Sources: World Bank (1982b, 1984).

the economy from the adverse changes in external conditions. Real GDP in 1973–7 grew at 7.6 percent per annum, an increase on the 6 percent growth achieved during the 1960s. As table 9.1 illustrates, this stemmed largely from the growth of investment. The annual growth rate of real fixed investment more than doubled from the 1968–72 period to reach 14.0 percent, with public investment increasing sharply from a 5.4 percent annual growth rate in 1968–72 to 19.8 percent in 1973–7.[2] The composition of investment, which emphasized the industrial sector and related infrastructure because of the industrialization policy, stayed largely unchanged. Although dramatic increases in production in the industrial and service sectors did occur, evidence of increased strains on the economy could be found in the declining efficiency of investment, as reflected in an increase in incremental capital-output ratios from 2.6 in 1968–72 to 3.8 in 1973–7 (Balassa, 1981). In contrast to the relative stability of the price level in the 1960s, inflation accelerated steadily during 1973–7 to reach an average of 20 percent annually. Total consumption grew at 8.5 percent a year. Although gross domestic savings grew at 8.8 percent annually in the 1973–7 period, it was not enough to finance the growth of investment, which was increasing at an even higher rate. Consequently, the investment–savings gap increased to 9.4 percent of GDP in 1977 from − 2.5 percent in 1972 and the very low net capital inflows of 1973 and 1974 were followed by a tremendous surge in foreign borrowing up to and including 1977. The resulting appreciation in the real exchange rate[3] was accompanied by a 3.7 percent per annum real decline in exports and an increase in the share of nominal imports in GDP from 11.1 percent in 1973 to 13.5 percent in 1977. Public-sector profligacy and heavy reliance on external resources during 1973–7 are important aspects of Turkey's performance to be analyzed later in this chapter.

The balance-of-payments situation reversed during the 1973–7 period. In 1973, while the balance of trade (goods and services) showed a deficit of $592 million, the substantial inflow of workers' remittances and net factor service income resulted in a $515 million current-account surplus. The subsequent rapid increase in imports illustrated in figure 9.1, coupled with a reduction in exports, increased the trade deficit to $3.9 billion in 1977 – a $4.5 billion reversal in just four years. The unfavorable balance of trade, together with a substantial decline in workers' remittances and net factor service income, led to a record high current-account deficit of $3.6 billion in 1977. To finance this deficit, the Turkish authorities relied on short-term international capital markets.

Table 9.2 shows the structure and growth of exports and imports according to the sectoral classification of the model used to analyze adjustment later in the chapter. In 1973, Turkey's exports consisted largely

Table 9.2 *Turkey: structure and growth of exports and imports, 1973–81 (based on value in US dollars)*

Sector	Percentage composition			Growth rate		
	1973	1977	1981	1973–7	1977–81	1973–81
Imports						
Agriculture	2.7	1.7	1.3	15.2	2.6	8.7
Consumer goods	5.1	5.0	4.9	27.2	10.8	18.7
Capital goods	37.5	30.3	20.1	21.7	0.3	10.5
Intermediate goods	32.7	29.7	24.7	25.3	6.2	15.4
Petroleum	9.3	22.6	39.1	60.5	27.5	43.0
Infrastructure	2.0	1.5	1.9	20.2	17.1	18.6
Services	10.8	9.3	8.0	23.7	7.0	15.0
Total	100.0	100.0	100.0	28.4	11.1	19.4
Growth in import prices				14.3	15.7	14.9
Exports						
Agriculture	20.9	24.0	21.7	12.9	23.2	18.0
Consumer goods	42.7	34.8	33.5	3.6	25.2	13.9
Capital goods	0.2	1.0	3.5	72.1	71.7	71.9
Intermediate goods	6.3	9.2	12.2	19.8	35.6	17.5
Petroleum	3.0	0.0	1.6	—	—	8.9
Infrastructure	4.8	9.7	6.1	29.9	12.9	21.1
Services	22.0	21.3	21.3	8.1	26.5	16.9
Total	100.0	100.0	100.0	9.0	26.4	17.4
Growth in export prices				15.2	3.6	9.1

Sources: World Bank (1982b, 1984).

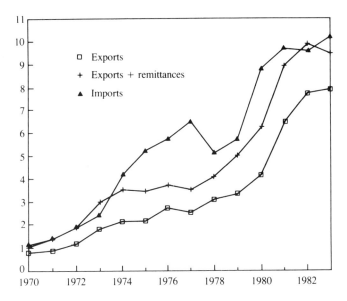

Figure 9.1 Trade and remittances, 1970–83 (billions of US dollars)

of food and livestock and light consumer goods, whereas its imports were mostly capital and intermediate goods. The export structure shows some movement toward capital goods and intermediate goods between 1973 and 1977, with the share of these goods increasing at the expense of consumer goods. For imports, the most significant change was the sharp increase in the share of petroleum products, which rose from 9.3 percent in 1973 to 22.6 percent in 1977. The small share of agricultural and consumer goods in total imports at this time indicates that Turkey had already passed through the "easy" stage of import substitution.

The performance of the Turkish economy at the end of 1977 was thus mixed. Despite the first oil shock and the stagflation in the industrial countries, the Turkish economy was growing rapidly. Some worsening of · the balance of trade was inevitable because of sluggish export demand abroad, the increased cost of imports due to higher oil prices, and higher import demand arising from sustained economic expansion. In addition, workers' remittances declined, a trend attributable in part to the recession in European countries. More disturbingly, however, the real exchange rate had become increasingly overvalued, reflecting the habitual drift in incentives against exports after each major devaluation episode, and the rapid increase in foreign indebtedness left the economy with little additional cushion when conditions worsened in 1978.

Confronting adjustment: crisis and reform, 1978–81

Considerable strains were evident in the Turkish economy even before the second oil shock. In responding to the first shock, the country had used up its credit line on international capital markets without undergoing any adjustment in economic structure. Instead, public spending had increased, exports had stagnated, and the steady march toward a foreign exchange crisis was slowed only by the cushion of higher workers' remittances. The world oil price increases of 50 percent in 1979 and 75 percent in 1980 which led to oil as a proportion of total imports rising from 9 percent in 1973 to nearly 40 percent in 1981 and to oil imports in 1980 representing over 80 percent of total export earnings, sufficed to push the economy over the edge. And the evolving foreign exchange crisis precipitated increasingly severe domestic economic disruptions.

In response to the growing foreign exchange crisis the government undertook a stabilization program early in 1978, which met with only mixed success. Although the current-account deficit improved markedly from $3.6 billion in 1977 to $1.7 billion in 1978, domestic inflation worsened as prices rose more than 50 percent. A new stabilization program was announced in March 1979 and amplified in the following months, culminating in a standby arrangement with the IMF in July 1979. Fueled by a 50 percent rise in the world price of petroleum, and in spite of the stringent stabilization measures, inflation accelerated to 64 percent in 1979. The balance-of-payments situation remained stable, with a $1.8 billion deficit on the current account.

On the trade side, as figure 9.1 illustrates, total exports stagnated in 1979, with a slight decrease occurring in merchandise exports. At the same time, the inflow of external capital, especially commercial borrowing, dried up. There was a sharp decline in the share of imports in GDP between 1977 and 1979. In dollar terms, imports of goods fell by 21 percent in 1978 and rose by only 10 percent in 1979, compared with 1977 levels. The volume of oil imports declined to 11.7 million tons in 1979 from 14.3 million tons in 1978. Non-oil imports – primarily capital goods and intermediate inputs – plunged to 59 percent and 55 percent of the 1976 volume in 1978 and 1979, respectively, reflecting a collapse of the earlier investment boom and a particularly rapid drop in private investment after 1977 due to lack of confidence in the political situation and economic management in the late 1970s and early 1980s. This sharp curtailment of imports led to their being rationed at a premium, to low capacity utilization in industry and to negative growth in GDP in 1979.

Early in 1980, a new government introduced extensive measures to address the deteriorating economic situation, and implemented a change in

Turkey's development strategy from inward-looking import substitution to export expansion. The new strategy which had been under discussion since 1978, involved opening up the economy by reducing the tariff and other barriers that had promoted import substitution and by dampening the existing bias against exporting. The measures announced in January 1980 included the devaluation of the Turkish exchange rate from TL 47 to TL 70; duty-free entry of imported inputs used in export production; simplification of the procedures for access to export incentives and import licenses; and streamlining of administrative regulations on investment incentives, with the reorientation of investment priorities and the creation of special incentives for export-oriented activities. In addition, certain State Economic Enterprises (SEEs) were permitted greater freedom in setting prices in an effort to improve their profitability and reduce deficits. In July 1980, the rediscount rate of the central bank on short-term notes was raised considerably and interest-rate ceilings on savings and loans were eliminated, allowing a rapid rise in nominal rates and resulting in positive real interest rates. In January 1981, the income tax system was reformed, import controls were liberalized, and additional export incentives were provided, to be supplemented by increases in export tax rebates in May 1981. Daily adjustments in the exchange rate were also introduced and, in July 1981, interest rates on bonds were freed and their indexation introduced.

Although the reforms undertaken in early 1980 had some immediate impact, their beneficial economic effects were limited by the unsettled internal conditions that existed prior to the September 1980 military takeover – conditions exacerbated by severe productivity declines in industry during the period. Although economic recovery accelerated in the final months of 1980 as the political situation stabilized, with exports, which were stagnant in the early part of the year, reaching levels 63 percent higher (in dollar value) than for the same period in 1979, 1980 was the second consecutive year of negative GDP growth. Buffeted by restrictive monetary policies and skyrocketing oil prices, domestic private investment in 1980 declined in real terms. The current-account deficit increased sharply with the $3.2 billion oil import bill larger than total commodity exports of $2.9 billion. Inflation surpassed 100 percent.

The situation improved markedly in 1981. Inflation came down to an annual rate of around 35 percent. Real imports of petroleum were restricted to a lower level than in 1980. Although the volume of non-oil imports increased substantially in response to the economic recovery, the aggregate dollar value of imports increased only by a moderate 13 percent. Workers' remittances picked up significantly, encouraged by the measures taken to protect their value. Exports continued to rise rapidly throughout 1981. Merchandise exports reached $4.7 billion, and industrial exports more than

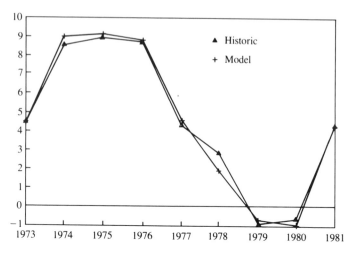

Figure 9.2 Historic versus model GDP growth (percent)

doubled. The Middle East became an important market not only for exports but also for Turkish contractors, with around $9 billion in outstanding contracts by the end of 1981. There was a marked improvement in the current-account deficit, which declined by 35 percent to about $2.1 billion. GDP increased by 4.2 percent, the first positive growth since 1978. While all sectors recorded growth, the 7.3 percent expansion in manufacturing output was especially noteworthy in that it indicated an upsurge in capacity utilization.

The external debt situation brightened in 1981 along with the general improvement in economic performance. The debt-service ratio declined to 13.1 percent in 1981 from 16.2 percent in 1980.[4] The improving debt situation was also reflected in a decline in the share of short-term credits in total debt from 49 percent in 1978 to 12 percent in 1981.

3 Tracking history

The historical run generated by the model of chapter 4 is first calibrated to Turkey's actual performance.[5] As figures 9.2 and 9.3 indicate, movements in real GDP have been very closely tracked, including the negative growth in 1979 and 1980. The model-generated shares of consumption, total investment, and private investment in GDP are also similar to actual values, as shown in figures 9.4 through 9.6.

Table 9.3 compares the structure of imports and exports generated in the historical run with their actual structure. Most structural changes evident

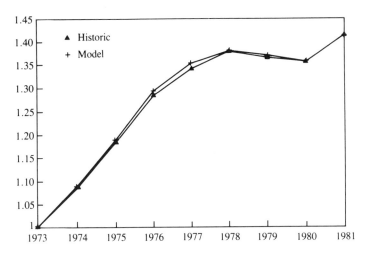

Figure 9.3 Historic versus model GDP (1973 = 1.0)

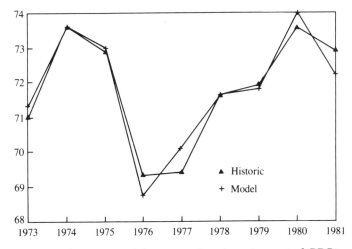

Figure 9.4 Historic versus model consumption share (percent of GDP)

in the actual data are reflected in the model results, including the tremendous increase in the share of petroleum in total imports and the declining importance of consumer-goods exports, which is matched by an increase in capital and intermediate-goods exports.

The model as applied to Turkey contains seven productive sectors. Six of the sectors are defined according to the aggregation scheme of chapter 4; the additional sector is petroleum, which has been separated from the

264   Adjustment in an inward-oriented economy: Turkey

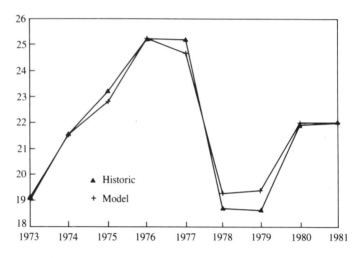

Figure 9.5 Historic versus model private consumption (percent of GDP)

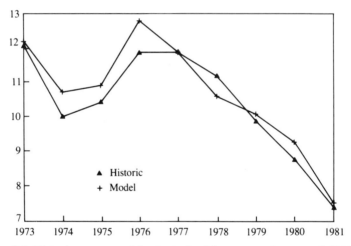

Figure 9.6 Historic versus model private fixed investment (percent of GDP)

intermediate-goods sector because of its prominent role in the foreign exchange crisis of the late 1970s. The world price of oil increased tenfold during the period (eightfold relative to other import prices), so that the increase in the domestic price of oil was substantial. This large relative price change should induce substitution away from oil imports and dampen demand. Actual Turkish experience, however, points to increased real oil imports throughout most of the period, and especially in the last few years

Table 9.3 *Turkey: structure of exports and imports – actual versus model (based on value in US dollars)*

Sector	1973	Actual 1977	Model 1977	Actual 1981	Model 1981
Imports					
Agriculture	2.7	1.7	2.9	1.3	2.6
Consumer goods	5.1	5.0	4.2	5.0	3.8
Capital goods	37.5	30.3	33.0	20.5	20.4
Intermediate goods	32.7	29.7	30.0	25.2	23.3
Petroleum	9.3	22.6	19.7	39.9	40.3
Infrastructure	2.0	1.5	1.2	1.9	1.3
Services	10.8	9.3	9.1	8.1	8.4
Exports					
Agriculture	20.0	12.8	20.8	21.7	22.5
Consumer goods	42.7	34.6	38.8	33.5	32.5
Capital goods	0.2	1.0	1.2	3.5	3.7
Intermediate goods	6.3	9.1	9.2	12.2	11.3
Petroleum	3.0	0.0	0.0	1.6	1.8
Infrastructure	4.8	9.6	10.0	6.1	6.4
Services	22.0	21.2	20.4	21.3	22.0

Sources: World Bank (1982b, 1984) and model results.

when prices reached their highest levels and economic activity was depressed. This increase in oil imports can be linked to two factors. First, since domestic petroleum production consisted almost entirely of refining imported crude petroleum, Turkey was almost completely dependent on imported oil; thus the short-run response of demand to price was quite low. Second, with the improving foreign exchange situation in late 1980 and 1981, the Turkish government began to rebuild petroleum stocks depleted in the early years of the crisis.

Two special instruments are used to track petroleum imports in the final three years of the period and counter the model's tendency to permit substantial substitution away from oil imports.[6] First, in 1979 and 1980, a substantial increase in the fixed coefficient representing imported intermediate inputs per unit of composite intermediate goods is imposed on the petroleum sector. This partly offsets the price-induced substitution away from petroleum imports that occurs in the intermediate demands in other sectors. Second, in 1980 and 1981, the government is assumed to import limited amounts of petroleum, which are added to domestic supply. This reflects the government's policy of slowly rebuilding its depleted petroleum stocks as foreign exchange became available.[7]

Table 9.4 *Historical run: aggregate price data*

Variable	1973	1974	1975	1976	1977	1978	1979	1980	1981	Growth
*Exchange rate (TL/$)	14.0	14.0	14.5	16.0	18.2	24.3	36.4	76.5	108.9	29.2
Premium rate (percent)	0.0	0.0	0.0	0.0	0.0	37.1	59.3	20.0	0.0	0.0
*Price level index	102.2	130.9	152.4	179.4	223.5	320.9	457.5	1,108.0	1,574.0	40.8
*Domestic inflation (percent)	0.0	28.1	16.4	17.7	24.6	43.6	70.6	102.4	42.1	40.8
*Average world inflation (percent)	0.0	27.3	9.8	8.8	9.0	9.0	20.1	24.4	-1.8	13.1
*Nominal depreciation (percent)	0.0	0.0	3.6	10.3	13.7	33.5	49.8	109.9	42.5	29.2
Real depreciation (percent)^a	0.0	-0.8	-3.0	1.4	-1.9	-1.1	-0.7	31.9	-1.4	1.5

Notes:
^{a} Real depreciation = nominal depreciation − (domestic inflation − world inflation).
*Indicates exogenous variables.

The principal elements of the historical run provides us with information about Turkey's economic performance from 1973 through 1981. Table 9.4 contains data on the exchange rate and the import premium rate that served to reduce import demand to match the available supply of foreign exchange, and aggregate prices. Movements in the latter reflect changes in the intensity of import rationing over the period. The time paths of domestic, import, and export inflation rates are all exogenous, and the nominal exchange rate is fixed exogenously as well. The final line in the table (real depreciation) measures movements in the real exchange rate.[8] Table 9.5 summarizes the balance of payments for 1973–81 while table 9.6 details the structure of GDP in the model-generated historical run.

4 Policy simulations

We now turn to some counterfactual policy simulations designed to illuminate the implications of alternative external conditions and policy responses. In each simulation, possible scenarios are examined by changing certain key exogenous variables while keeping most of the parameters and exogenous variables the same as in the historical run. In this way, answers are sought to five questions:

(1) Could more timely actions by policy-makers have alleviated or prevented the foreign exchange crisis of the late 1970s?
(2) What were the implications of the extreme year-to-year volatility of foreign capital inflows into the economy? How differently would the economy have performed if this inflow had been smoother, and had the import rationing of the 1978–80 period been avoided?
(3) Would the economy have continued to grow at the pace achieved during 1973–7 had the second round of oil price increases not occurred, or were the underlying strains in the economy sufficient to curtail growth even without further oil price increases?
(4) To what extent were Turkey's borrowing needs driven by external events, and how would resource inflows have been different without the oil price shocks?
(5) What would have been the impact of a more efficient allocation of investment during the adjustment period?

Simulations 1a and 1b Meeting shocks with positive policies
In the first pair of simulations, we address the question that lies at the heart of the analysis of Turkey's adjustment response to the external shocks of the 1970s: given the changing economic environment and external shocks, how would different choices by Turkish policy-makers in

Table 9.5 Historical run: foreign exchange earnings and expenditure (billions of US dollars)

Variable	1973	1974	1975	1976	1977	1978	1979	1980	1981	Growth rate (percent) 1973–81
Exports	1.80	2.07	2.05	2.71	2.50	3.03	3.37	4.27	6.27	16.9
*Remittances	1.18	1.43	1.31	0.98	0.98	0.98	1.69	2.07	2.49	9.7
*Foreign borrowing	0.14	0.20	1.34	1.90	2.39	1.14	0.81	3.16	1.01	28.4
Total earnings	3.12	3.70	4.70	5.59	5.87	5.15	5.87	9.50	9.77	15.3
Intermediate imports	1.02	1.58	1.89	2.27	2.56	2.55	3.01	3.53	4.08	18.9
Capital-goods imports	0.64	0.79	1.04	1.34	1.58	1.37	1.34	1.30	1.41	10.3
Consumption imports	0.73	1.76	2.19	2.09	2.33	1.12	1.41	3.35	3.33	20.8
*Residual oil imports	0.00	0.00	0.00	0.00	0.00	0.00	0.00	0.71	0.75	0.0
Total imports	2.39	4.13	5.12	5.70	6.47	5.04	5.76	8.89	9.57	18.9
Trade balance	−0.59	−2.06	−3.07	−2.99	−3.97	−2.01	−2.39	−4.62	−3.29	24.0
Current account	0.59	−0.63	−1.75	−2.01	−2.98	−1.02	−0.70	−2.56	−0.80	0.0
*Reserve increase	0.73	−0.43	−0.42	−0.11	−0.59	0.12	0.11	0.61	0.21	−14.6
Total oil imports	0.22	0.74	0.92	1.12	1.27	1.25	1.76	3.49	3.86	43.0
Oil as a percentage of total imports	9.3	18.1	18.0	19.6	19.6	24.9	30.5	39.2	40.4	20.2

Note: *Indicates exogenous variables.

Table 9.6 *Historical run: structure of nominal GDP, 1973–81 (percentage of GDP)*

Sectors	1973	1974	1975	1976	1977	1978	1979	1980	1981
Total consumption	83.8	85.5	85.7	81.8	83.5	84.5	84.7	87.1	84.3
Private	71.3	73.4	73.0	68.8	70.1	71.6	71.8	74.0	72.2
Government	12.5	12.1	12.7	13.0	13.4	12.9	12.9	13.1	12.1
Total fixed investment	20.1	18.5	20.5	23.4	23.9	22.5	21.7	19.8	19.0
Private	12.2	10.7	10.9	12.8	11.9	10.6	10.2	9.3	7.5
Government	7.9	7.8	9.6	10.6	12.0	11.9	11.5	10.5	11.5
Change in stocks	−1.1	3.0	2.4	2.0	0.8	−3.2	−2.3	2.2	2.9
Exports	8.6	7.0	5.7	6.4	5.1	5.8	5.9	8.4	11.9
Imports	−11.4	−14.1	−14.1	−13.5	−13.3	−9.6	−10.0	−17.5	−18.1
Total value added	96.9	96.7	96.0	96.0	96.0	97.0	97.1	95.3	95.4
Agriculture	25.2	25.2	24.2	23.6	23.6	24.3	24.3	25.8	26.0
Consumer goods	7.5	7.7	7.2	7.1	6.9	6.6	6.8	7.1	7.3
Capital goods	9.0	8.3	9.1	10.3	10.4	9.7	9.3	8.3	8.2
Intermediate goods and petroleum	8.9	8.9	8.2	7.7	7.0	6.7	6.8	5.6	6.6
Infrastructure and services	46.4	46.6	47.3	47.3	48.1	49.7	49.9	48.5	47.3

the earlier years have affected the economy's ability to rebound from the second round of shocks? In simulation 1a, we leave external conditions unchanged from the historical run, and examine the effects of alternative government policies regarding the exchange rate, public spending, and resource mobilization. We assume that the oil shocks of 1974–5 and 1979–80 are countered with real devaluations of the exchange rate. Although the cumulative real devaluation is slightly less than that occurring in the historical run, the key difference is in the phasing of the devaluation, which in the historical run occurred almost entirely in 1980. We further assume that public consumption and investment do not increase (as a share of GDP) so drastically, and that the falling marginal savings propensities exhibited by the private sector during the period are replaced by unchanged average savings rates throughout the period, indicating one possible response to the government's positive policy actions. In simulation 1b, we add to simulation 1a the assumption that the productivity declines of the latter half of the period are replaced by unchanged productivity.[9]

The reasonableness of the assumptions used to generate counterfactuals is, as always, a matter of judgment. Specifying the components of this particular counterfactual simulation requires judgments to be made about the effect of external economic events on domestic, political, and social conditions. For example, the foreign exchange crisis of 1978–80 played a clearly causative role in the productivity decline of these years. In addition, external events and their domestic economic impact also contributed to the turbulent political conditions in the country, although here the causative influence is less clear. While it is tempting to assume that, with proper economic policies, the productivity declines would have been replaced with positive growth at or near historic levels, such an assumption would neglect the possible role of political and social events (such as strikes) in the productivity decline. The approach here attempts to occupy the middle ground: the actual productivity declines are replaced by a counterfactual assumption of no change in productivity, rather than assuming a return to historic growth levels.

Table 9.7 summarizes the cumulative trade flows in the two simulations and the historical run. The discrete devaluations undertaken in simulations 1a and 1b evoke a substantial export response, with cumulative flows more than 20 percent higher. Although the real exchange-rate depreciation in the historical run is greater than that specified in the simulations, it occurs almost entirely in 1980 and so has little cumulative effect. In simulations 1a and 1b, the real devaluations undertaken in 1974 and 1975 in response to the first oil price increase produce a significant export supply response, which leads to the cumulative effect shown in the table. This increase in export earnings results in only a slight rise in imports. It appears instead

Table 9.7 *Simulations 1a and 1b: cumulative exports, imports, and borrowing (billions of US dollars)*

Variable	Historical run	Simulation 1a	Simulation 1b
Exports	28.09	34.64	34.48
Non-oil imports	38.45	39.01	39.61
Oil imports	14.63	14.10	14.46
Total imports	53.08	53.11	54.07
Balance-of-trade deficit	− 24.99	− 18.47	− 19.59
Foreign borrowing	12.09	5.58	6.70

Note: Simulations 1a and 1b are identical in the 1973–7 period.

mostly as a reduction in foreign borrowing requirements, with the cumulative net inflow in simulation 1a less than half that in the historical run. The elimination of negative productivity growth in simulation 1b has almost no effect on exports, but it does raise imports of both oil and non-oil products, reflecting the increased demand associated with faster output growth.

Table 9.8 summarizes economic performance in the historical run and the two simulations for the 1973–7 and 1977–81 periods. During 1973–7, aggregate GDP growth is not affected by the policy changes made by the government, although the composition of GDP is affected. Exports grow steadily in the simulations at 4.9 percent, compared to the steady decline associated with exchange-rate appreciation in the historical run. Although investment continues to lead the way, the curtailment of government investment coupled with the absence of any decline in private savings rates implies a more even split in investment growth between private and government components. The only negative feature of the policy changes is the decline in the growth rate of skilled labor employment, which is matched by a decline in the growth rate of urban labor household income (although all households share in the income decline).[10]

During 1977–81, differences among the simulations appear. GDP growth is 1 percentage point higher in simulation 1a than in the historical run, as policy-makers respond to the second oil price increase with further devaluation. In simulation 1b, where productivity declines are eliminated, GDP growth reaches 3 percent for the four-year period. Although export growth is slower in simulations 1a and 1b, this is because of the tremendous export surge during 1981 in the historical run; as table 9.7 shows, *cumulative* exports are substantially higher in the two simulations than in

Table 9.8 *Simulations 1a and 1b: growth of GDP and components, 1973–7 and 1977–81*

Variable	1973–7			1977–81		
	Historical	Sim. 1a	Sim. 1b	Historical	Sim. 1a	Sim. 1b
Private consumption	7.9	6.6	6.6	0.1	0.5	1.9
Government consumption	9.5	8.9	8.9	−2.4	−0.4	1.6
Private investment	7.4	12.8	12.8	−11.5	−6.3	−3.8
Government investment	19.9	11.5	11.5	−1.6	−3.2	−1.3
Exports	−5.7	4.9	4.9	22.2	15.5	15.2
Imports	14.2	11.4	11.4	−4.2	−2.5	−1.5
GDP	7.9	7.9	7.9	0.6	1.6	3.0
Capital stock	4.7	4.7	4.7	4.4	5.3	5.6
Skilled labor	2.6	2.0	2.0	−4.8	−4.0	−2.9
Unskilled labor	6.4	7.0	7.0	11.1	10.3	9.6
Value added in:						
Consumer goods	7.2	8.1	8.1	3.1	2.8	4.0
Capital goods	8.3	8.4	8.4	−1.9	−1.3	1.1
Intermediate goods and oil	8.1	8.3	8.3	1.4	2.1	4.1
Total household income	7.7	6.7	6.7	−1.8	−1.5	0.1
Rural households	5.3	4.7	4.7	1.8	2.3	3.6
Urban labor households	5.1	4.6	4.6	−0.5	0.4	1.5
Urban capitalist households	11.2	9.3	9.3	−6.1	−6.8	−4.6

Notes: Simulations 1a and 1b are identical in the 1973–7 period.
See also footnote 10.

the historical run. The investment decline evident in the historical run diminishes from simulation 1a to simulation 1b, with a corresponding positive impact on the growth rate of the capital stock and on value added in the capital-goods sector. The devaluation in simulation 1a seems to benefit labor households the most, and actually leaves capitalists worse off since the income they derived from import rationing in the historical run is eliminated. Elimination of productivity declines benefits capitalists more, although their income still drops sharply from its 1977 level.

Simulation 2 Smoothing capital inflows

One prominent feature of the balance of payments in the historical run data is the extreme variability of components of capital inflow into the economy. From very low initial levels in 1973–4, foreign borrowing rises rapidly, reaching a peak in 1977, after which it drops off substantially until 1980. After rapid early growth, remittances go through a similar recession in 1976–8. Indeed, remittances grow at 9.7 percent in nominal terms over the entire period, which corresponds to minimal real growth if deflated by the 9.1 percent growth rate in average export prices. It is the combination of these two events that so drastically squeezes the economy in 1978 when the second round of oil price increases hit.

Simulation 2 explores the extent to which this volatility influenced the economy. The pattern of remittances and foreign borrowing is altered, but the cumulative magnitude remains unchanged. Since such smoothing would have alleviated, although not necessarily eliminated, the acute foreign exchange shortage in 1978–9, we also assume that premium rationing of imports would have been eliminated, to be replaced with a flexible exchange rate, and also that the seesaw pattern of foreign reserve changes would have been replaced by more regular changes. In performing this simulation, we treat the variability of capital inflows into the economy as an "external shock" and examine the effect of eliminating that shock. This is not meant to imply, however, that the "smoothing" of an unchanged cumulative inflow was a viable policy option for Turkish authorities at the time.

Table 9.9 summarizes the current-account figures for the two runs. In the absence of any criterion for allocating the cumulative inflow optimally, somewhat arbitrary assumptions have been adopted.[11] The remittance and foreign borrowing figures have been left unchanged in 1973–4. In subsequent years, the sum of these two components has been chosen to maintain a constant real inflow for 1975–81, using the import price index as deflator; see figure 9.7 for the implied pattern. In allocating this total inflow between remittances and borrowing, a simple rule has been followed: nominal remittances grow at 5 percent, and borrowing is the difference between total

Table 9.9 *Simulation 2: capital inflows (billions of US dollars)*

Variable	1973	1974	1975	1976	1977	1978	1979	1980	1981	Growth rate (percent) 1973–81
Historical run										
Remittances	1.18	1.43	1.31	0.98	0.98	0.98	1.69	2.07	2.49	9.7
Foreign borrowing	0.14	0.20	1.34	1.90	2.39	1.14	0.81	3.16	1.01	28.4
Total capital inflow	1.32	1.63	2.65	2.88	3.37	2.12	2.50	5.23	3.50	13.0
Reserve increase	0.73	−0.43	−0.42	−0.11	−0.59	−0.12	0.11	0.61	0.21	−14.6
Real total capital inflow[a]	1.32	1.25	1.86	1.85	1.99	1.15	1.09	1.71	1.15	−1.7
Simulation 2										
Remittances	1.18	1.43	1.50	1.58	1.65	1.74	1.83	1.92	2.00	6.8
Foreign borrowing	0.14	0.20	0.63	0.75	0.88	1.02	1.59	2.63	2.55	44.1
Total capital inflow	1.32	1.63	2.13	2.33	2.53	2.76	3.42	4.55	4.55	16.7
Reserve increase	0.73	−0.06	−0.06	−0.06	−0.06	−0.06	−0.06	−0.06	−0.06	—
Real total capital inflow[a]	1.32	1.25	1.49	1.49	1.49	1.49	1.49	1.49	1.49	1.5
Import price index	1.00	1.30	1.43	1.56	1.70	1.85	2.29	3.04	3.04	14.9

Note: [a] Real total capital inflow figures were obtained by deflating the total capital inflow by the import price index.

Table 9.10 *Simulation 2: implications of smooth capital inflows*

	Ratio of value in simulation 2 to value in historical run		
Variable	1975	1978	1981
GDP	0.995	0.989	1.002
Absorption	0.940	1.024	1.058
Private consumption	0.978	0.988	1.021
Exports	1.314	0.963	0.826
Imports	0.902	1.174	1.075
Exchange rate	1.097	1.004	0.940
Skilled labor	0.967	1.021	1.026
Unskilled labor	1.037	0.982	0.986
Labor household income	1.000	1.042	0.995
Capitalist household income	0.912	0.941	1.125

Note: See footnote 10.

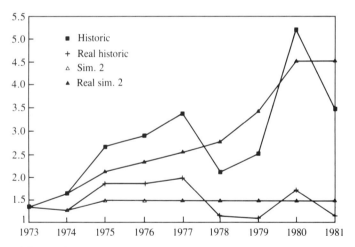

Figure 9.7 Nominal and real capital inflow patterns (billions of US dollars)

inflow and remittances. Since this nominal growth is slower than import inflation, the share of remittances in total inflow declines as time passes.

The implications of this alternative foreign capital pattern are summarized in table 9.10. Each entry is the ratio of the value in simulation 2 to the corresponding value in the historical run. GDP is only slightly higher in simulation 2 than in the historical run, implying that, if there are costs to the uneven pattern of real inflow, they do not show up in GDP.[12] Since the net effect of smoothing is to make more foreign capital available in 1978–81, it is not surprising that most other variables indicate that the simulation run outperforms the historical run in 1978 and 1981, while the reverse is true in 1975. One interesting result concerns exchange-rate movements: in 1978, the exchange rates are nearly identical in the two scenarios. The major difference lies in the fact that, in the historical run, there is an additional import premium of 37 percent. By providing the economy with a real inflow in 1978 equivalent to the average real inflow for 1975–81, premium rationing can be eliminated. This supports the hypothesis that the severity of the 1978–9 crisis can be linked to a certain extent to swings in real capital inflows. By 1981, the smoothed inflow pattern would have implied a 6 percent appreciation of the exhange rate compared to the historical run.

As for the distribution of household income, the changes are attributable to the different division of capital inflows between borrowing and remittances. Although this is of little macroeconomic importance, it does affect distribution since remittances flow to labor households and borrowing is undertaken by capitalists. Because the simulation smooths the path of remittances, labor household income is higher in 1978, when actual remittances were low, and lower in 1981, when actual remittances were quite high. But because employment of skilled labor is higher throughout most of the period in simulation 2 than in the historical run, labor incomes rise even when changes in remittances are taken into account.[13]

If the relatively small difference between the two scenarios seems surprising, it must be remembered how little has been changed. Only the *pattern* of inflow differs, not the real amount, and none of the other shocks that shaped the economy in the historical run (such as oil price increases or declines in total factor productivity) has been altered. The next three policy simulations are designed, therefore, to explore several of these features.

Simulations 3a and 3b Eliminating the second oil price shock

We now introduce a more significant counterfactual change in exogenous conditions by eliminating the second round of oil price increases. Instead of petroleum import prices rising 50 percent in 1979 and 78 percent in 1980, these increases are reduced in simulations 3a to 14 and 11 percent, respectively.[14] In the absence of the second oil price shock, net capital inflow into the economy would probably have been lower since the high borrowing levels of the early 1970s could not have been sustained indefinitely and the inflow of remittances from the Gulf economies would have been reduced. We therefore assume that workers' remittances grow more slowly during 1978–81, so that cumulative remittances in this period

Table 9.11 *Simulations 3a and 3b: cumulative balance of payments, 1978–81 (billions of US dollars)*

Variable	Historical run	Simulation 3a	Simulation 3b
Total earnings	30.29	29.91	30.30
Exports	16.94	19.33	19.72
Remittances	7.23	5.78	5.78
Foreign borrowing	6.12	4.80	4.80
Imports	29.27	28.99	29.39
Trade balance	− 12.33	− 9.66	− 9.67
Current account	− 5.08	− 3.88	− 3.88
Reserve increase	1.05	0.92	0.92

are 20 percent lower than historical levels. Furthermore, we assume that annual foreign borrowing remains constant at $1.2 billion during 1978–81, which implies a 20 percent reduction in cumulative borrowing as well. Finally, the uneven shifts in world export demand that characterized the calibrated historical run are replaced by a smoother pattern of demand growth in the four major export sectors, with one-half the average growth of the historical run in each sector.[15] Simulation 3b goes a step further and replaces the 1978–80 historical run productivity declines with the assumption that productivity growth rates are zero.[16]

Prior to 1978, these two simulations are identical to the historical run. Our interest in them is in examining the 1978–81 performance of the economy in the absence of this second external shock, and particularly in considering whether the rapid growth of the earlier period could have been sustained. We conclude that even with the more favorable assumptions about productivity in simulation 3b, the growth of GDP falls roughly halfway between the economy's actual performance in 1973–7 and 1977–81.

Tables 9.11, 9.12, and 9.13 contain information on these two policy simulations. Table 9.11 shows the implications for the balance of payments of eliminating the second oil price shock and the productivity declines. With a flexible exchange rate and cumulative remittances and foreign borrowing 20 percent lower than in the historical run, cumulative export earnings in the simulations are $2.4–2.8 billion higher, offsetting the decline in foreign capital inflow. As a result, the $2.7 billion decline in the cumulative trade deficit is matched by the increase in export earnings, so that cumulative imports (in dollars) are roughly unchanged from the historical run. Furthermore, since lower petroleum prices imply lower

Table 9.12 *Simulations 3a and 3b: real exchange-rate depreciation*
(*percent*)

Year	Historical run	Simulation 3a	Simulation 3b
1978	−1.1	12.0	12.3
1979	−0.7	−5.7	−4.3
1980	31.9	9.2	10.2
1981	−1.4	−6.5	−6.3
Total	28.7	9.0	11.9

Table 9.13 *Simulations 3a and 3b: real GDP growth rates, 1977–81*
(*percent*)

Variable	Historical run	Simulation 3a	Simulation 3b
GDP	1.1	2.3	3.6
Private consumption	0.1	1.5	2.7
Total fixed investment	−6.2	−3.7	−2.3
Exports	22.2	18.9	20.4
Imports	−4.2	−2.2	−1.8
Value added in:			
Consumer goods	3.1	3.8	5.1
Capital goods	−1.9	0.2	2.1
Intermediate goods and oil	1.4	2.6	4.4
Total household income	−1.8	0.8	1.8
Rural households	1.8	3.8	5.1
Urban labor households	−0.5	1.8	2.7
Urban capitalist households	−6.1	−2.7	−1.7

Note: See footnote 10.

average import prices, the cumulative import bill of $30.3 billion in simulation 3b buys 16 percent more in real terms than the same nominal amount would in the historical run.

Table 9.12 summarizes the movements of the real exchange rate that underlie the balance-of-payments figures in table 9.11. The simulations have different implications for the real exchange-rate movements necessary to achieve external balance. The cumulative real depreciation in the historical run was 28.7 percent, which occurred entirely in 1980 as part of the major trade policy liberalization and reforms. The cumulative real depreciations in the two simulations are substantially smaller (9.0 and 11.9 percent, respectively) than that of the historical run, even though total foreign capital inflow is 20 percent lower. This reflects both the increased availability of foreign exchange resulting from lower oil prices, and the earlier, more sustained export "boom."

Table 9.13 shows how GDP growth is affected by removal of the two shocks. Setting world oil price growth equal to the growth of other import prices adds 1.2 percentage points to the growth rate of GDP. It is interesting, however, that removal of the productivity declines has a larger impact (1.3 percentage points) than the oil price reduction. This points again to the conclusion, which was also reached in earlier studies by Dervis and Robinson (1982) and Lewis and Urata (1984), that external shocks played a large but not exclusive role in derailing the Turkish economy from its earlier growth path. Although the productivity loss was not unrelated to the oil price rise, much of it stemmed from domestic policies and political conditions that were amplified, but not caused, by changing external conditions. It is interesting to note that real export growth is lower in simulations 3a and 3b than in the historical run, even though cumulative exports are higher. The dollar value of exports in 1981 was $0.5 billion lower in the simulation runs, thereby yielding the lower average growth rate. In neither of the two simulations is export growth sufficient to allow positive growth in real imports, but this reflects in part the 1977 base for the calculation, when massive borrowing and the overvalued exchange rate fueled import demand.

In distributional terms, urban capitalists are the gainers and rural households the losers in simulation 3a, compared with the historical run. With a 2.6 percentage point change in the growth rate of total income, the income of capitalists improves by 3.4 percentage points while that of rural households improves by only 2.0 percentage points. The distributional effect of moving from simulation 3a to simulation 3b appears neutral, with all three income groups benefiting about the same.

Simulations 4a and 4b External shocks and borrowing requirements

A common perception about how Turkey responded to the external changes of the 1970s is that it placed undue reliance on foreign borrowing instead of undertaking more positive policies of adjustment. In simulations 4a and 4b, we use the model to examine this issue by asking how the economy's borrowing needs would have differed in the absence of the two oil price shocks.

Simulation 4a removes both shocks and instead lets petroleum prices

Table 9.14 *Simulations 4a and 4b: capital inflow and import capacity (billions of US dollars)*

Variable	1973	1974	1975	1976	1977	1978	1979	1980	1981	Cumulative 1973–81
Historical run										
Foreign borrowing	0.14	0.20	1.34	1.90	2.39	1.14	0.81	3.16	1.01	12.09
Balance-of-trade surplus	−0.59	−2.06	−3.07	−2.99	−3.96	−2.01	−2.39	−4.63	−3.29	−24.99
Real foreign borrowing	0.14	0.15	0.94	1.22	1.41	0.62	0.35	1.04	0.33	6.20
Real balance of trade	−0.59	−1.59	−2.15	−1.92	−2.33	−1.09	−1.04	−1.52	−1.08	−13.31
Import price index	1.00	1.30	1.43	1.56	1.70	1.85	2.29	3.04	3.04	—
Total imports	2.39	4.13	5.12	5.71	6.46	5.04	5.76	8.90	9.57	53.08
Oil imports	0.22	0.74	0.92	1.12	1.27	1.25	1.76	3.49	3.86	14.63
Non-oil imports	2.17	3.39	4.20	4.59	5.19	3.79	4.00	5.41	5.71	38.45
Simulation 4a										
Foreign borrowing	0.14	−0.38	0.05	0.60	0.81	−0.12	−0.61	0.38	−0.22	0.65
Balance-of-trade surplus	−0.59	−1.11	−1.42	−1.64	−1.86	−0.92	−0.75	−2.04	−1.74	−12.07
Real foreign borrowing	0.14	−0.35	0.04	0.48	0.59	−0.08	−0.35	0.20	−0.12	0.55
Real balance of trade	−0.59	−1.02	−1.22	−1.30	−0.91	−0.29	−0.44	−1.06	−0.95	−5.88
Import price index	1.00	1.09	1.16	1.26	1.38	1.50	1.72	1.92	1.83	—
Total imports	2.39	3.50	4.19	4.78	5.30	4.83	5.72	7.86	7.53	46.10
Oil imports	0.22	0.37	0.43	0.53	0.59	0.57	0.72	1.15	1.13	5.71
Non-oil imports	2.17	3.13	3.76	4.25	4.71	4.26	5.00	6.71	6.40	40.39
Simulation 4b										
Foreign borrowing	0.14	−0.30	0.24	1.11	1.55	0.84	−0.78	2.30	1.73	8.39
Balance-of-trade surplus	−0.59	−1.19	−1.61	−2.15	−2.59	−1.88	−2.14	−3.96	−3.69	−18.62
Real foreign borrowing	0.14	−0.28	0.21	0.88	1.12	0.56	0.45	1.20	0.95	5.23
Real balance of trade	−0.59	−1.09	−1.39	−1.71	−1.88	−1.25	−1.24	−2.06	−2.02	−12.05
Import price index	1.00	1.09	1.16	1.26	1.38	1.50	1.72	1.92	1.83	—
Total imports	2.39	3.53	4.27	4.94	5.51	5.07	6.05	8.41	8.10	48.26
Oil imports	0.22	0.37	0.43	0.54	0.61	0.59	0.75	1.21	1.19	5.91
Non-oil imports	2.17	3.16	3.84	4.40	4.90	4.48	5.30	7.20	6.91	42.35

grow at the same rate as those for capital and intermediate goods. In the absence of sharp oil price increases, it seems unlikely that the foreign exchange scarcity that led to the major devaluation in 1980 would have occurred, so we hypothesize that the real exchange rate appreciates 1 percent annually from 1973 to 1981.[17] The real exchange rate in 1973 still reflected the real devaluation of 1970, which had led to a sizeable export supply response by reducing the anti-export bias. Historically, Turkish policy-makers had allowed a steady real appreciation of the exchange rate after the periodic maxi-devaluations that followed foreign exchange crises, so that assuming a 1 percent annual appreciation is not unreasonable. Premium rationing of imports is eliminated, and foreign borrowing adjusts endogenously to achieve external balance. Remittances are set to their historic levels through 1978; from 1979 to 1981 they are reduced by 20 percent (as in simulations 3a and 3b). The swings in foreign reserve changes that appear in the historical run are replaced by the even time path used in simulation 2. Growth in world export demand between 1973 and 1981 is smoothed and reduced to half the average of the historical run for the main export sectors.[18]

Simulation 4b assumes a more rapid real appreciation of 2 percent annually and reduces by half the growth rates of world export demand used in simulation 4a. All other features of simulations 4a and 4b are the same.

Table 9.14 compares the profile of borrowing and imports in simulations 4a and 4b with that in the historical run. The net flow of resources into the economy (as measured by the trade balance) in simulation 4a is less than half that in the historical run, and cumulative borrowing over the entire period is less than $1.0 billion, as contrasted with over $12.0 billion in the historical run. From the perspective of balance-of-payments management, the scenario is quite attractive, since it implies that slow appreciation of the real exchange rate, coupled with moderate growth in export demand, would have permitted the economy to avoid increased foreign indebtedness.

When one considers the more pessimistic assumptions of simulation 4b, the scenario changes. The 2 percent annual appreciation, together with slower export demand growth, imply that borrowing requirements rise steadily throughout the period, with cumulative borrowing of $8.4 billion, only one-third less than in the historical run. Deflating the borrowing and trade deficit figures to allow for the lower import prices of simulation 4b results in cumulative real borrowing and trade deficit figures close to those of the historical run.

Unfortunately, the available information does not permit us to identify either of these two scenarios as more realistic than the other, had the oil shocks not occurred. What these results do suggest, however, is that the

Table 9.15 *Simulations 4a and 4b: no oil price shocks (percentage deviation from historical run)*

Variable	Simulation 4a			Simulation 4b		
	1975	1978	1981	1975	1978	1981
GDP	0.9	0.6	10.9	0.9	1.2	12.4
Absorption	−6.2	−1.2	16.3	−4.8	3.9	26.1
Private consumption	−1.3	−2.3	10.3	−0.7	0.5	15.6
Exports	53.6	42.1	−3.2	44.4	10.3	−31.4
Imports	−6.3	16.6	20.6	−4.4	22.6	29.8
Skilled labor	1.0	5.1	19.2	1.5	6.8	22.9
Unskilled labor	−1.1	−4.3	−10.6	−1.7	−5.8	−12.6
Total household income	−0.2	0.3	16.9	0.8	3.9	24.0
Rural households	7.2	5.9	17.2	7.2	6.2	18.7
Urban labor households	2.7	6.2	17.9	3.0	7.8	20.9
Urban capitalist households	−9.5	−9.5	15.3	−7.1	−1.5	32.8

Note: See footnote 10.

high borrowing requirements of the Turkish economy cannot be attributed solely to the impact of oil price increases. The results of simulation 4b indicate that, with reasonable hypotheses about exchange-rate management and export demand growth, the Turkish economy could have required nearly as many external resources as it actually did receive in the aftermath of the oil price shocks.

The data on imports in table 9.14 indicate what factors underlie the different borrowing requirements in the simulations. Some $8.5 billion of the $12.0 billion increase in the cumulative trade deficit in the historical run is attributable to increased spending on oil imports. In the historical run, cumulative oil imports represented 28 percent of total imports during the period, while in simulations 4a and 4b, the share was only 12 percent. The cumulative dollar costs of imports of all other commodities ("non-oil imports" in the table) are slightly higher in the historical run than in simulations 4a and 4b in the early years, but significantly lower in the 1977–80 crisis period. Since the price index of non-oil imports is the same in all simulations, this corresponds to a real reduction in import availability; in 1979 and 1980, real non-oil imports are 20 percent lower in the historical run than in simulation 4a.

Table 9.15 summarizes the performance of various macroeconomic aggregates in the two simulations. In the first half of the period, GDP in both simulations differs only slightly from that in the historical run. The main benefits from the absence of any oil price shock appear in the last few years, and yield an 11–12 percent increment in GDP by 1981. The export differences are more striking, however; real exports are more than 53 percent higher in simulation 4a than in the historical run in 1975, and 42 percent higher in 1978. By 1981, however, the steady appreciation of the exchange rate and slower demand growth mean that the export "boom" of the historical run surpasses the export levels achieved in simulation 4a. In simulation 4b, the faster appreciation of the exchange rate means that export performance fades more rapidly, so that in 1978 real exports are only 10 percent higher than historical run levels, and by 1981 they are more than 30 percent lower.

The outlook for skilled labor improves in both simulations, with skilled employment 19–23 percent higher in 1981 than in the historical run. But this improvement in relative performance masks the fact that, with productivity declining, the absolute number of skilled laborers rises slowly (1 percent annually in simulation 4a, 1.3 percent in simulation 4b) while the real wage of unskilled labor continues to fall. From a distributional standpoint, labor households are better off in all years, with their position relative to the historical run improving steadily. Rural households also gain. Capitalists are the biggest losers until the rapid growth of the final few years.

Simulation 5 Reallocating investment

The results of replacing the constant proportions method of allocating investment sectorally, which is used in the historical run, by a more "market-oriented" allocation scheme related to sectoral rates of return as described in chapter 4, are summarized in tables 9.16, 9.17, and 9.18.[19] In table 9.16, we see that the pattern of investment changes dramatically when the allocation becomes responsive to rental rates. The service sector is the big loser in 1973 with a 32 percentage point decline in the share of investment; all other sectors gain from 4 to 7 percentage points. The impact of these changes in investment allocation on the structure of the economy is given in table 9.17, which contrasts sectoral composition in simulation 5 with that in the historical run for 1981, the last year of the period. The capital stock structure changes significantly, with all sectors except services gaining relative to the historical run; total capital stock increases by 3.3 percent. Changes in output and value added are also quite striking, although more moderate than the capital stock changes, with aggregate increases of around 2 percent in each, and sectoral changes ranging from −12 to +30 percent for value added and from −10 to +10 percent for output. As the last column indicates, the increased output in all

Table 9.16 *Simulation 5: rental rates and investment allocation*

Sector	Rental rate 1973	1981	Investment share 1973	1981
Historical run				
Agriculture	19.4	25.3	10.8	11.5
Consumer goods	14.4	9.7	9.3	5.2
Capital goods	53.6	40.6	3.4	3.1
Intermediate goods	12.2	5.3	18.4	19.6
Petroleum	18.7	15.2	1.8	4.3
Infrastructure	10.2	11.7	10.3	19.3
Services	17.4	15.8	46.1	37.0
Total	17.6	15.8	100.0	100.0
Simulation 5				
Agriculture	19.4	21.3	15.2	21.7
Consumer goods	14.4	6.8	15.1	10.2
Capital goods	53.6	23.6	9.1	6.2
Intermediate goods	12.2	4.8	25.1	17.0
Petroleum	18.7	7.7	5.8	5.3
Infrastructure	10.2	11.5	16.0	14.6
Services	17.4	24.9	13.8	25.0
Total	17.6	17.1	100.0	100.0

Table 9.17 *Simulation 5: structure and investment reallocation, 1981 (percentage deviation from historical run)*

Sector	Capital stock	Value added	Output	Exports	Imports	Output price
Agriculture	31.6	12.0	9.9	28.9	1.0	−8.1
Consumer goods	43.7	13.9	7.0	14.1	5.6	−4.3
Capital goods	59.8	23.7	9.9	13.2	3.2	−11.7
Intermediate goods	15.0	6.8	2.6	3.3	1.1	−1.2
Petroleum	36.4	30.4	3.0	30.4	−0.8	−23.7
Infrastructure	10.8	9.1	9.1	7.3	0.0	−6.9
Services	−23.8	−12.5	−10.5	−39.1	0.5	17.9
Total	3.3	2.2	2.1	4.3	1.4	0.0

Table 9.18 *Simulation 5: GDP and foreign trade, 1981 (percentage deviation from historical run)*

Variable	Deviation
GDP	1.5
Private consumption	1.1
Fixed investment	9.4
Dollar value of exports	1.3
Dollar value of imports	0.6
Cumulative borrowing, 1973–81	1.8

sectors except services means that all domestic prices except those for services drop relative to the historical run. Since domestic prices directly affect export competitiveness, lower prices yield higher exports in all sectors except services, with an aggregate increase of 4.3 percent.[20] Imports also increase, with the largest increases occurring in consumer and capital goods. The low price elasticity for petroleum products is evident in the fact that a 3 percent rise in petroleum output permits a 24 percent decline in the domestic price, although the domestic petroleum price still remains substantially higher than other output prices in relative terms.

Table 9.18 shows the effect of the reallocation on GDP and other aggregates in 1981. GDP increases by 1.5 percent as a result of the more efficient allocation of investment, and private consumption increases by 1.1 percent. Real fixed investment rises substantially, even though the nominal share of investment in GDP is nearly identical in the two simulations. This large increase in real investment occurs because of the decline in the relative price of capital goods, which forms the main (around 90 percent) component of increases in the capital stock. Thus the 12 percent decline in the price of capital goods permits real investment to increase by 9 percent over the historical run with the same nominal investment effort.

5 Conclusions

Turkey's policy response to external shocks was typical of many developing countries. It attempted to postpone adjustment to the first round of oil price increases, and for a time it succeeded, since favorable growth in remittances and easy access to external capital permitted the economy to finance increased imports through additional external financing. Growth averaged nearly 8 percent a year between 1973 and 1977, but the resource gap (imports minus exports) increased from less than 3 percent to more than 8 percent of GDP during the same period. When the second round of oil price increases hit in 1979–80, the economy was unable to postpone adjustment any longer since remittances fell and the supply of external capital declined. The result was several years of painful adjustment, with low or negative growth in GDP. The oil price rises dominated developments in the external sector in the economy. Oil imports rose to more than 40 percent of total imports by 1981, and the increased cost of these imports absorbed 80 percent of the large amount of borrowed funds.

Analysis of the interaction between external factors and government policies supports the following conclusions:

(1) Timely adjustment to the two oil price increases consisting of real devaluations, reduced public-sector spending, and higher private savings, rather than postponement would have improved GDP growth by about 1 percentage point and avoided the severe balance-of-payments squeeze that occurred in the late 1970s. Eliminating the decline in industrial productivity experienced during the latter part of the 1970s, without necessarily returning to historical rates of productivity growth would have added another 1.4 percentage points to the growth rate of GDP, but it must be recognized that the link between economic policy-making and the productivity declines caused by turbulent political conditions is tenuous.

(2) Eliminating the "shock" of a highly volatile pattern of workers' remittances, foreign borrowing, and reserve changes, while keeping the cumulative amount unchanged would not have made a significant difference to GDP over the period as a whole nor would it have avoided the severe balance-of-payments squeeze that occurred in the late 1970s.

(3) The strategy of growth without adjustment pursued in 1973–7 could not have been sustained in the later years of the decade even if the second round of oil price increases had not occurred. Even with the elimination of the 1979–80 oil price rise, GDP growth from 1977–81 would have been higher by only a little more than 1 percentage point. Underlying strains in the economy and the tremendous increase in foreign indebtedness would still have required an eventual adjustment.

(4) The high borrowing requirements of the Turkish economy could not be attributed solely to the oil price increases. Indeed, with assumptions about exchange-rate management and export demand growth consistent with historical experience, the economy would have required nearly as many external resources as it actually did even if there had been no oil price shocks.

(5) Improved allocation of historical levels of investment in response to sectoral profitability would have channeled resources away from services and toward agriculture and manufactured goods and led to an improvement in GDP growth.

Notes

1 Celasun (1983) undertakes a detailed analysis of structural change in the Turkish economy in the pre-1973 period.

2 It is important to note that Turkish national income accounts were substantially revised around 1986. Since the revised data were used wherever possible, the numbers cited here may not be directly comparable to those cited in earlier analyses, such as Dervis and Robinson (1982) and Lewis and Urata (1984).

3 Balassa (1981b) claims that the real exchange rate between Turkey and its major trading partners appreciated by 13.2 percent between 1973 and 1977.

4 The debt-service ratio used here is defined as total debt service (payments and interest) as a percentage of goods, non-factor services, and workers' remittances.

5 For a description of the methods used for tracking, see chapter 4.

6 Such strong substitution responses were not observed in the separate studies by Dervis and Robinson (1982) and Lewis and Urata (1984) of each oil price episode. In part, this difference can be attributed to the departure from the strict "Armington" assumption on the demand side, which in the earlier models implied a single low substitution elasticity for petroleum. In the current model, more costly intermediate imports induce substitution at all levels of the production structure. A second, more technical, reason for the difference stems from the inclusion in the current model of both oil price increases, so that, by the end of the period, relative prices change by a factor of around 8 or 9, instead of a factor of around 3 as in the two earlier studies. The second price increase therefore pushes substitution processes further up the isoquants and brings about more drastic changes in factor proportions than when the increases are viewed as two distinct episodes, each starting from a price ratio of unity.

7 An alternative way to accomplish this result would be to fix the input coefficient for petroleum into each sector's production process, and to make the quantity of oil imports an explicit government policy instrument.

8 The "real" exchange-rate measure used here is the price-level-deflated exchange rate, which indicates whether nominal exchange-rate movements offset the difference between domestic and world inflation rates. Throughout this chapter, the term "real exchange rate" applies to this measure. A constant real exchange rate implies no change in aggregate incentives to export or produce for the domestic market.

9 Since the negative productivity growth rates for the industrial sector averaged about −2.5 percent a year from 1978–80, whereas the positive growth rates averaged about +2.5 percent annually in 1973–7, the specification of zero growth rates in simulation 1b implies that in the latter simulation roughly half of the 1978–80 productivity loss (relative to 1973–7) is eliminated.

10 In all household income data reported in this section, skilled and unskilled labor households have been combined into a single category entitled "urban households." Rural households include both agricultural laborers and agricultural capitalists (or landowners).

11 Optimal borrowing experiments are reported for Thailand in chapter 7, but no similar experiments were done for Turkey.

12 An unanswered question that influences this result is whether there are costs associated with the existence of premium rationing in the historical run. If one accepts the existence of rent-seeking behavior, then the elimination of these rents in simulation 1 would result in more of a productivity gain. There are however no empirically based estimates of resources used for rent-seeking in Turkey.

13 Total urban employment (skilled and unskilled) is exogenous in each year. Since skilled labor has a fixed real wage that is higher than the endogenous unskilled wage, higher skilled employment (and thus lower unskilled employment) will always be associated with higher real labor incomes because of the shift in skill composition.

14 These are the import inflation rates of non-oil industrial imports (capital and intermediate goods) in each of these years.

15 The resulting pattern of growth rates corresponds approximately to elimination of the large exogenous increase in export demand associated with the 1980-1 export boom in Turkey.

16 Thus simulation 3b differs from simulation 3a in the same way that simulation 1b differs from simulation 1a.

17 One must specify exogenously a time path either for the exchange rate or for foreign borrowing. As in the India study reported in chapter 6, it would be possible to undertake an analysis of Turkish borrowing during the period, eliminate all funds clearly associated with adjustment to oil price increases, and use the resulting figures in the policy simulations. In practice, this is difficult, so instead we make assumptions about Turkish exchange-rate policy in the absence of the shocks and then allow borrowing to adjust endogenously.

18 The annual export demand growth rates used in simulation 4a are: agriculture, 5 percent; consumer goods, 5 percent; intermediate goods, 9 percent; and services, 4 percent. The annual rates used in simulation 4b are half of those in simulation 4a.

19 Unlike the simulations in chapters 6 to 8, the investment reallocation simulation is run in "savings-driven" mode here.

20 Exports of capital goods, intermediate goods, and infrastructure are fixed exogenously in dollar terms and unchanged between the historical run and simulation 5. The increase in export quantities shown in table 9.18 for these sectors occurs because lower domestic prices mean lower dollar prices received for exports, and thus higher export volumes to keep nominal dollar values unchanged. It should be recalled that exports from these three sectors are very small.

10 Conclusions

1 Introduction

Developing countries were wracked by a series of external shocks in the 1970s and early 1980s: (i) the quadrupling of petroleum prices in 1973–4, corresponding to a real increase of 150 per cent, a real decline during 1974–8, and an 80 percent increase in real terms between 1978 and 1980; (ii) the concomitant stagflation in the OECD countries in 1973–4 and 1979–80, punctuated by a strong recovery; and (iii) the increase in nominal interest rates, deflated by developing-country export prices, from −10 percent in 1979 to 20 percent in 1981. To those must be added other fluctuations in the external environment, for example, a boom in a number of primary commodities, such as cocoa, coffee, phosphate, and uranium in the mid 1970s followed by a collapse of their prices in the early 1980s to levels not seen since the Second World War. But that was not all. There was a devastating succession of droughts in the Sahelian countries in the early 1970s and more isolated episodes of harvest failure, such as in Korea in 1978–9 and in India in 1979–80.

There is much analytical merit in distinguishing among different types of shocks and appropriate responses entailed by each of these. But the above description of events shows that countries were in practice required to react to a multiplicity of shocks, in some cases simultaneously and in others sequentially, that often pulled in opposite directions. This alone would have made the formulation of coherent adjustment policy difficult. When it is further realized that the countries thus responding to conflicting policy imperatives constituted a very diverse group, the task of imposing analytical order on the richness of country experience, in order to elicit policy-relevant lessons, is made more complicated.

And yet that has defined the agenda for this study. It has been twofold. First, an analytical method deriving from the absorption-cum-switching framework of open economy macroeconomics was implemented on data from thirty-three developing countries (i) to classify them into groups

289

according to the degree of reliance on different modes of adjustment, and (ii) to draw general conclusions about patterns of adjustment (chapter 2). Second, these conclusions were examined in greater depth by describing the structure and workings of a general equilibrium-based policy framework (chapter 4), identifying four oil-importing developing countries – India, Thailand, Kenya, and Turkey – where the framework was to be implemented (chapter 5) and using the four models to study the adjustment experience of those countries (chapters 6–9). The transition from the method of chapter 2 to that of chapter 4 was eased in chapter 3 by constructing a half way house that relies on a data base typically employed in general equilibrium analysis – a Social Accounting Matrix for Kenya – to probe a number of the hypotheses suggested by the method of chapter 2, using partial equilibrium analysis.

2 External shocks

The terms-of-trade losses arising from the oil price shocks have been seen to be very large for the oil-importing developing countries. They were, however, also accompanied by considerable external financing. Much of that was due to the recycling of petrodollars that would not have occurred in the absence of the oil price shocks. How then does a scenario of no external-shocks-cum-associated borrowing compare with historical developments? This was explored in the country studies as follows.[1] In India, a scenario of no external shocks, together with no external assistance in the form of borrowing from the IMF's Oil Facility, the oil-exporting countries, the IMF's Extended Fund Facility, and workers' remittances, would have led to mostly higher investment and output up to 1976/7.[2] The elimination of both the oil shocks as well as the coffee and tea booms in Kenya, together with the setting of annual external borrowing at "normal" levels so as to eliminate its boom and oil shock-induced components, would have benefited the economy: terminal capital stock, which is a proxy for future growth potential, the import capacity of the economy (in all years except 1978), and export volumes would all have been higher. The debt-service burden would have been very much lower. The corresponding policy simulation in Turkey removes both external shocks and, in the absence of any readily available benchmark regarding "without shock" foreign borrowing, postulates that policy-makers manage the economy so as to achieve a rate of appreciation of the real exchange rate of 1 percent, a figure consistent with historical experience. Such an assumption about the real exchange rate leads to a lower level of foreign borrowing, so that the experiment shares broad similarities with the India and Kenya policy simulations described above. At the same time, premium rationing of imports is eliminated, remittances set to approximate historic levels, and growth in world export demand smoothed, and reduced to half of that in the historical run. GDP, consumption, and imports are all substantially higher in 1981 compared to the historical run. And, finally, it was seen that external shocks, net of favorable exogenous developments, were indeed positive in Thailand, so that, in their absence, real GDP in 1982 would have been almost 14 percent higher than its actual value.[3]

The above evidence indicates that the absence of external shocks, and such foreign borrowing as the data allow to be associated with them, would indeed have left the economies in question better off in terms of the leading macroeconomic indicators. The comparative analysis of chapter 2 did not however find any statistical association between the size of external shocks, expressed as a proportion of GNP, and country performance as measured either by the rate of growth of GNP or the deviation from its pre-shock value. This does not contradict the evidence on the damaging effects of external shocks suggested by the country studies, which are based on comparisons with "no shock" scenarios; indeed growth rates over the 1973–81 period were in general lower than in 1963–73. Instead, the lack of a statistical association implies that the magnitude of external shocks cannot account for differences in growth performance across countries. In particular, the analysis of chapter 2 indicated a significant correlation between economic growth and the importance of export expansion in adjustment to external shocks, as well as a particularly strong correlation between export expansion and public resource mobilization in response to those shocks. This lends support to the desirability of classifying countries on the basis of modes of adjustment, as is done in that chapter, rather than by structural characteristics or the magnitude of external shocks. Furthermore, the most successful adjustment, featuring export expansion and public resource mobilization, occurred in countries which faced among the most severe external shocks.

3 Fiscal adjustment

The need to retain a sense of perspective about the importance of external shocks is confirmed by a comparison of their role *vis-à-vis* those of internal policy failures. Thus, an important finding emerging from the study of thirty-three developing countries, and made possible by the application of an analytical framework that incorporates both fiscal and trade adjustment, is that public-sector profligacy was in many cases at least as important as external shocks in worsening their balance of payments. This took many different forms. Internal upheavals in Jamaica and Portugal led to a significant expansion in the role of the public sector and in fiscal deficits. In Brazil there was an (eventually) unsuccessful attempt to pursue growth without adjustment in the face of heightened popular expectations. And in the Southern Cone of Latin America – in particular, Argentina and Uruguay – exchange-rate adjustment was held hostage to inappropriate domestic monetary and fiscal policy, a situation that was to prove unsustainable.

This attention to fiscal adjustment is important for two reasons. *First*, it focuses on the critical role of tax intensification and public consumption restraint in bringing about the disabsorption required to effect a transfer to oil-exporting and creditor countries. The emphasis is timely, given the importance attached to switching policies and, in particular, export expansion in earlier applied work.[4] This is certainly not to suggest the unimportance of trade adjustment, a position that in any event could not be supported by the statistical analysis of chapter 2, but simply to remind that fiscal and trade adjustment are both important and complementary elements of a package of policy responses to external shocks. Indeed, the theory of adjustment argues that switching without disabsorption is likely to lead to inflation without any improvement in the balance of payments.

Although fiscal adjustment is important, attention must also be paid to the methods employed in bringing it about. Thus, one of the counterfactual policy simulations on Kenya (see chapter 8) explores the consequences of substituting domestic resources for external borrowing, while maintaining fixed investment at its historical levels. Specifically, the ratio of external borrowing to investment is fixed at 35 percent, a crude approximation to its "normal" long-term level, while domestic tax rates and government consumption are scaled uniformly upwards and downwards respectively. This ensures that a transfer of income from the private to the public sector enhances national savings, which is precisely what is needed to finance investment fixed at historical levels following a decline in external borrowing. However, the transfer of income to the public sector is deflationary and reduces GDP, consumption, and government revenue sharply *vis-à-vis* the historical run. This sacrifice, while maintaining the economy's growth potential, leads to lower levels of external indebtedness. However, it would have been preferable if the reduction in absorption were to be more flexibly implemented, so as not to impose unacceptable costs on consumption in years when it was already quite low.

The importance of promoting national savings is also brought out in one of the policy simulations in chapter 9 on Turkey which explores the consequences of a policy package comprising unchanged (rather than falling) marginal savings propensities in the private sector, a moderate (rather than drastic) increase in the share of public consumption and investment in GDP, and real exchange-rate devaluation (as opposed to appreciation up to 1980). Such a package leads to an increase in GDP growth compared to the historical run in the period 1977–81, a very significant increase in exports, more than halving of the cumulative net inflow of foreign capital, and an increase in the capital stock brought about, as a result of the above assumptions, through a more even split in the growth between private and public investment.

Needless to say, the above policy simulations are more useful in identifying broad orders of magnitude than in describing exactly how fiscal adjustment should take place. There are two points to be made. First, the relative dependence on external versus domestic resources should emerge from an intertemporal cost–benefit calculation of the kind that explicitly incorporates the tradeoff between foreign borrowing and domestic savings. The former permits more current consumption, while the latter increases future consumption because of lower debt-service payments. Such an optimization experiment done for Thailand in chapter 7 shows that much more investment and borrowing in the early years after the first oil price shock and much less in the later years would have maintained Thailand's growth potential with a lower external debt burden.

Second, fiscal adjustment would not typically take the form of across-the-board tax intensification and reduction of public consumption. During the period under consideration, much of Kenya's tax revenue was derived from a turnover tax system, so that intensification of tax rates on raw materials and capital goods would have exacerbated tax-induced cascading and production inefficiency in the economy. Hence, tax intensification would preferably have taken the form of reforming the tax system in the direction of taxation of consumption, implemented, as in many other countries, via the value-added technique, so as to reap some efficiency gains. Similarly, certain public expenditures, usually those on infrastructure and poverty alleviation, are socially more productive than others and should not be subject to across-the-board reductions. Identifying those expenditures requires detailed microeconomic and sectoral analysis.

The *second* reason for the importance of fiscal adjustment arises because, with the very considerable difficulties in obtaining additional external financing that currently prevail, it is clear that fiscal adjustment will have to play an even more important role in developing-country adjustment to future external shocks. Thus, model-based calculations adapted from Mitra and Go (1990) on India, one of the countries severely affected by the 1990/1 Gulf crisis, suggest that, in the absence of foreign borrowing, an increase in oil prices – from pre-crisis levels of $16 to $21 a barrel, the average price facing India in fiscal year 1990/1 – together with a cessation of workers' remittances from Iraq and Kuwait, would have required *either* a 12 percent increase in the average tax rate *or* an average expenditure reduction of 3 percent, together with a real depreciation in the exchange rate of the order of 1.5 percent in order to maintain existing levels of investment. Additional foreign financing equaling 1 percent of the pre-shock current-account deficit would bring the tax and expenditure adjustment numbers down to 11 percent and 2.5 percent respectively and the real exchange-rate adjustment to around 1 percent.

4 Commodity booms

The analysis of thirty-three developing countries shows that many of the primary producers experienced peaks and troughs in terms of trade, mainly caused by fluctuations in primary commodity prices. This made it difficult to formulate and maintain a coherent set of adjustment policies to oil shocks and concomitant recessions in the OECD countries. Indeed, there seemed to be a widespread perception (a) that unfavorable shocks (oil price increases) were temporary and could therefore be met through borrowing, and (b) that favorable shocks (coffee, cocoa, phosphate, and tin price increases) were more than transitory and therefore justified increased public spending.

Unfavorable shocks are temporary

Notwithstanding variations in initial conditions and policy packages, the impression (shared in a number of developed countries) that the 1973–4 oil price increase was temporary and could therefore be met by short-term borrowing was widely prevalent. Thus, Turkey did not undertake fiscal and trade adjustment in response to the first round of oil shocks, relying instead on external borrowing to tide her over balance-of-payments difficulties. Chapter 9 demonstrates that the strategy was unsustainable and would have been derailed even in the absence of the 1979–80 round of external shocks. The discussion of chapter 7 shows that Thailand used foreign borrowing to postpone adjustment to the first oil price shock. In India, likewise, the oil price rise was thought of as a temporary phenomenon. While the domestic monetary-fiscal policy stance was tightened very considerably, leading to rapid balance-of-payments adjustment at the expense of investment and growth, this, as chapter 6 argues, was undertaken more to combat inflationary pressures arising out of harvest failure and other domestic disturbances than in response to terms-of-trade shocks.

Favorable shocks are permanent

The link between commodity booms and stepped-up public spending was brought about by the fact that the boom often occurred in a sector with which the government either had direct fiscal ties or which was a source of export tax revenue. The pattern is discouragingly familiar in a large number of countries. Thus, the coffee and cocoa boom fueled an extremely ambitious investment program in the Ivory Coast and it is estimated that earnings foregone as a result of relaxing investment criteria used prior to the boom amounted to 5 percent of GDP in the early 1980s. Faced with increases in energy and metal prices, Bolivia stepped up public investment on projects, a number of which had low returns. In Morocco, the phosphate boom encouraged public investment in capital-intensive structures and, more generally, a pattern of government expenditure from which retrenchment was difficult when the commodity boom collapsed. Finally, the case study of Kenya in chapter 8 shows clearly how any sense of urgency arising out of the need to adjust to the first round of oil price shocks was undermined by the overborrowing – and associated large increases in consumption and imports – made possible by the primary commodity boom of the mid 1970s.

A policy rule

This pattern of policy responses suggests that it might be desirable for the purposes of economic management to regard favorable shocks as temporary and therefore not to permit difficult-to-reverse increases in public consumption and investment and, correspondingly, to regard unfavorable shocks as permanent and therefore requiring adjustment rather than financing. No doubt, the pursuit of such a rule in an ideal world would lead to costly mistakes. But given the tendency to optimism and the aversion to undertaking painful adjustments displayed by many of the countries analyzed in this book, it may serve as a useful device for restraining excesses in the public sector. It deserves serious consideration in guiding developing-country adjustment to future external shocks.

5 Growth-oriented adjustment

By itself, a low current-account deficit reveals little about the success of adjustment. This is because it is consistent with both low saving and investment as well as with high saving and investment. Only the latter is likely to be associated with growth-oriented adjustment. Broadly speaking, given a current-account deficit, adjustment will be more growth-oriented if it is consumption rather than investment that has borne the brunt of disabsorption. But the argument needs to be qualified, since an increase in efficiency and improved sectoral composition can support the same or higher growth with lower levels of investment. Indeed, the discussion on the

Ivory Coast and Bolivia in chapter 2 highlights the dubious nature of public investments financed by windfall gains arising out of the primary commodity boom.[5]

Investment reallocation

Growth-oriented adjustment therefore requires careful reprioritization of public expenditure and investment programs in the light of their benefits. While this will call in practice for a more microeconomic analysis, a rough indication of the efficiency gains made available by a better targeted investment program is provided by examining the consequences of reallocating investment even within the six sectors singled out for analysis in the four country studies.

Since the sectoral allocation of investment in the historical run is given, there is no tendency for sectoral rates of return to investment to come together over time. In order to help answer the question posed above, the country models are asked the question: what would be the consequences of reallocating the same amount of investment as in the historical run in response to differences in sectoral rates of return? The results are instructive. Thus, in Kenya, the average gain in gross output as a result of implementing this investment rule is 2.2 percent compared to the historical run, with the largest increases occurring in the consumer-goods and intermediate-goods producing sectors. The corresponding gain in the "no-external-shock-cum-terms-of-trade-induced-borrowing" simulation mentioned above, compared to the historical run, is 2.3 percent. This comparison shows that the output losses from external shocks were comparable to those arising from not pursuing a more "market-" based system of investment allocation. Furthermore, the latter would not have generated any obviously undesirable distributional outcomes. The same is the case in Thailand, where implementation of the above investment rule would have led to increases in outputs of all sectors except services and improved the lot of all groups in the population except the best off, viz., white-collar workers who derive most of their income from the service sector. The results are, however, less clear-cut in the case of India. While GDP and consumption are higher, there is a deterioration in the balance-of-payments on two counts. First, the intermediate-goods producing sector which, being part of manufacturing, is one of the beneficiaries of the investment reallocation, is an above-average user of imported intermediates. Second, the extra income raises domestic demand for agricultural and consumer goods and, hence, their prices. Since consumer goods account for the vast majority of Indian exports, this erodes their competitiveness in world markets and leads to a marked decline in exports.[6]

While the results emerging from these policy simulations are interesting, it is important not to attach a great deal of significance to the actual numbers emerging from the investment reallocation simulations for the four countries. First, data on investment and its sectoral allocation in the historical run are among the less reliable parts of the data base assembled for each country. Second, the particular investment rule implemented here, though simple and therefore policy-implementable, focuses entirely on short-run profitability. It would therefore be instructive to look at other, more forward-looking rules for reallocating investment, a task that would, however, be computationally very expensive with even a moderate disaggregation of sectors of the kind used here.

The above caveats notwithstanding, since reshuffling the allocation of investment is an important part of growth-oriented supply-side adjustment to shocks, and since the efficiency gains from the investment reallocation examined here are sufficiently large, it may be concluded that countries should pay serious attention to introducing greater market orientation in the allocation of investment across different sectors of the economy.

Savings through taxation

Adverse terms-of-trade movements, by imposing income losses, reduce savings. The increasing savings necessary to support growth-oriented adjustment can then be expected to come from the public sector in the form of revenue increases through taxation. This raises the question: will domestic savings be increased through taxation? Or might the private sector reduce its savings by the same amount as public savings are increased? Empirical evidence suggests otherwise; the private sector reduces its saving by only a fraction of the amount raised through additional taxes.[7] Hence, increased taxation accompanied by restraint on government expenditure can indeed raise domestic saving.

Comparing India and Korea

Patterns of growth-oriented adjustment of the kind discussed here were, however, generally not observed in the countries analyzed in this study. This was no doubt in part because lessons available with the benefit of hindsight were not readily appreciated at the time. But it was also because countries were subject to numerous different shocks either more or less simultaneously or over time. Thus, for example, the first oil price shock occurred at a time when India was suffering from a 17 percent rate of inflation brought on by a severe drought in 1972–3 and steeply rising defense expenditures. The need to arrest inflation was perceived to be more important than that of adjusting to external shocks and triggered a stiff dose of demand management. The resulting domestic price stability and underutilized capacity in the manufacturing sector however made possible a strong export response resulting in rapid balance-of-payments adjustment. Although imports in general went up throughout the seventies compared to the previous decade because of some trade liberalization, there was a slowdown in intermediate- and capital-goods imports and concomitant stagnation in the ratio of investment to GNP. In fact, public investment was not increased for fear of generating inflationary pressures, notwithstanding accumulating reserves of food due to bumper harvests in the mid 1970s and of foreign exchange due to workers' remittances from the Gulf countries.

The 1979–80 shocks thus occurred against a background of substantial food and foreign exchange reserves. They did however coincide with a severe drought; real income fell by 15 percent from the record level of the previous year. Adjustment policy was somewhat bolder. The maintenance of export orientation was encouraged through further import liberalization to ensure that domestic producers were exposed to international competition. The government stepped up real public investment as well as imports of food, edible oil, and fiber to help contain inflation. Domestic oil exploration efforts were increased substantially. The enlarged current-account deficit resulting from these developments was met by continuing private remittances and an Extended Fund Facility from the IMF.

Thus, while India's deflationary adjustment policy to the first round of external shocks had negative consequences for investment and growth, it was partly responsible for creating very substantial food and foreign exchange reserves which permitted an altogether bolder and potentially more growth-oriented adjustment to the second round of external shocks.[8] Indeed, a more growth-oriented response to the first round of shocks, underwritten by greater external borrowing and supplemented by selective imports of wage goods to combat inflationary pressures, would have resulted either in a significantly higher external debt burden or, what is very similar, a much lower level of foreign exchange reserves. Policy-makers would then have found themselves with less room for maneuver on the eve of the second round of shocks. Whether that would have necessarily triggered a more cautious response must remain a matter of judgment.

A somewhat contrasting example is provided by Korea's adjustment to the two rounds of external shocks. Adjustment to the first involved a vigorous export expansion drive that was aided by a devaluation in 1974, as well as subsidies and various other export incentives. Indeed, the method of chapter 2 shows that the balance-of-payments effect of export expansion exceeded that of external shocks very significantly. Although public consumption was expanded, this was more than offset by tax intensification, resulting in a stepping up of public resource mobilization. The growth of private consumption was also held in check during this period and real wages were restrained relative to the consumer price index in 1974 and 1975, although this was to be reversed in later years. This powerful export and domestic resource mobilization effort allowed Korea to finance an investment boom with comparatively limited recourse to external borrowing over and above the historical trend of the latter.

The contours of adjustment to the second round of external shocks, which comprised not only terms-of-trade losses but also adverse interest-rate movements on external debt, were however quite different. What is most striking is the diminished role of export expansion and very significant reliance on external financing. The reasons are to be sought in differences in initial conditions, in turn partly caused by the policies pursued after the first oil price shock. First, the investment boom referred to above was encouraged by a massive expansion in domestic bank lending, and led to overheating of the economy in 1977, 1978, and early 1979. The resulting pressure on the labor market caused a steep rise in wages in excess of productivity gains and a gradual erosion of competitiveness in export markets. This fact, together with the slowdown in growth in the developed-country trading partners, accounted in 1979 for the first decline in Korean exports in fifteen years. Second, an extremely bad harvest in 1978–9 fueled cost–push inflationary pressures, with deleterious consequences for competitiveness. The need to finance temporary shortfalls caused by the poor harvest explains part of the additional external borrowing undertaken in these years. Contractionary demand management, credit limits, and devaluation helped stabilize the economy and restore export growth again.

This discussion of sequences of deflationary and growth-oriented adjustment in India and Korea suggests, with the benefit of hindsight, that there were intertemporal tradeoffs between the modes of adjustment to the first and second round of shocks. Judgments regarding the appropriateness of growth-oriented adjustment therefore need to take into account not only the standard considerations of absorption and switching but also the fact that a particular mode of adjustment to one shock creates initial conditions that, *inter alia*, shape adjustment to a subsequent one.

6 Equity-oriented adjustment

The question of the impact of adjustment to external shocks on poverty and income distribution has been the subject of much discussion.[9] While all four country studies in this book have focused on this question, it receives the most systematic attention in the India study. That study exploits all the data in the national accounts as well as in the National Sample Survey (1) to allocate production-related and transfer income to fifteen rural and fifteen urban classes, (2) to map the income of those groups into consumption expenditure of five rural and five urban groups, using estimates of savings behavior, and (3) to disaggregate the consumption expenditure of those groups into those for individual items, using econometrically estimated complete demand systems. This allows an extensive investigation of the consequences of any policy package, not only on macroeconomic and sectoral aggregates, but also on the position of the ten groups of households (five rural and five urban) as well as on summary measures such as the Gini coefficients of income or consumption inequality. A detailed discussion was presented in chapter 6.

The question of whether an economy's adjustment to various shocks has a satisfactory or adverse distributional impact is not well posed. This is because, faced with terms-of-trade and other changes, an economy must adjust. The more interesting exercise is then to compare the distributional consequences of the adjustment policies actually adopted in a country with those that would have resulted from alternative policies. This is precisely the approach taken in the four country studies.

The historical run of the India study shows no particular change in the evolution of inequality over the period 1973–4 and 1983–4 among the five rural and five urban groups identified by the study, a development that was noted to be broadly consistent with available empirical evidence. Furthermore, comparisons of the historical run with a large range of counterfactuals reveals hardly any change either in the Gini coefficients, in the cost-of-living indices for the various groups, or in the share of the bottom 40 percent of the population in income and consumption. And, although data for the other three countries did not permit a similarly detailed attention to distribution, the relatively limited distributional impact of macroeconomic policy changes is found there as well.

The reasons for this have to do with the structure of the labor markets as well as with the level of aggregation at which the studies are conducted. Starting with the former, the "full employment" character of the models employed implies that returns to all households from different sources roughly offset each other.[10] Moreover, as argued in chapter 4, general equilibrium analysis, by taking into account a wider class of substitution mechanisms working through factor markets than is typically the case with partial equilibrium analysis, tends to dampen movements in the distribution of income. Since the assumption of a segmented and fully employed labor market does not appear unreasonable, it is necessary to accept its implications for income distribution as well.

Turning to the latter, since the six-sector scheme is derived from a considerably more disaggregated input–output table, it is clear that the analysis could be conducted at such a level.[11] The data do not however permit any further significant disaggregation of households, so that it is not possible to study the effect of policies at a high level of disaggregation with respect to both commodities and households.[12] And yet, variations in the consumption and employment characteristics of households can be expected to be important only at a very disaggregated level. This implies that distributional effects will be noticeable only for policies that can be aimed at household or income groups on the basis of such variations, for example, highly targeted expenditure reductions or tax increases, rather than broad macroeconomic policies. Or, to put it another way, what is critical for the distributional impact of adjustment is the way in which policy-makers give concrete expression at the microeconomic and sectoral level to broad macroeconomic policies. More positively, careful targeting of tax and expenditure changes has the potential for minimizing the adverse distributional impact of adjustment policies.

Finally, it must be stressed that the above insensitivity would not hold if the range of policy alternatives explored included redistribution of endowments, such as land and capital. Policies that did this would certainly change the distribution of income and consumption. However, such redistribution was not an element of policy discussions of adjustment in any of the four countries considered in this study. It is therefore unnecessary to consider the effects of such policies here.

7 Lessons

Iraq's invasion of Kuwait in August 1990 led to the price of oil doubling from \$16–\$17 to around \$30 a barrel, the drying up of workers' remittances and adverse effects on tourism in a number of countries in the Middle East. Ten countries – Bangladesh, Egypt, India, Jordan, Pakistan, Philippines, Sri Lanka, Sudan, and Turkey – were classified by the World Bank as being "most immediately impacted" by those developments. While OPEC crude oil prices fell back to pre-crisis levels by the second quarter of 1991, the episode highlighted the vulnerability to disruption in the oil market that attends the world's increasing dependence on oil supplies from OPEC in general and, within OPEC, on a few countries – Saudi Arabia, Iran, the United Arab Emirates, Iraq, and Kuwait – in particular. This latest episode, together with the other convulsions experienced by the international economy in the last two decades prompt the question: how should oil-importing developing countries respond to such terms-of-trade shocks in the future?

To summarize the lessons of experience:

It would be advisable for oil-importing developing countries to treat adverse terms-of-trade shocks as permanent in terms of the adjustments required on the demand side. It is then preferable to implement the necessary disabsorption and switching policies, rather than to rely mainly on external financing. Expensive supply-augmenting public investment, for example in domestic energy sources, should however be delayed till the nature and duration of a shock becomes clearer.

Given that investments in a number of countries have experienced poor returns, their reduction would effect disabsorption while actually improving efficiency. Beyond that, disabsorption should as far as possible be directed at consumption while protecting public expenditures oriented toward poverty alleviation.

Switching policies should not be accompanied by import tariffs and other restrictions that bias the incentive structure against exports, weaken links with the world economy, and reduce flexibility in responding to subsequent shocks. Indeed, adjustment in countries characterized by such restrictions should include import liberalization and export expansion.

Oil price increases should in general be passed on except where the existing price to users includes a large tax component. Incomplete pass-through will worsen the budgetary situation and call for absorption and switching policies.

Greater market orientation should be introduced in the allocation of investment across different products and sectors.

Every country must adjust to external shocks, for the observation that investment is the sum of domestic and foreign savings is no more than an accounting identity. Our study demonstrates that policies can however determine whether that adjustment is achieved with growth or stagnation. The above summary of applicable lessons, based on the experience of the two major oil price shocks, shows what needs to be done. We recommend them as a guide to adjustment policy for the future in the developing world.

Notes

1 For details, see chapters 6 to 9.
2 This was to be reversed later in the period following the substantial external borrowing that occurred after the second round of external shocks.
3 Since Thailand did not borrow from special oil facilities, the simulation makes no adjustment for foreign borrowing.

4 See, for example, Balassa (1981a, 1984).

5 Thus, World Bank (1983) estimates that the return on investment – defined as the average annual growth of real GDP divided by the average investment rate at current prices – fell from 26.8 percent during 1960–70 to 20.5 percent during 1970–80 in developing countries. In sixteen countries of twenty-two requiring debt rescheduling during 1982–3, the rate of return on investment had declined below 20 percent in the late 1970s and early 1980s. The report also notes that the decline in the return on investment was even more marked in the industrialized countries over the same period.

6 Results essentially similar to those for the other countries hold for Turkey, but the investment reallocation simulation for that country is not strictly comparable, as it holds foreign savings constant and allows total investment to vary in order to satisfy the savings–investment balance for the economy as a whole.

7 See Haque and Montiel (1987).

8 This was not the only reason for the bolder response. For a fuller discussion, see chapter 6.

9 See, for example, Development Committee (1988), Cornia, Jolly, and Stewart (1987).

10 The "full employment" assumption refers to no open unemployment of laborers. In fact, those who cannot find high-paying employment drift into low-productivity occupations where the wage must move to clear the market. For details, see chapter 4.

11 Thus, for example, the input–output table underlying the India study distinguishes 115 sectors.

12 In fact, the data base for India permits a study of the five rural and five urban households at a nine-sector level of disaggregation but this, from the point of view of distribution, makes little difference compared to the six-sector disaggregation chosen in chapter 6.

References

Ahluwalia, I. (1985), *Industrial Growth and Stagnation in India*, Oxford University Press.

Ahluwalia, M. (1986), "Balance of Payments Adjustment in India, 1970–71 to 1983–84," *World Development*, 14(8), pp.937–62.

Ahamed, L. and W. Branson (1983), "Kenya: Short Run Macroeconomic Policies," World Bank, Initiating Memorandum (April).

Aitchison, J. and J.A.C. Brown (1969), *The Lognormal Distribution*. New York: Cambridge University Press.

Allen, R. and C. Hayden (1980), "The Revised Kenya Social Accounting Matrix (1976)," ODA, University of Warwick (December, processed).

Ansu, Y. (1985), "External Shocks, Domestic Policies and Structural Changes: Kenya 1971–82," World Bank, processed.

Balassa, B. (1981a), "The Newly Industrializing Developing Countries After the Oil Crisis," *Weltwirtschaftliches Archiv*, 117(1), pp. 142–94.

(1981b), "Growth Policies and the Exchange Rate in Turkey," in *The Role of Exchange Rate Policy in Achieving the Outward Orientation of the Turkish Economy*, Meban Securities Brokerage and Finance Corporation, Istanbul.

(1983), "The Adjustment Experience of Developing Economies After 1973," in J. Williamson (ed.), *IMF Conditionality*, Washington, DC: Institute for International Economics, pp. 145–74.

(1984), "Adjustment Policies in Developing Countries: A Reassessment," *World Development*, 12, pp. 955–72.

(1984), "The Policy Experience of Twelve Less Developed Countries," in G. Ranis, R.L. West, M. Leiserson, and C. C. Morris (eds.), *Comparative Development Perspectives: Essays in Honor of Lloyd Reynolds*, Boulder: Westview Press.

(1985), "Exports, Policy Choices, and Economic Growth in Developing Countries after the 1973 Oil Shock," *Journal of Development Economics*, 18, pp. 23–35.

(1986), "Policy Responses to Exogenous Shocks in Developing Countries," *American Economic Review*, 76, pp. 75–78.

Balassa, B. and F. McCarthy (1984), "Adjustment Policies in Developing Countries, 1979–83: An Update," World Bank Staff Working Paper No. 675.

Bank of Thailand (1977), *Annual Economic Report*.

Bevan, D., P. Collier, and J. Gunning (1987), "Consequences of a Commodity Boom in a Controlled Economy: Accumulation and Redistribution in Kenya," *World Bank Economic Review*, 1(3), pp. 489–513.

——— (1989), "Fiscal Response to a Temporary Trade Shock: The Aftermath of the Kenyan Coffee Boom," *World Bank Economic Review*, 3(3), p. 359–78.

Bhagwati, J. and P. Desai (1970), *India: Planning for Industrialization*, London: Oxford University Press.

Bhagwati, J. and T.N. Srinivasan (1975), *Foreign Trade Regimes and Economic Development: India*, New York: National Bureau of Economic Research.

Bhalla, S. and P. Vasistha (1988), "Income Redistribution in India: A Reexamination," in T.N. Srinivasan and P. Bardhan (eds.), *Rural Poverty in South Asia*, New York: Columbia University Press.

Brooke, A., D. Kendrick, and A. Meeraus (1988), *GAMS: A User's Guide*, Scientific Press, Redwood City, California.

Bruno, M. (1982), "Adjustment and Structural Changes Under Supply Shocks," *Scandinavian Journal of Economics*, 84, pp. 199–221.

Bruno, M. and J. Sachs (1985), *Economics of Worldwide Stagflation*, Massachusetts: Harvard University Press.

Buffie, E. (1986), "Input Price Shocks in the Small Open Economy," *Oxford Economic Papers*, No. 38, pp. 551–65.

Celasun, M. (1983), "Sources of Industrial Growth and Structural Change: The Case of Turkey," World Bank Staff Working Paper No. 614.

Chamratrithirong, A. (1979), *Recent Migrants in Bangkok Metropolis: A Follow-Up Study of Migrants' Adjustment, Assimilation and Integration*, Mahidol University, Institute for Population and Social Research.

Chenery, H., S. Robinson, and M. Syrquin (1986), *Industrialization and Growth: A Comparative Study*, London: Oxford University Press.

Chu, Ke-Young (1987a), "External Shocks and Fiscal Adjustment in Developing Countries: Experiences During 1962–82," IMF Staff Working Paper No. WP/87/48.

——— (1987b), "External Shocks and the Process of Fiscal Adjustment in a Small Open Developing Economy," IMF Staff Working Paper No. WP/87/11.

Cline, W. et al. (1981), *World Inflation and the Developing Countries*, Washington, DC: Brookings Institution.

Condon, T., S. Robinson, and S. Urata (1985), "Coping with a Foreign Exchange Crisis: A General Equilibrium Model of Alternative Adjustment Mechanisms," in A.S. Manne (ed.), *Economic Equilibrium: Model Formulation and Solution*, Mathematical Programming Study No. 23, Amsterdam: North-Holland Publishing Company.

Corbo, V. and J. de Melo (1987), "External Shocks and Policy Reforms in the Southern Cone: a Reassessment," in G. Calvo (ed.), *Debt, Stabilization and Development*, Oxford: Basil Blackwell.

Corden, M. (1985), *Inflation, Exchange Rates and the World Economy*, Oxford University Press.

Cornia, G., R. Jolly, and F. Stewart (1987), *Adjustment with a Human Face*,

London: Oxford University Press.

Deaton, A. and J. Muellbauer (1980), *Economics and Consumer Behavior*, New York: Cambridge University Press.

Dell, S. and R. Lawrence (1986), "Balance-of-Payments Adjustment in the 1980s," *World Development*, 14, pp. 873–1105.

Dervis, K. and S. Robinson (1978), "The Foreign Exchange Gap, Growth and Industrial Strategy in Turkey: 1973–1983," World Bank Staff Working Paper No. 306.

(1982), "A General Equilibrium Analysis of the Causes of a Foreign Exchange Crisis: The Case of Turkey," *Weltwirtschaftliches Archiv*, 118(2), pp. 259–80.

Dervis, K., J. de Melo, and S. Robinson (1982), *General Equilibrium Models for Development Policy*, New York: Cambridge University Press.

Devarjan, S. and H. Sierra (1986), "Growth Without Adjustment: Thailand, 1973 to 1982," Country Policy Department, Discussion Paper No. 1986–5. Washington, DC: World Bank.

Development Committee (1988), *Protecting the Poor During Periods of Adjustment*, World Bank.

Dick, H. and S. Gupta (1984), "Effect of Oil Price Increases on Four Oil-Poor Developing Countries: A Comparative Analysis," *Energy Economics*, 6, pp. 59–70.

Dornbusch, R. (1980), *Open Economy Macroeconomics*, New York: Basic Books.

(1990), "From Stabilization to Growth," Paper presented to the Conference on Development Economics, World Bank (April).

Dunkerley, J. (1979), "Adjustment to Higher Oil Prices," Working Paper for Discussion at the July 10th, 1979 meeting of Ford Energy/LDC Group.

Edwards, S. (1989), "Temporary Terms of Trade Disturbances, the Real Exchange Rate and the Current Account," *Economica*, 56, pp. 343–57.

Edwards, S. and S. van Wijnbergen (1989), "Structural Adjustment and Disequilibrium," in H. Chenery and T.N. Srinivasan (eds.), *Handbook of Development Economics*, Amsterdam: North-Holland.

Fried, E. and C. Schultze (eds.) (1975), *Higher Oil Prices and The World Economy: The Adjustment Problem*, Washington, DC: Brookings Institution.

Gelb, A. (1989), *Oil Windfalls: Blessing or Curse*, London: Oxford University Press.

Ghanem, H. and H. Kharas (1985), "Foreign Borrowing and the Real Exchange Rate in LDCs," World Bank CPD Discussion Paper No. 1985–4.

Government of India (1984), *Economic Survey 1983/84*, Ministry of Finance.

Government of Thailand (1960), *Population Census*.

(1973), *Labor Force Survey*.

(1977), *Survey of Migration in Bangkok Metropolis*, National Statistical Office, Bangkok.

Gupta, S. and S. Togan (1984), "On Managing Adjustment to External Shocks in Oil Importing Developing Countries," *Journal of Policy Modeling*, 6(1), pp. 95–109.

Haque, N.U. and P. Montiel (1987), "Ricardian Equivalence, Liquidity Constraints and the Yaari-Blanchard Effect: Tests for Developing Countries," IMF Working Paper No. WP/87/85.

Hideshima, K. and Y. Inoue (1982), "Impact of the Oil Crisis on the Economic Growth of Developing Countries – Case Studies for the Philippines & Thailand," International Development Center of Japan, Working Paper Series No. 22.

Hoffmann, L. and L. Jarass (1983), "Impact of Rising Oil Prices on Oil-Importing Developing Countries and the Scope for Adjustment," *Weltwirtschaftsliches Archiv*, 119, pp. 297–316.

Khan, M. and M. Knight (1983), "Determinants of Current Account Balances of Non-oil Developing Countries in the 1970s," IMF Staff Papers, 30(4), pp. 819–42.

Khan, M. (1986), "Developing Country Exchange Rate Policy Responses to Exogenous Shocks," *American Economic Review*, 76, pp. 84–7.

Kharas, H. and H. Shishido (1986), "Thailand: An Assessment of Alternative Foreign Exchange Borrowing Strategies," *Journal of Policy Modelling*, 8, pp. 1–26.

Killick, T. *et al.* (1984), *The Quest for Economic Stabilization*, Vol. II, "Kenya, 1975–81," London: Heinemann, Chapter 5.

Lewis, J. and S. Urata (1984), "Anatomy of a Balance-of-Payments Crisis: Application of a Computable General Equilibrium Model to Turkey, 1978–1980," *Economic Modelling*, 1(3), pp. 281–303.

Lin, Ching-yuan (1981), *Developing Countries in a Turbulent World: Patterns of Adjustment Since the Oil Crisis*, Praeger Publishers.

Little, I., T. Scitovsky, and M. Scott (1970), *Industry and Trade in Some Development Countries: A Comparative Study*, London: Oxford University Press.

Marion, N. and L. Svensson (1984), "Adjustment to Expected and Unexpected Oil Price Increases," *Canadian Journal of Economics*, 17, pp. 15–31.

Martin, R. and M. Selowsky (1984), "Energy Prices, Substitution, and Optimal Borrowing in the Short Run: An Analysis of Adjustment in Oil Importing Developing Countries," *Journal of Development Economics*, 14, pp. 331–50.

McCarthy, F. and A. Dhareshwar (1992), "Economic Shocks and the Global Environment," PRE Working Paper No. 870, The World Bank.

Mitra, P. (1986), "A Description of Adjustment to External Shocks: Country Groups," in D. Lal and M. Wolf (eds.), *Stagflation, Savings and the State*, London: Oxford University Press.

"Adjustment to External Shocks in Selected Semi-Industrial Countries, 1974–1981," in P. Ferri and G. Ragazzi (eds.), *Adjustment to Shocks: A North-South Prospective*, Supplement to the *Journal of Banking and Finance*, Amsterdam: North-Holland.

"Adjustment to External Shocks in Selected Less Developed Countries," CPD Discussion Paper No. 1986–38, World Bank.

(1992), "The Coordinated Reform of Tariffs and Domestic Indirect Taxes," *World Bank Research Observer*, 7(2), pp. 195–218.

Mitra, P. and D. Go (1990), "Exploring Fiscal Adjustment to the Third Oil Price Shock, India 1990–91," (World Bank, processed).

(1993), "Trade Liberalization, Fiscal Adjustment and Exchange Rate Policy: A

Methodological Illustration using Indian Data," (World Bank, processed).

Mitra, P. and S. Tendulkar (1986), "Coping with Internal and External Exogenous Shocks: India, 1973–74 to 1983–84," World Bank, CPD Discussion Paper No. 1986–21.

Pearce, D. and R. Westoby (1985), "World Oil Prices and Output Losses in Developing Countries," Department of Political Economy, University College London, Discussion Paper No. 85–02.

Pyatt, C. and J. Round (eds.) (1985), *Social Accounting Matrices: A Basis for Planning*, World Bank Symposium.

Reserve Bank of India (1985), *Report of the Committee on the Working of the Monetary System*, Bombay.

Sachs, J. (1981), "The Current Account and Macro-economic Adjustment in the 1970s," *Brookings Papers on Economic Activity*, 1, pp. 201–82.

Sanderson, W. and J. Williamson (1985), "How Should Developing Countries Adjust to External Shocks in the 1980s: An Examination of Some World Bank Macroeconomic Models," World Bank Staff Working Paper No. 708.

Sierra, H. and T. Condon (1987), "An approximation technique for computing optimal dynamic paths," *Journal of Economic Dynamics and Control*, 11, pp. 405–23.

Sussangkarn, C. (1983), "Government Employment and Alternative Labor Market Closures in an Economy-wide Setting: Applications to Thailand," (World Bank, Development Research Department, processed).

Svensson, L. (1984), "Oil Prices, Welfare and the Trade Balance," *Quarterly Journal of Economics*, 99, pp. 649–72.

Tanzi, V. (1986), "Fiscal Policy Responses to Exogenous Shocks in Developing Countries," *American Economic Review*, 76, pp. 88–91.

Taylor, L. and F. Lysy (1979), "Vanishing Income Redistribution: Keynesian Clues About Model Surprises in the Short Run," *Journal of Development Economics*, 6, pp. 11–29.

van Wijnbergen, S. (1984), "Oil Price Shocks and the Current Account: An Analysis of Short Run Adjustment Measures," *Weltwirtschaftsliches Archiv*, 120(3), pp. 460–80.

(1985), "Oil Price Shocks, Unemployment, Investment and the Current Account: An Intertemporal Disequilibrium Analysis," *The Review of Economic Studies*, 52, pp. 627–45.

Verghese, S.K. (1984), "Management of Exchange Rate of Rupee Since Its Basket Link: Part I," *Economic and Political Weekly*, 19(28), pp. 1096–1105.

Westoby, R. (1984), "A Survey of Methods and Models Used to Assess the Macroeconomic Impact of Oil Price Rises," Department of Political Economy, University College London, Discussion Paper No. 84–17.

World Bank (1980a), *World Development Report*.

(1980b), *Thailand: Income Growth and Poverty Alleviation*, Report No. 2566-TH.

(1981a), *Thailand: Managing Resources for Structural Adjustment*, Report No. 4366-TH.

(1981b), *World Development Report*.

(1982a), *Growth and Structural Change in Kenya: A Basic Economic Report*, Report No. 3350-KE.

(1982b), *Turkey: Industrialization and Trade Strategy*, Report No. 3641-TU.

(1982c), *World Development Report*.

(1983), *World Development Report*.

(1984), "Turkey-Data Information System (1984, third quarter)," unpublished mimeo (November 1).

(1985), *Thailand: Perspectives for Financial Reform*, Report No. 4085–TH.

(1988), *A Visual Overview of World Oil Demand*, Industry and Energy Department Working Paper, Energy Series Paper No. 8.

(1990), *World Development Report*.

Index

absorption, 17, 292, 302
  excess absorption schedule, 10–13
  restraining, 35, 292
  Turkey, 275, 282
accounting in general equilibrium models,
  74–80
Africa, drought, 34
agriculture
  India 151, 153, 154, 155, 167, 169–70,
    170–89 passim
  India, shocks, simulation, 182–7
  Kenya, 50–5, 228, 245, 249–50
  Korea, 299
  share of labor force, 200
  technology, India, 149
  Thailand, 193, 195, 198–202, 210–11
Ahamed, L., 226, 227, 252
Ahluwalia, I., 191
Ahluwalia, M. S., 151, 161
aid to India, 147
Aitchinson, J., 132
Allen, R. M., 72, 253
Ansu, Y., 252
Argentina, adjustment patterns, 22–35
armaments see defense
autarky of Turkey, 255

balance of payments, 17
  and external shocks, 24–5, 149–51
  India, 146–7, 149–51, 159, 298
  and investment, 19
  Kenya, 222–4
  Korea, 298
  and public resource mobilization, 31
  and public sector profligacy, 35
  and savings, 19
  Thailand, 195, 196
  Turkey, 257, 259, 268, 271, 273, 277,
    280, 281, 286

Balassa, B., 8, 20, 30, 35, 44, 257, 287, 303
bank lending to developing countries, 3
barter terms-of-trade, India, 159
Benin, adjustment patterns, 22–35
Bevan, D., 253
Bhagwati, J. N., 191
Bhalla, S., 163
Bolivia, adjustment patterns, 22–35
borrowing, 3, 219, 290–1, 293, 296, 213
  Bolivia, 33
  India, 170–7
  Kenya, 48–9, 222, 224, 237, 238, 240,
    247, 252
  Korea, 299
  pro-cyclical borrowing, 32
  Thailand, 193, 194, 196, 197–8, 211–16
  Turkey, 254, 257, 268, 270–1, 273–4,
    277, 279–83, 285, 286
  see also debt
Branson, W., 226, 227, 252
Brazil, adjustment patterns, 22–35
Brooke, A. D., 74, 145
Brown, J. A. C., 132
Bruno, M., 44
Buffie, E. F., 7

calibration of general equilibrium models,
  109–10, 113–14
capital
  flows
    from Argentina, 32
    from Guatemala, 34
    Kenya, 222
    Turkey, 254, 257, 271, 273–6, 277, 280
    Uruguay, 32
  formation
    India, 154, 160
    Kenya, 225–6, 238
    in general equilibrium models, 108

310

316   **Index**